Code Enforcement
A Comprehensive Approach

Joseph M. Schilling
and James B. Hare

Solano Press Books
Point Arena, California

Code Enforcement
A Comprehensive Approach

August 1994

Solano Press Books
Post Office Box 773
Point Arena, California 95468
Phone (707) 884-4508/Fax (707) 884-4109

Cover design by Design Site, Berkeley, California
Book design by Canterbury Press, Berkeley, California
Index by Paul Kish, Mendocino, California
Photographs by Joseph M. Schilling, except where noted
Printed by Braun-Brumfield, Inc., Ann Arbor, Michigan

ISBN 0-923956-21-2

Trees are one of nature's renewable resources.
To preserve this invaluable resource for future
generations, Solano Press Books makes annual
contributions to the *American Forests Global
Releaf Program*. *American Forests* is the nation's
oldest nonprofit citizens' conservation organization.

⊕ Printed on partially recycled paper.

NOTICE

Before you rely on the information in this book,
be sure you have the latest edition and are aware
that some changes in statutes, guidelines, or case
law may have gone into effect since the date of
publication. The book, moreoever, provides
general information about the law. Readers
should consult their own attorneys before
relying on the representations found herein.

We live in a regulatory society, with government at all levels promulgating rules that limit or control our conduct and affairs. These regulations are widely used as the means to respond to community issues, solve problems, or carry out duly adopted public policies.

Nowhere is this more evident than when public agencies control the use of land. A host of federal, state, and local regulations may apply to a particular parcel, depending on the transaction. These transactions may include zoning and conditional use permits or the processes governing accessory uses, tentative maps, exactions, and mitigation banking. Whether these regulations are effective or necessary is part of a continuing debate; but their enactment at the local level has been found to have a direct impact on the quality of our neighborhoods and, at times, on the patterns of land usage and the value of real estate.

Adopting regulations, however, is only the first part of a larger cycle that includes both enactment and enforcement of laws. For all of the lofty objectives regulations may be designed to achieve, the means by which they are enforced become the test of their utility in addressing community issues and needs.

Code Enforcement: A Comprehensive Approach seeks to establish the nexus between the enactment of regulations and the practice of enforcement. This book includes observations and guidance on the legal foundations of regulatory controls, writing enforceable regulations, managing code compliance programs, and employing administrative remedies as an alternative to criminal and civil litigation. The discussion of cases and examples used in this book illustrate the difficult circumstances associated with the practice of code enforcement and the use of alternative methods for handling cases. The authors and their associates learned much from these experiences, and it should be emphasized that the examples cited throughout are presented with the intent to share knowledge gained, rather than to criticize the way any particular case was handled at the time.

This book, like others, could not have been written without the assistance of many and the influence of a few. Joe would like to acknowledge his dedicated staff in the San Diego City Attorney's Code Enforcement Unit: Senior Deputy City Attorneys Diane Silva-Martinez, Makini Hammond, and Mary Jo Lanzafame; legal secretaries Linda DeGreef, Michele Richards, and Lena Swindle; Litigation Investigators Dennis Smith and Michael Hart; and Legal Assistant Dave McKean. Joe would also like to recognize the contribution and support of the Center for Municipal Dispute Resolution, especially Susan Quinn, Donna Silverberg, and Marcia Foreman. The rosters of local government are not static, and both authors thank some of Joe's former staff for their help in the early days of the Code Enforcement Unit, including Pete Grover, Barret Brown, Linda Anthony, Lulu Barcelona, Cindy Lane, and the always enthusiastic and dedicated Art Weatherford.

Jim would like to acknowledge his debt to the Rancho Santa Fe Association, including the Association Manager Walt Ekard and staff, Building Commissioner Carol Dick, Senior Planner Keith Behner, and Assistant Planner Chester Hunter. Further acknowledgement goes to Mike Meeker, the Association's primary enforcement agent, who has demonstrated on countless occasions his understanding of the necessary balance between customer service and the ultimate goal of achieving regulatory compliance.

Both authors would like to express their appreciation to the City of San Diego and its staff for their contributions of reference materials and forms and to acknowledge the support from individuals who donated their time to pose for photographs that appear in the book. The creative book design skills and ceaseless energy of Pat Shell gave this book life which has made it a very workable guide for practitioners.

Special recognition is in order to the City of San Diego's code enforcers, including Sheri Carr, Bonnie Contreras, Joseph Flynn, Frank Hafner, Chief Monica Higgins, Tony Khalil, Bill Nelson, Sam Oats, Ty Rogers, Jan Rowland, Bob Vacchi, and Randall Ward for initiating those complex enforcement questions and nightmare cases that helped to develop the fabric of comprehensive code enforcement. During the preparation of this book, and over many years, both authors have received advice and encouragement from one of the city's most accomplished writers of land use polices and regulations, Betsy McCullough. The authors are also indebted to Warren Jones and Jaimie Levin of Solano Press Books, the publisher, for their patience and assistance in helping us translate our code enforcement experiences into a more understandable form.

Finally, we both would like to thank the owner of Les Girls Adult Theater for maintaining more than a dozen signs in violation of San Diego's sign regulations. It was this high profile case that caused us to join forces and to establish the connection for this book.

Contents

Figures, Graphs, and Flow Charts

Introduction

The code enforcement official is a unique public servant whose responsibility lies squarely between policy making and the realms of law enforcement and litigation.

Regulatory Foundations

Local Regulatory Implementation

Managing Code Enforcement

Investigating Cases

Selection of Remedies

Administrative Remedies

Criminal Prosecution

Using Civil Injunctions

Defenses to CE Actions

Introduction

Introduction

Code enforcement is a function local governments* perform that citizens consider important for accomplishing community goals, such as protecting property values and the environment. Others view code enforcement as an annoying intrusion into the free use of private property. Traditionally, it has been a process whereby local governments use various techniques to gain compliance with duly-adopted regulations such as land use and zoning ordinances, health and housing codes, sign standards, and uniform building and fire codes. In recent years, federal and state regulations governing air and water quality and the transport and storage of hazardous wastes, and requirements for implementing the Americans with Disabilities Act have come into play. Local governments are now obliged to include enforcement of these rules and regulations in the array of responsibilities they assume for protecting the public health and welfare.

Contemporary code enforcement involves local enforcement officials in the job of ensuring compliance with policies, codes, rules, regulations, and permits in a proper, timely fashion within the limits of the law. Consequently, enforcement officials must be fully acquainted with the adoption process and the thinking behind the regulations they enforce as well as the legal limits placed on them. Conversely, those who write the laws must understand the problems particular to enforcement and administration as the codes and regulations are implemented.

Enforcement officials must be fully acquainted with the adoption process and thinking behind the regulations they enforce and the legal limits placed on them.

In this context the code enforcement official is a unique public servant whose responsibility lies squarely between policy making and the realms of law enforcement and litigation. The U.S.

---

* Cities, counties, municipalities, local agencies—these are the terms referring to local governments used interchangeably throughout this book. Many of the practices discussed also apply to federal and state enforcement agencies.

Congress, state legislatures, and city councils and county boards of supervisors adopt policies, codes, rules and regulations to solve problems or respond to federal, state, or community mandates. Enforcement applies these laws to specific properties, either by using warnings and notices to persuade voluntary compliance or by filing court actions, all under the rubric of 'police powers'. Local enforcement officials and those who write the policies, codes, rules, and regulations are obligated to understand the management of the code enforcement function and the entire complex process that is the subject of the following chapters.

A. Defining Comprehensive Code Enforcement

Code enforcement is defined as the process by which public agencies gain compliance with those laws, regulations, and permits over which they have authority.

By itself, code enforcement is defined as the process by which public agencies gain compliance with those laws, regulations, and permits over which they have authority. Comprehensive code enforcement goes beyond this basic definition to encompass an awareness of the public policy basis for codes and the case resolution alternatives to achieve compliance. Both aspects add perspective to and improve the results of local enforcement efforts.

Most local agencies start the enforcement process after a citizen files a complaint with the local building inspection or planning department. An enforcement agent visits the property to determine if a code violation exists; and, if a violation is discovered, a notice is issued to the property owner or tenant. Since most violations exist through simple, unintentional ignorance of a regulation, the majority of cases are resolved soon after this initial notice. Compliance is accomplished when the owner or tenant obtains proper permits, makes necessary repairs, or abates the conditions which constitute the violations. Where the owner fails to comply voluntarily, the municipality can pursue a variety of administrative enforcement actions or take the owner to court.

The Tough Ten Percent

An enforcement agency eventually gains voluntary compliance in approximately ninety percent of its code enforcement cases by issuing the initial notice of violation. However, for the remaining ten percent, an agency may use nearly all of its resources to bring these properties into compliance. This rule of the Tough Ten Percent and the techniques enforcement agencies can use to gain compliance is the primary focus of Chapters Six through Nine.

If every case was limited to these simple events, the job of an enforcement official would be easy; but, for code enforcement to support community goals, officials must go beyond inspecting private property, issuing a notice, and filing an enforcement action in court. Code enforcement issues start earlier, when the planner or municipal attorney drafts an ordinance and permit. Intertwined in the development and management of land use policies and programs, enforcement considerations also arise when municipalities issue use permits and when the enforcement agency monitors compliance with underlying permit conditions.

A comprehensive approach to enforcement means that anyone who works in the code enforcement environment—city and county planners and district attorneys, code enforcement personnel, managers and administrators, private practitioners and consultants—is increasingly obligated to understand the connections between traditional code enforcement activities and such topics as constitutional law, property rights, economics, policy and plan implementation, and decision-making processes.

B. Principles of Comprehensive Code Enforcement

Although compliance is the primary objective, the road to compliance may be complex. Taking a comprehensive route is recommended. The case for a comprehensive approach to code enforcement begins with becoming familiar with its principles—

- **Establish measurable goals based on identified community needs.** Identifying needs and translating them into measurable goals to be attained through enforcement is primary. While a mandate to protect basic health and safety drives the enforcement of building and fire codes, local agencies also have the discretion to respond to the priorities of neighborhoods and the community. Impressive case closure statistics are far less valuable if they do not represent a concerted attack on violations the community most abhors.

- **Evaluate enforcement issues before drafting ordinances and designing programs.** Code enforcement starts before a particular parcel is found in violation of a land use regulation. Elected and appointed officials, including planning commissioners and city council members, should consider the possible impact of code enforcement before adopting regulations that others will be assigned to enforce. A comprehensive view can help identify enforcement issues early in the process.

- **Integrate implementation with enforcement.** Municipalities often assign one part of an organization to implement regulations and another to conduct enforcement. Implementation is how municipalities put a regulation into action: zones are established, planners and building inspectors review proposals, process permits, and inspect final development. Enforcement comes into play when a specific property, previously the subject of implementation, is found to violate a regulation. Enforcement is therefore the method by which an agency assures that the use of land continues to comply with local regulations after permits are issued. Thus, interaction between those assigned to implement and those assigned to enforce is critical to long-term success.

- **Monitor land use plans, permits, and zoning ordinances for their effectiveness after formal adoption.** The enforcement agency

The Regulatory Cycle

Many local agencies separate the processes of enacting, implementing, and enforcing regulations. The person who drafts the ordinance may not be the one who issues subsequent permits, who may in turn be someone other than the person who investigates cases or files enforcement actions. Whether or not they are understood or managed by the agency, the interrelationships among these functions tend to act upon each other in a cycle composed of the elements shown in the adjacent figure.

Community Needs. Most new regulations start with a community concern which is either brought to the organization by its constituency or identified and experienced by its own staff.

Goals. Having identified an issue or community need, agencies then try to identify the objectives that will be met when the matter is resolved.

Budgeting and Organization. Either in response to particular issues or as a part of ongoing operations, agencies devote staff and resources to preparing, im-

plementing, and enforcing regulations.

Regulations. An agency must sometimes enact a new law, ordinance, or policy to resolve a matter.

Implementation. Once a regulation is adopted, the agency implements the law by reviewing applications and issuing permits.

Portion of the cycle most subject to authorities and constitutional constraints

REGULATIONS
IMPLEMENTATION
BUDGET AND ORGANIZATION
GOALS
INVESTIGATIONS
NO ISSUE
DISPUTE RESOLUTION
ADMINISTRATIVE PROCESS
COMMUNITY NEEDS
LITIGATION
PROSECUTION
RESULTS ASSESMENT
COMPLIANCE

Portion of the cycle most subject to policy and budgetary constraints

ILLUSTRATION BY
LISA GOEHRING

Investigation. The bridge between implementation and enforcement starts with the investigation of alleged code violations to determine whether or not a violation exists.

Remedies, Responses, and Enforcement Actions. If initial con-

tact during investigation does not persuade the violator to correct a violation, the agency must evaluate a number of enforcement remedies and select one that is most appropriate to the facts of the case. To achieve compliance the agency can either employ dispute resolution to reach a mediated settlement, use its own administrative procedures of abatement and permit revocation, or pursue litigation through criminal prosecution and civil injunction.

Assessment of Results. This last step completes the cycle. Assessment of results links the enactment of regulations with enforcement. Most agencies do not routinely measure for effectiveness by determining whether a particular regulation was clearly understandable, readily enforceable, and provided an acceptable level of compliance. If constituents do not complain, decision makers are left to assume that the law is meeting community needs. But if the regulation does not work or has unintended results, the agency should start the regulatory cycle anew.

should monitor compliance with the conditions imposed by development and use permits on a specific parcel, building or use. By using a comprehensive approach from the beginning, combining the theory of land use planning with everyday implementation and enforcement techniques, city planners will be able to draft permits and ordinances that will be more enforceable.

By using a comprehensive approach from the beginning, city planners will be able to draft permits and ordinances that will be more enforceable.

■ **Coordinate implementation and enforcement of state and local land use regulations.** Enforcement responsibilities are often spread among different municipal departments as well as various state agencies. Comprehensive code enforcement evaluates all applicable land use regulations (under California law this includes predominately among others the Uniform Building and Fire Codes, State Housing Law, Subdivision Map Act, California Coastal Act, and California Environmental Quality Act), and coordinates the independent enforcement agencies empowered to administer and investigate these regulations.

■ **Evaluate all available enforcement options and remedies to resolve enforcement cases effectively.** In the practical realm of code enforcement, the agency must evaluate all options to gain compliance, including informal notices, office hearings, mediation, administrative hearings, criminal prosecution, and civil injunctions. Comprehensive code enforcement can assist officials in the field and municipal attorneys and prosecutors in the courts. Enforcement must contain a certain degree of flexibility to address unique enforcement situations.

■ **Compliance is the primary objective of comprehensive code enforcement; penalties and punishment are secondary.** Public policy goals, implementation of adopted regulations, and resolution of enforcement cases are accomplished through compliance. While the imposition of penalties, punishment, and incarceration may be justified as a deterrent to crimes involving personal behavior, a code enforcement official is usually more interested in correcting a physical deficiency in a place or structure. Comprehensive code enforcement never loses sight of compliance as the means to achieve community goals and the agency's mission.

Public policy goals, the implementation of adopted regulations, and the resolution of enforcement cases are accomplished through compliance.

C. The Complexities of Code Enforcement

The responsibility of an agency and its enforcement personnel is often more complex than simply issuing a stop work order to a property owner who fails to obtain proper permits. In many respects, code enforcement is a specialized form of law enforcement, subject to all of the legal standards and constitutional limitations that law enforcement entails. In this sense, code enforce-

Code Enforcement and Community Attitudes about Neighborhood Deterioration: The 'Broken Window Theory'

Developing a sense of order which results from effective and timely code enforcement can help to curb the physical deterioration of our cities. If we strive for an orderly urban environment through such measures as repairing dilapidated buildings, removing trash and junk from vacant lots, and replacing broken windows, we might improve our opportunities as a community to manage the more complex social and economic problems of homelessness, crime, and poverty.

How individuals respond to property maintenance has been cleverly demonstrated in an experiment by social scientists to test the hypothesis of the 'Broken Window Theory'.* They left an inoperable car parked on a public street in a high crime neighborhood in New York City. During the next few hours they observed a number of people vandalize and steal parts from the car; and within forty-eight hours the car was nothing more than a shell.

They repeated the experiment in a more affluent neighborhood in Palo Alto, California, near Stanford University. Although more time elapsed, the social scientists observed the same behavior: people

destroying property perceived to be neglected and abandoned. Because it was an easy target, abandoned property attracted criminal behavior, and the socioeconomic level of the neighborhood seemed to have no appreciable impact.

Describing the theory in the *Atlantic Monthly* in 1982, James Q. Wilson and George L. Kelling wrote that "social psychologists and police officers tend to agree that if a window in a building is

broken and is left unrepaired, all the rest of the windows will soon be broken." Neglected property allowed to remain in such a condition is a signal to the community that no one cares. Wilson and Kelling go on to suggest that disorder and crime are inextricably linked with the physical environment at the community level. As they explained in a more recent article in 1989—

"[A] lot of serious crime is

adventitious, not the result of inexorable social forces or personal failing. A rash of burglaries may occur because drug users have found a back alley or an abandoned building in which to hang out. In their spare time, and in order to get money to buy drugs, they steal from their neighbors. If the back alleys are cleaned up and the abandoned buildings torn down, the drug users will go away. They may even use fewer drugs, because they will have difficulty finding convenient dealers and soft burglary targets."

This relationship between crime and neighborhood deterioration is one of the leading justifications for a comprehensive code enforcement program. If left unabated, abandoned buildings, substandard apartments, and even graffiti can rapidly develop into public nuisances threatening the public's health and safety. An aggressive code enforcement program can help to reduce the likelihood that properties with minor violations will contribute to a neighborhood becoming worse. Code enforcement can also help contain the possibility that more dilapidated properties will spread throughout a neighborhood or community.

* "Broken Windows," by James Q. Wilson and George L. Kelling, *Atlantic Monthly*, March 1982.
** "Making Neighborhoods Safe," by James Q. Wilson and George L. Kelling, *Atlantic Monthly*, February 1989.

ment officials are the police officers of the land use process. Building inspectors—together with zoning investigators, fire inspectors, city planners, sanitarians, and code compliance officers—must not only understand the legal concepts of due process, rights of privacy, and unreasonable searches and seizures, but must judiciously apply these constitutional principles in the field.

Many code enforcement cases involve aspects of larger economic, social, and political issues within the community, including drugs, gangs, homelessness, graffiti, substandard housing, environmental protection, and the preservation of historic buildings. Code enforcement problems are as diverse as the communities in which they exist. An illegal sign may be the worst problem in one neighborhood while another may have to contend with dilapidated buildings infested with rats and vermin.

Code enforcement officials are often thrust into complex problems with a variety of conflicting interests. When enforcement officials issue a notice for maintaining a substandard apartment building, the interests of tenants and landlords are at stake. Neighbors may feud over barking dogs or auto repair businesses in residential zones. Disputes between a developer and environmentalists surface when the planner attempts to monitor compliance with federal, state, and local permits. Elected officials and community groups may pressure enforcement officials to punish violators swiftly, while in some cases these same groups may complain that officials are harsh, overzealous, and bureaucratic.

Enforcement officials must balance all this against their duties to enforce municipal, state, and federal regulations to protect the general public welfare. A comprehensive approach can help to resolve enforcement cases while maintaining a balance between competing interests.

D. Conclusion

Over the years many members of local government and the community have not appreciated the complexities and challenges confronting code enforcement officials. Some have viewed code violations as technicalities involving minor regulations—overheight fences, abandoned or inoperable vehicles, excessive storage—while others have complained that enforcement is an impediment to small business development or yet another example of stifling bureaucracy. As a result, many code enforcement programs have been subject to budget cuts, based on the reasoning that the enforcement of land use regulations is not as critical to the public's general health and safety as are other more visible services.

In many respects, code enforcement is a specialized form of law enforcement, subject to all of the legal standards and constitutional limitations that law enforcement entails. Supreme Court Justice William Brennan wrote, "After all, if a policeman must know the constitution, then why not a planner?" (*San Diego Gas and Electric v. City of San Diego*, 450. U.S. 621 (1981))

Code enforcement officials are often thrust into complex problems with a variety of conflicting interests.

Notwithstanding these misconceptions and setbacks, over the past fifteen years code enforcement has developed into a critical municipal service to provide for the orderly and productive growth of livable communities. The impact of floods, fire, earthquakes, landslides, and windstorms on the built environment has alerted the public to the need for a higher standard for regulating land use, both to minimize damage and destruction caused by natural disasters and to ensure that communities are well-built and sustainable. Additionally, the public's growing desire to live in diverse, attractive, and well-managed communities demands more creative strategies to enforce proper and effective land use regulations.

The public now places a high priority on the commitment and ability of local agencies to enforce regulations through permits and discretionary approvals to maintain neighborhoods, protect property and property rights, and preserve the value of public and private investments. Consequently, many municipalities recognize code enforcement as an important tool to help sustain and protect the health, safety, and welfare of their cities, towns, and neighborhoods. Partially through this broader commitment, code enforcement itself has become a recognized profession, spanning the entire organization of city and county government. Enforcement responsibilities are vested with an array of specialized code compliance officers, city planners, environmental monitoring agents, fire prevention and building inspectors, and other public employees. And professional organizations similar to the California Code Enforcement Council (CCEC) and the American Association of Code Enforcement (AACE) have organized chapters throughout the country.

A comprehensive framework—that includes the steps of assessing community needs, developing goals, adopting regulations and issuing permits, enforcing the law, and evaluating the overall effectiveness of a program from beginning to end—can help clarify how local governments implement, administer, and enforce state and local land use regulations. Practitioners, politicians, and policymakers may also benefit from using this comprehensive approach to respond to, evaluate, and resolve code enforcement issues in their communities.

CCEC = California Code Enforcement Council

AACE = American Association of Code Enforcement

Introduction

Regulatory
Foundations

Local Regulatory
Implementation

Managing Code
Enforcement

Investigating
Cases

Selection of
Remedies

Administrative
Remedies

Criminal
Prosecution

Using Civil
Injunctions

Defenses to
CE Actions

Regulatory
Foundations

*Since a valid law, regulation, or ordinance
is the prerequisite to code enforcement,
this chapter takes a brief look at the
entire land use regulatory system.*

Regulatory Foundations

Regulations are evoked to respond to a wide array of urban problems such as homelessness, gangs, and graffiti, as well as the pressures of suburban growth such as traffic congestion, public facilities financing, and a deteriorating infrastructure. Municipalities often respond to these complex problems by using their police power to enact a variety of zoning and other land use regulations.

Since a valid law, regulation, or ordinance is the prerequisite to code enforcement, this chapter takes a brief look at the entire land use regulatory system. We start with the constitutional authority of local agencies to enact regulations and continue with a discussion of zoning laws, uniform codes, and relevant state land use statutes such as the California Environmental Quality Act (CEQA) and the California Coastal Act. Although the courts have generally supported this contemporary expansion of municipal land use regulations, new ordinances are frequently subject to legal challenge. Thus, it is important to understand these principles as they may relate to the legal defense of a challenged regulation. Moreover, to ensure that regulatory powers do not unreasonably infringe on the rights of property owners and are exercised within constitutional boundaries, both the planner who writes the ordinance and the field agent who enforces it should have a general understanding of the underlying legal principles that empower governments to regulate and the procedural regulations which deliver that power.

By necessity the following paragraphs stress legal terms and jargon. Remember that code enforcement is a specialized type of 'law' enforcement, and the courts have given each definition a special meaning. While volumes have been written about 'Preemption', 'Municipal Affairs,' and other legal concepts, our

CEQA = California Environmental Quality Act

To ensure that regulatory powers are exercised within constitutional boundaries, both the planner and the field agent should have a general understanding of the underlying legal principles.

13

purpose is only to provide a broad framework of the legal principles and terms pertaining to municipal land use regulations and to explain how the implementation and enforcement of regulations can respond to identifiable community problems.

A. Overview: General Regulatory Authority

Municipalities in California derive their governmental powers from the state constitution which creates two basic types of cities, General Law and Charter. Also known as 'Home Rule' cities, Charter Cities come into existence after a majority of the electors adopt a charter as prescribed by provisions of state law. In states such as California that provide for home rule in the constitution, Charter Cities are free to enact regulations that govern their own 'municipal affairs'. A Charter City, however, must also act consistently with the terms of its own charter, for the courts have concluded that a charter limits local power in the same way a constitution limits state or federal powers. Those municipalities not operating under a charter are considered 'General Law' cities and must follow regulations as provided for in state statutes. Although counties can also operate under a charter (California Constitution article XI, §§ 3 & 4), counties are designated political subdivisions of the state and are therefore subject to state laws in the same manner as General Law cities.

1. Municipal Affairs Doctrine

Article XI, section 5(a) of the California Constitution allows Charter Cities to make and enforce all ordinances and regulations that involve 'municipal affairs'. When a city acts within this mandate, its ordinances are considered superior to state law and may conflict with state law as long as the matter is not of statewide significance. However, because the term 'municipal affairs' has no precise definition, such matters have traditionally been decided by the courts on a case-by-case basis. Thus, the concept of 'municipal affairs' is subject to constant change, and what may at one time be considered the sole domain of Charter Cities at a later time may become an issue of statewide concern.

The courts continue to determine whether a situation involves a municipal affair by applying the framework established in the leading case of *Bishop v. City of San Jose*, 1 Cal.3d 56, 62-63 (1969). Cases which provide further discussions of Charter City powers include *Committee of Seven Thousand v. Superior Court*, 45 Cal.3d 491, 505-506 (1988) (construction of local roads considered a 'municipal affair', but construction

For further discussion of 'municipal affairs' doctrine please consult *The California Municipal Law Handbook* (1994), published by the League of California Cities, Section V, Police Powers, pages 7-10.

of major highways is a matter of statewide concern). *See also,*
Brown v. City of Berkeley, 57 Cal.App.3d 223, 230-231 (1976)
(Police Review Commission).

2. Police Power Doctrine

Both a General Law and a Charter City possess the
powers granted in California Constitution Article XI, section 7,
to "make and enforce within its limits all local, police, sanitary,
and other ordinances and regulations not in conflict with general laws," (counties also have the same police powers). Conflicts
exist when an ordinance duplicates, contradicts, or enters into a
field fully occupied by the general state law.

What Is Preemption?

Preemption is the legal concept courts apply to determine whether
a state law is superior to a local ordinance. Generally associated
with the police powers doctrine, preemption can also occur under
the 'municipal affairs' doctrine. While the courts may reach the
same conclusion, judges ask slightly different questions.

Under 'municipal affairs', the question is whether the subject area
is one of statewide concern or a municipal affair. The courts do
not inquire as to whether the local ordinance conflicts with state
law. This is somewhat different from the traditional police power
doctrine where the courts evaluate whether a conflict exists. A
conflict is present if the subject matter is fully occupied by the
state. While the courts appear to perform an academic exercise in
distinguishing between the form of these two questions, the critical issue under either doctrine is whether the area under scrutiny
is one of statewide importance. If statewide importance is found,
the local law is considered to be preempted by the state statute.

For more details about the legal nuances of preemption, please con-
sult "Charter Cities Financing in California—A Growing
'Statewide Concern'?" by Richard Hiscocks and Marie Backes,
University of San Francisco Law Review, Vol. 16 (Summer, 1982).

---

3. Scope of Police Power within Land Use Regulatory Authority

Municipal authority to regulate land and enact zoning
and building ordinances is derived from the police power.
Particularly as it relates to land use actions, however, the state
legislature can enact statutes which apply to both Charter and

Municipal authority to regulate land and enact zoning and building ordinances is derived from the police power.

Absent conflict with state law, the courts generally view land use ordinances as valid exercises of the municipal police power as long as they are reasonably related to the public's health, safety, and welfare.

Police Power Expansions

As with 'municipal affairs', what constitutes a valid enactment under the police power continues to evolve. Recent court decisions have taken the notion of police power into such wide-ranging land use areas as aesthetics, blight caused by an adult businesses, and rent control.

▓ **Municipalities have** the power to declare what uses or activities constitute a public nuisance; this police power is not limited to those items listed in state law. *People v. Johnson*, 129 Cal.App.2d 1,6-7 (1954).

▓ **A ban on the** posting of signs on public property is another valid ordinance supported by aesthetics. *Members of City Council of Los Angeles v. Taxpayers for Vincent*, 466 U.S. 789, 805-807 (1984).

▓ **Zoning regulations** that govern the location of 'adult' businesses are justified by the substantial governmental interest in preventing the urban deterioration caused by the secondary effects of 'adult entertainment'. *City of National City v. Wiener*, 3 Cal. 4th 832, 845-847 (1992).

▓ **Municipalities have** a legitimate governmental interest in the enactment of regulations that establish local rent control regulations as a means to counteract the harms emanating from a housing shortage. *Birkenfield v. City of Berkeley*, 17 Cal. 3d 129, 159-161 (1976).

General Law cities. Therefore, municipalities must carefully analyze existing laws and each year's crop of new enactments.

Absent conflict with state law, the courts generally view land use ordinances as valid exercises of the municipal police power as long as they are reasonably related to the public's health, safety, and welfare. Further, the means adopted to accomplish those purposes must also be appropriate.

Zoning and Building Regulations

Through their police powers municipalities can establish zoning and other related land use regulations. *Miller v. Board of Public Works*, 195 Cal. 477, 490 (1925) (first California Supreme Court decision approving police power to establish zoning); *Agnew v. City of Los Angeles*, 190 Cal.App.2d 820, 828 (1961) (approved municipal authority to require building permits as a precondition to build on private property); *Associated Home Builders etc., Inc. v. City of Livermore*, 18 Cal. 3d 582, 609 (1976) (growth management initiative that restricted issuance of building permits).

Zoning laws that limit the number of unrelated people living together in single-family zones was approved by the U.S. Supreme Court in *Village of Belle Terre v. Borass*, 416 U.S. 1, 10 (1974); Under California law, however, such zoning laws cannot infringe on the California Constitution's Privacy Clause absent a compelling governmental interest. See *Adamson v. City of Santa Barbara*, 27 Cal.3d 123, 130 (1980).

4. Enforcement Authority

Implicit in the authority to enact land use regulations through the police power is the ability to implement and enforce these ordinances and regulations. This principle is often illustrated in enabling ordinances and regulations which are solely dedicated to establishing the means of enforcement and penalties. The California Supreme Court, for example, has recognized the state's enforcement power to enact statutes which impose civil penalties as a necessary consequence of its police powers. *See Hale v. Morgan*, page 17.

B. California's Land Use Regulatory Scheme

1. Overview

As a result of the broad grant of the police powers to control the use of land and buildings, state and local governments in California have developed an elaborate system of land use regulations. For purposes of this book, our focus is on those elements of California's land use scheme which have implications for code enforcement.*

Land use regulations in California are generally addressed to one or more of the following purposes—

■ **Procedures and Processes.** To create the procedures that property owners must follow to develop and build on their land (for example, the Subdivision Map Act and the California Environmental Quality Act) or to establish the process that local governments use to enact regulations and apply zoning designations to specific areas of a city.

■ **Regulations.** To establish the underlying ordinances that govern how land and buildings are used; these are the actual zoning and building code regulations which create the list of permitted uses and minimum construction requirements.

■ **Enforcement Ordinances.** To empower enforcement agencies and outline the enforcement process and possible remedies.

Most land use ordinance and statutes include one or more of these aspects. For example, while the Subdivision Map Act primarily establishes the rules for developing and subdividing large tracts of land, Government Code Section 66499.31 outlines the enforcement consequences should a property owner fail to follow the procedural rules. The California Coastal Act is another land use regulation which creates special land development procedures within the designated coastal zone and also incorporates the local building and zoning regulations that can limit the development as well as restrict the use itself.

The overlay of state and local land use regulations on the same property or development project also creates a maze of multiple regulations which the property owner must simultaneously follow. Thus, while the owner seeks to develop land within the coastal zone, the project's review could include questions such as whether the underlying zone permits the proposed use, whether the structure meets the criteria of the local building code, and whether the use and the structure satisfy the specialized requirements of the Coastal Act; if the land contains sensitive habitat (coastal sage scrub or maritime chaparral), CEQA could require further environmental analysis.

---

* For more detailed information about land use concepts and regulations such as general plans, the Subdivision Map Act, redevelopment, and CEQA, we would refer our readers to References and Suggested Readings at the end of this book.

Enforcement Cases

■ **Ordinances which** establish reasonable enforcement procedures and penalties are a logical extension of a municipality's police power. *Ex Parte Green*, 94 Cal. 387, 390 (1892) (power to assess fines includes the power to incarcerate as a means to collect fines).

■ **A municipality can** select the particular mode for enforcing any valid police, sanitary, or other regulations within its territory. *City of Stockton v. Frisbie & Latta*, 93 Cal.App. 277, 289 (1928).

■ **City has authority** to declare a building a public nuisance if it violates the local building code and threatens the public's health and safety; city can also abate this nuisance by demolition. *City of Bakersfield v. Miller*, 64 Cal.2d 93, 104 (1966).

■ *Hale v. Morgan*, 22 Cal.3d 388, 398 (1978) (court invalidated mandatory $100 per day penalty as excessive, but acknowledged the creation of a civil cause of action as an appropriate enforcement remedy). The same reasoning the court applied in the *Hale* decision can equally apply to the police power of municipalities to enact land use enforcement and penalty ordinances.

■ **Criminal prosecution** is permissible even though statute also authorizes civil penalties for violation of statute. *People v. Oatas*, 207 Cal.App.3d Supp. 18, 23 (1989) (enforcement of Department of Motor Vehicles regulations).

Before any regulations can be enforced, a system of law must exist which creates the regulating agency and provides for its ability to regulate.

Procedures and Process. Before any regulations can be enforced, a system of law must exist which creates the regulating agency and provides for its ability to regulate. In some instances, these laws do not establish any direct regulation of their own, but empower a local government to set up agencies or authorize the adoption of ordinances. The primary example of enabling legislation includes all of those sections comprising the State Planning and Zoning Law (California Government Code sections 65000, *et seq.*).

Enabling laws can also be enacted at the local level, usually taken in the form of adopting the broader framework of the local municipal code. The initial adoption or radical revision of a zoning code, often attendant to the incorporation of a city, has the effect of establishing the enabling regulations. More routinely, however, local agencies incrementally institute new enabling regulations through day-to-day revisions.

Permits. Another part of the California land use scheme is legislation that provides for uniform processes of permission or restriction. While they may allow for refinement at the local level, laws such as the California Subdivision Map Act and the California Environmental Quality Act firmly provide minimum standards of conduct and procedure. For example, the Subdivision Map Act prescribes fairly specific standards of application, notice, conduct of hearings, findings, and time limitations on decision making; and CEQA contains similar standards for controlling the environmental review process.

2. Scope of Local Zoning Code

State law gives cities and counties fairly broad latitude to establish zoning regulations which rely on the notion of 'police powers' exercised in the interest of the public's health, safety, and welfare. Most municipal zoning codes start as enabling legislation adopted at the local level, with a zoning ordinance primarily composed of a catalogue of use districts or zones, each such zone being no more than a list of permissions and/or restrictions of land use and building placement. The existence of this catalogue enables the city or county to choose and assign zones to properties. Given the wide variability of land use patterns, local conditions, and community preference throughout the state, the flexibility and local control of this system is critical.

For the purposes of a code enforcement scheme, there are two components to the local zoning code. The first of these is the basic enabling sections and regulations. Second, and dis-

Appendix B contains examples of zoning enabling ordinances.

tinctly separate, is the establishment of districts, generally in the form of a zoning map which applies the regulations to the various land areas of the jurisdiction. The basic enabling component of the zoning code provides—

- **Authorities of regulation,** including the general purpose of the zoning code in support of the public's health, safety, and welfare
- **Regulations that apply** to all of the zones
- **A catalogue of zones,** including uses and development criteria
- **Process and criteria** for the issuance of special permissions such as zoning variances, conditional use permits, and planned unit development permits
- **Definitions of terms**

Of particular importance to code enforcement are those elements of the basic zoning code which include—

- **Definitions used specifically for nonenforcement matters.** These might include definitions of common land use terms such as 'hotel' or 'junkyard'. By defining these terms in an objective fashion, the enforcement agency is provided with concrete terms instead of leaving the matter to interpretation by field staff or the courts.
- **Clarification of nonconforming status and rights.** Changes in zoning codes or districts almost invariably result in the creation of structures or uses which do not comply with the newly established rules. The means by which rights to such nonconforming structures or uses can be maintained, transferred, or expanded is a critical factor in the eventual conformance of an area to a rezoning action.
- **Establishment of an enforcement process with a clear statement of remedies, penalties, and rights.** A prescribed system of enforcement—with authority specifically delegated to designated officials, procedures for notice and due process, and a clear statement of penalties and rights—supports the notion of fairness and equal treatment. In addition, this element of the code can contain such matters as the enforcement agency's right to enter property or to abate.
- **Standards of measurement for criteria such as height, floor area, and general nuisance.** In order to be applied consistently and not lead to adverse interpretation by

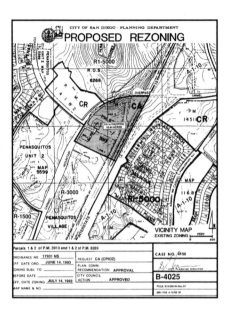

The 'Duck Test'

Remember the 'Duck Test' when considering the definition of terms. The test is derived from the quote by former New York City Mayor Fiorella La Guardia, "If it looks like a duck, walks like a duck, and quacks like a duck, it must be a duck." This is the kind of common sense process brought to bear when a term is otherwise undefined. To the extent that such common sense works for the term wherever it appears in the code, by all means use it. However, if a specific meaning is needed, the term should not only be defined, but used consistently. Capitalizing a specific term suggests that the term is used as defined.

the courts, terms of measurement must be clearly established. Such measurements should not require instru-
ments which are not commonly available, nor should
they be defined in terms which are not intuitive.

These sections serve as the foundation for enforcement.
The code enforcement official should, through practice, identify
where clarification of the basic enabling sections of the local land
use code could provide more straightforward information for field
purposes and a clearer line of reasoning for purposes of litigation.

3. Building Regulations:
Uniform Codes and Statutes

State and local building codes, together with zoning regulations, form the code enforcement foundation of California's land use scheme.

State and local building codes, together with zoning regulations, form the code enforcement foundation of California's
land use scheme. As with zoning ordinances, the protection of
health and safety is also the primary issue in the adoption of
building codes that regulate the construction, repair, and occupancy of buildings and other structures.

Building codes perform a variety of purposes. Building
codes generally—

- **Classify the occupancy** of buildings according to use
- **Establish the engineering** and structural standards depending on the type of building materials
- **Create the building permit process** and the requirements for submission of plans, etc.

As a result of these building code complexities and the
need for regional consistency, most municipalities adopt uniform
codes prepared by regional or professional trade associations.
Uniform Codes are industry-wide standards which have been
developed and tested by the construction industry and engineering professionals.

Appendix B contains an example of an ordinance adopting the Uniform Building Code.

Historically California municipalities were free to adopt
these uniform codes or enact their own local building, plumbing,
or mechanical code. Although Government Code section 38660
et seq. authorizes municipalities to regulate building construction, in 1970 the legislature amended the State Housing Law
which limits local authority—

- Health and Safety Code section 17921 empowers the
  Department of Housing and Community Development (HCD) to set the standards for dwellings,
  hotels, and apartments, and the State Fire Marshal to
  set statewide standards for fire regulations and panic
  hardware.

HCD = Department of Housing and Community Development

Local Flexibility and Building Regulations

In recent years, the amount of flexibility municipalities have to modify the uniform codes has been very confusing. California Health and Safety Code section 17958 seems to give municipalities some limited degree of flexibility. The state Attorney General, state legislature, and the courts have further refined the ability of municipalities to deviate from the uniform codes—

- Municipalities can impose additional building requirements not found in the uniform codes. 55 Ops. AG 157, 160 (1972).

- Municipalities cannot adopt more stringent fire and panic safety requirements than those promulgated by the State Fire Marshal as authorized by Health and Safety Code section 13100. 72 Ops. AG 180, 182 (1989); by contrast, Health and Safety Code section 13143.5 was subsequently enacted by the legislature to permit municipalities to enact more stringent fire requirements if they can satisfy the unique regional criteria set forth in Health and Safety Code section 18941.5.

- Municipalities cannot make any changes to the California Building Standards Code unless such modifications are reasonably necessary to offset some unique local geographical conditions. Health and Safety Code section 17958 and 17958.5; *see Briseno v. Santa Ana*, 6 Cal.App. 4th 1378, 1382-83 (1992) (local occupancy standard declared invalid for being more restrictive than statewide codes).

HCD issued Information Bulletin 94-2 on January 3, 1994, declaring that all local abatement procedures for substandard residential dwellings must conform with California Code of Regulations, Title 25, Division 1, Chapter 1 §48. Apparently, HCD now wants municipalities to submit local abatement ordinances for its review. This Bulletin is currently under review by many municipal attorneys throughout the state.

- Health and Safety Code section 17922 requires HCD to adopt the building standards consistent with the model codes as part of the California Building Standards Code.
- Health and Safety Code section 17958 requires municipalities to impose the same requirements as contained in section 17922.

Some sources of uniform codes include—

- ICBO Uniform Codes, including the Uniform Building Code, Uniform Plumbing Code, Uniform Housing Code, and Uniform Mechanical Code promulgated by the International Conference of Building Officials (ICBO)

ICBO = International Conference of Building Officials

- Uniform Fire Code developed by the Western Association of Fire Chiefs

- National Electrical Code developed by the National Fire Protection Association

- BOCA Codes: The various codes promulgated by the Building Official and Code Administrator, International (BOCA) are used primarily in states outside the west. (BOCA is in the process of consolidating the requirements of the uniform codes into one code.)

Compared to zoning and planning ordinances, local flexibility is greatly limited in the enactment of building codes. If local governments were permitted to establish their own structural requirements and substantially modify the uniform building and fire codes, public safety could be seriously threatened by having inconsistent building specifications which might in turn increase the municipality's exposure to civil liability. Moreover, local governments are also limited in their legal authority to make their local building and fire codes more restrictive than the uniform codes. This limitation on local government power avoids the confusion that could plague building industries if they were forced to interpret and apply different standards within the same general region.

4. State Statutes with Land Use Enforcement Consequences

While municipal ordinances generally govern the implementation and enforcement of local zoning and building regulations, several California land use statutes also involve code enforcement provisions. The State Housing Law, for example, imposes a mandate on local governments to enforce state standards. These statutes may also authorize different enforcement remedies or control the ongoing enforcement of permits.

a. State Housing Laws. California Health and Safety Codes sections 17910 *et seq.* are concerned with the regulation of buildings and uses designed for human habitation. Together with Titles 24 and 25 of the California Code of Regulations, these provisions establish the minimum rules, regulations, and authorities for residential dwellings. Health and Safety Code section 17920.3 is the primary enforcement provision of the State Housing Law, through its establishment of the criteria to declare a building 'substandard'.

Pursuant to section 17964, localities must designate an enforcement department to be responsible for enforcement of the State Housing Law. If municipalities fail either to designate or adequately enforce the State Housing Law, per Health and Safety Code section 17965, the California Department of

Housing and Community Development would become the enforcement agent of the state.

b. Public Nuisance. Civil Code section 3480 codifies the traditional common law definition of a public nuisance. Civil Code section 3493 outlines the three remedies which a municipality can use to remove or 'abate' the activity which caused the public nuisance. Code of Civil Procedure section 731 permits the city attorney or district attorney to file a civil action in superior court in the name of the People of California to abate a public nuisance. If the nuisance continues after written notification, Penal Code section 372 permits the filing of a criminal complaint. Government Code sections 25845, 38771, and 38773.5 authorize counties and cities to enact local enforcement ordinances that would establish administrative procedures to abate public nuisances.

Code of Civil Procedure section 731 permits the city attorney or district attorney to file a civil action in superior court in the name of the People of California to abate a public nuisance.

Special public nuisance statutes which relate to the use of real property and buildings include Health and Safety Code sections 11570 to 11587 (Drug Abatement Act), Penal Code sections 11225 through 11235 (Red Light Abatement Law), and Penal Code sections 11200 through 11207 (Unlawful Liquor Sales Abatement Law). These statutes permit a private citizen, City Attorney, or the district attorney to file a civil action in superior court that seeks an injunction to abate continuous activities involving illegal drugs, prostitution, gambling, bathhouses, and liquor.

c. CEQA: Mitigation Monitoring. CEQA establishes the statewide procedures for the assessment of environmental impacts that may be generated by proposed development projects. (California Public Resources Code sections 21000 *et seq.*) CEQA is another state regulatory scheme where local governments are the designated agents to implement and enforce state standards. Public Resources Code section 21082 requires every city to adopt local guidelines and procedures to evaluate projects and administer the city's responsibility under CEQA. All local guidelines must be consistent with state CEQA guidelines found in California Code of Regulations, Title 14, § 15000 *et seq.* Where the review finds environmental impacts, the municipality may impose mitigation measures as a condition of project approval.

Public Resources Code section 21081.6 now requires that all environmental mitigation components be monitored by local agencies. Mitigation conditions added during the discretionary review process may have a specific regulatory effect on the project. Mitigation conditions are similar to normal con-

See Christward Ministry v. County of San Diego, 13 Cal.App. 4th 31 (1993) (evaluating adequacy of mitigation monitoring program).

ditions that may attach to permits, such as conditional use permits which are issued as part of the discretionary review process.

d.   Redevelopment Law. Redevelopment law in California is largely directed toward creating redevelopment agencies to eliminate blight within the boundaries of a specially designated area of the municipality. The Community Redevelopment Law is found in California Health and Safety Code section 33000.

Redevelopment agencies are empowered to enter into contracts, exercise the extraordinary power of eminent domain, and use funding mechanisms not generally available to other municipal agencies. Redevelopment agencies may also establish design controls to implement redevelopment plans. Generally redevelopment agencies coordinate enforcement efforts with municipal planning and building departments operating under their municipal codes and regulations; thus, code enforcement activities can occur either through the redevelopment agency enforcing the underlying municipal codes or through the municipal enforcement agency acting within the redevelopment area. Although the rules are the same, protecting the public investment in redevelopment's success gives additional impetus to enforcing health, safety, and aesthetic codes. Moreover, new investment in redevelopment areas must be assured of the continuing interest in the maintenance of their surroundings.

e.   California Coastal Act. The California Coastal Act, Public Resources Code section 30000 *et seq.*, regulates the use and development of coastal resource areas and establishes additional land use objectives which must be incorporated into plans, regulations, and permits adopted by local agencies. The Coastal Act not only establishes the underlying regulations, but also provides special procedures for implementation and enforcement.

The primary responsibility for enforcement has now shifted from the state to local governments. Public Resources Code section 30500(a) requires each local government in the coastal zone to prepare a Local Coastal Plan (LCP). Ultimately, therefore, implementation of much of the Coastal Act becomes the responsibility of local agencies operating with their own enforcement regulations and remedies.

Before development can occur within the coastal zone, the local agency must first issue a coastal development permit per Public Resource Code section 30600(a). During the last decade, this process has led to local permits which contain criteria and conditions differing greatly from what had previously

New investment in redevelopment areas must be assured of the continuing interest in the maintenance of their surroundings.

LCP = Local Coastal Plan

been the case. Matters such as siltation control, hours of operation, and maintenance of access, which might never have been written into a permit in the 1970s, today have become commonplace. These special conditions create new and unique enforcement responsibilities for the local agency as it assumes the responsibility for issuing coastal permits.

Enforcement of Coastal Act violations may take place under either of the following scenarios—

- A private party or state Attorney General files a civil action for injunction, declaratory relief, and recovery of civil penalties, per Public Resource Code sections 30803 and 30805.

- The Coastal Commission's executive director issues a cease-and-desist order, pursuant to Public Resource Code section 30809. A negligent or intentional violation of a cease-and-desist order may be punished by a maximum civil penalty of $6000, per section 30821.6.

2 Local Regulatory Implementation

Enforcement as a government service is an outgrowth of an agency's mission to implement policy through the application of its laws and regulations.

Defenses to
CE Actions

Using Civil
Injunctions

Criminal
Prosecution

Administrative
Remedies

Selection of
Remedies

Investigating
Cases

Managing Code
Enforcement

Regulatory
mentation

Regulatory
Foundations

Introduction

Local Regulatory Implementation

After the basic constitutional authority and land use regulatory scheme are in place, the next step for an agency is to apply these statutes and ordinances when responding to specific community issues. This step is commonly referred to as regulatory implementation.

At the moment an issue or need requiring a new regulation is identified, the local legislative body has the combined responsibility to provide both the law—through the enactment of a regulation or group of regulatory amendments—and the enforcement resources to meet the defined need. Since in any given situation politics may run high, a thoughtful approach is necessary to achieve success for the organization, its leaders, and its constituency.

Since in any given situation politics may run high, a thoughtful approach is necessary to achieve success for the organization, its leaders, and its constituency.

A. Assessing Local Regulatory Needs

Needs are identified in one of two ways. The first results from the agency's own planning and strategic self-assessment. In the past, this form of internally produced problem identification has been referred to as 'proactive'. The second, often called 'reactive', is when a party outside the agency identifies the need. An agency which has a strong planning and land use enforcement agenda, with its mission well-tuned to the community, will attempt to build such consensus in establishing its strategic plans that little distinction between these sources will exist.

Some Sources of Agency-Generated Needs—
- Residual issues from planning and legislative hearing processes
- Legislator's election promises and platform issues
- Issues identified during the budget process
- Observations of agency field staff and management

Some Sources of Neighborhood-Generated Needs—

- Cataclysmic community event
- Unmet public issues identified during the planning and budget processes
- Issues identified by the media

B. Regulatory Response

Regulations represent a response by an agency to an identified need. While directed at a specific issue or event, a regulatory response must still fit within the framework of the enabling and policy documents which provide for the response.

1. Agency Mission

A well-developed and publicly involved planning and policy process will lead naturally to the promulgation of regulatory controls anticipating a community's needs.

A well-developed and publicly involved planning and policy process will lead naturally to the promulgation of regulatory controls anticipating a community's needs. But even when this is not the case, a proposed regulatory response must be tested against the long-range planning and budgetary goals of the agency. Adopting special purpose regulations inconsistent with the overarching aims of an agency will diffuse and weaken the ability to meet its goals.

2. Local Policy

Enforcement as a government service is an outgrowth of an agency's mission to implement policy through the application of its laws and regulations. Often, local policy is enacted on an issue-by-issue basis, simultaneously with the passage of new laws or in response to a singular crisis event. However, key policies which lead to enforcement often come from goals and directions contained in a comprehensive policy statement, such as a local General Plan.

California State Law (Government Code section 65300) requires that municipal level governments prepare comprehensive long term General Plans. General Plans are primarily used to depict future land use and community development objectives. In this respect, code enforcement is not usually a primary aim of a General Plan. However, the General Plan is integral to the enforcement process. This occurs initially in establishing the policy background for regulations, subsequently in providing justification for enforcement activities to violators, and finally in demonstrating to the court that a necessary community interest is at stake when an enforcement case is brought forward.

Local Policy Statements and Code Enforcement

Policies are not regulations. Nevertheless, local policy statements can have a marked effect on neighborhood preservation activities and code enforcement programs. These effects can result from the establishment of general plan directives, goal statements, and the derivatives of specific implementing actions.

General Plan Elements. Both mandated and optional general plan elements often create policy for neighborhood preservation which can serve as the mandate for code enforcement activities. Housing element policies may place a premium on the maintenance of the existing affordable housing stock. Similarly, redevelopment elements may seek to bolster capital investments through a parallel enforcement and maintenance program.

Goals Statements. Policies are, essentially, statements of community aspiration in the form of goals and objectives. Some of these goals are either generally or specifically directed to code enforcement. A General Plan housing element goal statement might generally seek the maintenance of a particular location or type of dwelling unit through inspection and enforcement. A more specific conservation element objective might call for the establishment of an enforcement program dedicated to dealing with illegal dumping in designated wetlands.

Implementation Impacts. With each subdivision, each street vacation, each redevelopment action, and each housing project decision, the local agency implements its general plan and dictates its priorities. The ability to establish the linkage between a development project condition and the general plan policy, for example, gives additional credence and background to any subsequent enforcement action. In making choices between competing objectives, the agency also demonstrates its commitment to stated priorities.

Litigation Impacts. The policy statements of a General Plan can have a marked effect on litigation. The General Plan articulates a public policy standard in a manner which casts a particular enforcement action in the light of an action taken to further a necessary public interest. Policy language directed at aesthetics and the removal of blight, for example, may have utility in a court case involving the abatement of an obsolete sign.

3. Legislative Framework

New legislation must be consistent with the regulatory framework. This is especially true when an established scheme of regulation enforcement exists, extending beyond the written format of the existing regulatory code to—

- **Use of Terms**, in a manner consistent with the terms defined in the local code

- **Processing Provisions**, which provide for application, notice, permit issuance, and enforcement not in conflict with those provisions outlined in the code (primarily relating to the administrative transactions between applicants and the agency)

- **Procedures**, which are a logical extension of existing practice and do not confuse members of the public or practitioners who are accustomed to a routine of notice and appeal (primarily relating to decision making on the applications filed)

4. Minimum Reach

Because the local legislative response will apply a new regulation to actual circumstances, the agency at this point must account for the rights of the regulated. The person drafting the regulation must always ask, "Does this regulation do the minimum to meet the intent of the legislative body without interfering with private property rights?"

Does this regulation do the minimum to meet the intent of the legislative body without interfering with private property rights?

Agency staff are often tempted to expand a relatively narrow request for draft legislation into a work program aimed at a broad range of solutions. A question about the city's fence ordinance, say, becomes an opportunity to revise that entire section dealing with gates, materials, design, and all manner of topics not included in the original request. The result? New regulations which impose enforcement on matters which were never at the heart of the legislature's initial discussion. In a sense, a new class of violators are created in response to the agency's intent. The process of incrementally going beyond the stated policy and legislative direction when formulating a legislative response dilutes the enforcement of regulations which are intended merely to respond to a community's key issues and needs.

In a desire to be more precise in controlling land and buildings, a regulation sometimes raises the threshold of willing participation. Where a reasonable, simple, and intuitive regulation may achieve willing compliance and cooperation, as the requirements and general level of difficulty increases, people who would otherwise be willing to comply do not subject themselves to the process. And while the process meets certain legitimate public objectives—in this case, an applicant-funded design review for all structures—the writer of regulations must always understand the ramifications of a given process from the point of view of future applicants.

When drafting regulations, the goal is to meet an expressed need. The regulation itself does nothing. Only in combination with implementation does the legislative response meet a community need. To fulfill this requirement, the process of investigation and analysis must contain the following steps—

Clear Articulation of the Project Goal. A single statement of the need which the regulatory response is designed to meet. It should be a single, written, declarative statement containing an objective measurement of success. For example, "The goal of this project is to reduce neighborhood clutter by the elimination of junk vehicles parked in front yards." Setting attainable goals and meeting them works for both the elected official and the agency staff.

Identification of Interested Parties. Since people and organizations inside and outside the agency will have an interest in the outcome of any legislative effort, all players must be incorporated into the process.

Determining Magnitude. Laws are routinely written without regard for the magnitude of resulting case loads. If the goal is to reduce the number of derelict vehicles in front yards to zero, it is important to know whether the number of such occur-

When drafting regulations, the goal is to meet an expressed need. The regulation itself does nothing. Only in combination with implementation does the legislative response meet a community need.

Who Should Be Involved in a Process to Adopt a Derelict Car Regulation?

- The requestor (a community group)
- The adopting authority (the city council)
- The drafter (the planning department)
- The funding evaluator (the city manager)
- The enforcement agent (the codes compliance department)
- The prosecutor (the district attorney)
- The potential violators (residential property owners)

Involving these parties should not stop with a simple referral. Since these are the parties who will be regulated, it is essential that the agency promote active involvement.

Developing a Team Approach

The adjacent figure is a matrix which addresses the need to provide a regulatory response which involves all necessary interest groups to achieve a project goal. The matrix is a complete planning cycle.

Beginning with the identification of an issue and proceeding through implementation and enforcement to final evaluation, this matrix suggests the scope and timing of involvement. Code enforcers work with those who draft the regulations, attorneys work with interest groups, and the council addresses potential violators with a single goal in mind. If one player works in isolation, the likelihood of successful regulatory response is jeopardized.

In this process, understanding and mutual cooperation are possible. A matrix such as this not only can be adapted to any regulatory response to form the road map for the process, but also alerts all parties to the existence of the larger picture.

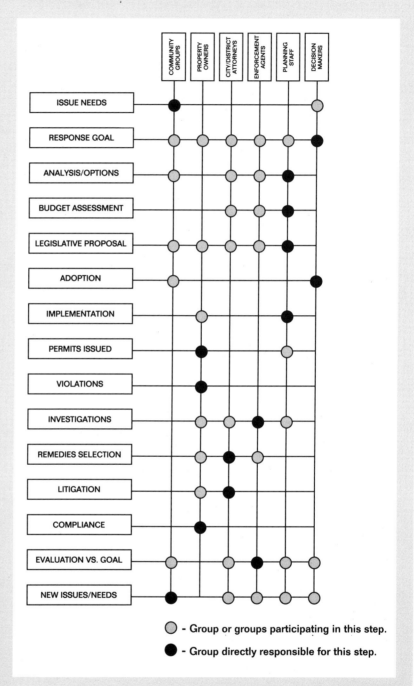

○ - Group or groups participating in this step.

● - Group directly responsible for this step.

rences is 7 or 700. While often written in the interest of "giving code officers another tool," a law not encompassing the magnitude of the problem can only lead to inadequate budgeting for enforcement or the potential abuse of enforcing selectively.

C. Regulatory Criteria

After assessing needs and formulating a scheme of regulatory response comes the actual drafting and adoption of a regulation. It is beyond the scope of this book to provide a detailed primer on regulation writing. However, enforcement agents may find it helpful to understand the principles necessary for well-crafted regulations—not only for an appreciation of comprehensive code enforcement, but also to understand the genesis of the rules they enforce.

Enforcement agents may find it helpful to understand the principles necessary for well-crafted regulations—not only for an appreciation of comprehensive code enforcement, but also to understand the genesis of the rules they enforce.

The scheme for classifying municipal regulations is especially useful, in particular the distinction between 'remedial' and 'prospective' regulations.

1. Remedial Regulations

In some cases newly adopted regulations seek to limit or otherwise regulate uses or structures already in existence. These regulations are usually established to remedy the impacts of an existing use. In this instance, the non-conforming use and structures are not given full, permanent, legitimate status. Some remedial regulations contain abatement procedures whereby, after a specified period within which the value of the use or structure is amortized, the use of the structure must cease. A sign regulation which contains abatement provisions is an example of a remedial regulation. Similarly, building codes requiring the reinforcement of older, unreinforced masonry buildings prior to a set deadline have a remedial effect in increasing the earthquake safety of these structures.

2. Prospective Regulations

Most regulations are prospective. That is, the regulation acts on those uses and structures which are begun after the adoption of the regulation. Examples of prospective regulations abound, and include the rezoning of property or the establishment or revision of permit processes.

Within the family of prospective regulations, three basic paths exist: discretionary permit processes, ministerial permit processes, and matters where permits are not required but where the agency retains the authority to regulate.

Discretionary Permit Process. A discretionary process exists where the local agency establishes and retains or delegates the authority to approve, conditionally approve, or disapprove a use or structure based on both objective and subjective criteria within a publicly accessible process. Out of necessity, a discretionary process must also contain the findings upon which the issuing entity will judge the application. These findings are declarative statements of anticipated future facts, such as: "The proposed use will be consistent with the General Plan," or "The proposed center will not create an over-concentration of similar facilities in the immediate neighborhood."

Rezoning of property and the subdivision of land are common forms of legislative and quasi-judicial discretion. The discretionary actions which are usually at the center of a code enforcement matter, however, are those in which a conditioned permission is given, such as a planned unit development or a conditional use permit. Discretionary approvals allow for flexibility and public discussion, which in turn often lead to tailored conditions responding to issues raised by a particular use, structure, or locale. These tailored permits are granted in accordance with procedures established in the enabling legislation. Within pre-established parameters, the issuing authority is left to determine one, several, or all of the following—

- **Where** or to what site within the jurisdiction the permission is granted
- **What** use the permission allows
- **When** or the life span of the permission and under what conditions it may be halted or discontinued
- **Who** may operate or occupy the use or building and whether the permission is transferable
- **How** the use may be conducted in terms of its site plan, building design, and performance conditions

To the extent that the enabling legislation does not pre-establish any of these areas of discretion, if the permit is to be enforceable, the issuing authority must specifically address the determination of that criteria.

Before initiating a discretionary process, a note of caution is necessary. An agency will occasionally defer final regulation and put a discretionary process in place as a quick fix because the broad processes afford latitude. Wherever possible, a straightforward ministerial process, backed by objective criteria, is a much stronger and ultimately fairer approach than issuing a number of unique permits under varying degrees of case-by-case discretion.

Objective, ministerial control is usually a much stronger and ultimately fairer approach than issuing a number of unique permits under varying degrees of case-by-case discretion.

Avoiding the Beaver Cleaver Trap

When a zoning regulation is written, most planners envision an 'average' circumstance to which the regulation will apply. For example, if an ordinance amendment is proposed for a single-family zone, everybody sees Beaver Cleaver's house. We imagine a two-story house—with a detached garage, on a flat rectangular mid-block parcel fronted by a standard curb and gutter—or some closely related variant. While this is not an unreasonable premise, the person responsible should test the draft regulation against a random batch of plans from the building department—a half dozen will do if the plans show some variety. Better yet, ask the plan checkers in the department to measure the regulation against the plans. Many surprising, unintended results of regulation can be avoided by such real-world testing.

Ministerial Permit Process. In a ministerial process, permission results from a simple applicant-to-agency transaction involving objective or quantitative criteria which, when met, obligates the issuance of permission. A commonly cited ministerial process is the issuance of a building permit where the structure and use conforms in all respects to the criteria of the zone and the applicable building codes. In land use matters, ministerial process relies on the existence of established and universally measurable objective standards which speak generically to the questions WHERE, WHAT, HOW, and (infrequently) WHO, as those terms are described above. Since little opportunity will exist for site-by-site consideration, objectivity in ordinance provisions requires a precise understanding of the regulated operation. A measurement becomes absolute: a setback of 10'-0" both guarantees the right to build at that or a greater distance and also guarantees at least the technical enforceability of the ordinance against any construction which does not meet that dimension.

Carefully written language establishing a ministerial process for the agency is probably the most secure enforcement position for two reasons—

    ▪   Unlike discretionary actions, the criteria are measurable and discrete, and are not as likely to be subject to misapplication by a decision-making body

    ▪   Unlike nonpermit matters where an act of permission is not required, the transaction of issuing a permit allows for agency involvement prior to the establishment of a structure or use

Shall or Should?

The word 'should' has almost no place in an ordinance or permit. Should represents a statement of policy, as in: "Houses in this district should be built no nearer to the street than ten feet from the curb line." Compare this to the implementing ordinance which might state: "Street setbacks, measured perpendicularly from face of curb, shall be 10'0". Note that the ordinance statement contains a defined term (setback), the method of measurement (perpendicularly from face of curb), and an unambiguous way of writing ten feet (10'0"). And most importantly, the implementing ministerial provision uses the word, 'shall'.

Recision

Because it is most important from an enforcement perspective, and the least often addressed, special attention should be focused on the 'When' criteria. To be effective, a special permit process should establish three horizons of recision: voiding, or recision prior to the exercise of the permit by the applicant; non-compliance, or recision during the exercise of the permit by the agency; and closure, or recision after the exercise of the permit by the applicant. Terms and conditions for each of these three horizons are needed to answer the 'what if' questions in a contractual fashion.

The recision of a permission is a powerful enforcement tool. When evoked, it adds to the charges that may be brought against a violator, and provides for an administrative remedy which may be employed within an agency without having to enter the court system. The recision of a permission also adds to the charges against a violator when the matter proceeds to litigation. If the enabling regulation provides, recision can be a part of a remedial regulation or a ministerial process. However, recision is most often an element of enforcement within the realm of discretionary permits.

To be effective, a discretionary permit process should establish three horizons of recision: voiding, or recision prior to the exercise of the permit by the applicant; non-compliance, or recision during the exercise of the permit by the agency; and closure, or recision after the exercise of the permit by the applicant. Terms and conditions for each of these three horizons are needed to answer the "what if" questions in a contractual fashion.

"What if"...the approval is given and not exercised by the applicant in a timely manner? Then the permit is voided.

"What if"...the applicant does not perform the functions permitted in the manner prescribed by the terms and conditions? Then, with due process the permit can be rescinded for non-compliance.

"What if"...the applicant establishes the permitted activity and then goes out of business or wishes to change locations? Then certain procedures of site clearing or reuse adaptation or recording of closure documents with the agency are required.

Nonpermit Process. The final category of prospective regulation involves those uses or structures for which the agency does not require a permit to be issued, but for which some form of objective standard is established. For example, most agencies regulate the height and location of fences within various zones, but do not require a permit for constructing the fence. Similarly, the establishment of a particular use on a property often occurs without the issuance of a permit and relies on the due diligence and judgment of the individual establishing the use to conform to requirements of the zone. When a property owner constructs a building or uses the property contrary to local regulations, the agency's first transaction with the owner or user is usually by way of code enforcement. In these instances, it is critical that the agency adopt regulations that are both reasonable and intuitive. Following commonly practiced community standards, a reasonable individual should have a high probability of intuitively meeting the standards of a nonpermit process regulation. The regulation should screen for clear abuse, not for subtle non-conformity.

A regulation should screen for clear abuse, not for subtle non-conformity.

D. Enforceability vs. Defensibility

In reviewing the proposed regulatory response, a regulation should be looked at from the perspective of defensibility and enforceability. Defensibility speaks to the ability of the ordinance to withstand the challenge of constitutional or statutory litigation. Besides including all of the standards of reasonableness and a relationship to the provisions of higher-level enabling and controlling legislation, defensibility means that the new regulatory response is not challengeable on the basis of constitutionality or preemption.

Enforceability also refers to an agency's ability to achieve the aims of a regulation when faced with an enforcement action. Enforceability speaks to the ease with which an agency can enforce a regulation on its own terms in the field so that the regulation will prevail in those case-by-case matters which may eventually have to be litigated.

Enforceability also refers to an agency's ability to achieve the aims of a regulation when faced with an enforcement action.

For purposes of field enforcement, clean and objective standards are crucial. Knowing the purpose and intent of a regulation, which derives from a clearly established goal, will also help in field enforcement, since the reason for a regulation can be straightforwardly presented to the violator.

E. Agency Organization and Budget: Calculating the Cost of Regulation

How an adopted regulation affects an agency's budget ought to be of primary concern. But, somewhat astoundingly, one large municipal jurisdiction once calculated the fiscal impact of each new regulation in just this fashion—

Preparation of Ordinance	$1,700
Notice and Process	750
Review by city attorney	1,000
TOTAL	$3,450

This estimate was, alas, only for placing a law on the books. Arriving at some useful suppositions which will allow a legislative authority to know what costs are associated with a regulatory act is not that difficult. The form below contains an expanded list of cost centers which must be evaluated by all parties to the legislation, filled in with some reasonable estimates, and totalled.

A factor to consider when estimating the cost of enforcement is that the few most difficult cases require the greatest expenditures. The costs of preparing legislation vary greatly depending on the issue. For the purpose of a minor and non-controversial item,

---

Cost Estimation Form for a New Regulation

Initiation Costs (One-time Expenditures)

Issue Analysis	$_____
Statement of Goal	$_____
Formulating Alternatives	$_____
Preliminary Approach/Proposed Regulation	$_____
Assessment of Impact	$_____
Tests on Plans	
Calculation of Recurring Costs	
Legal Review	$_____
Administrative Costs: Hearings and Notice	$_____
TOTAL =	$_____

Recurring Costs (Continuing Expenditures)

Permit Volume Anticipated (_____)

Unit Cost to Process and/or Issue	$_____
Unit Cost to Monitor and/or Enforce	$_____
Unit Costs x Volume = Permit Subtotal	$_____

Violations and/or Non-Conformings
    Anticipated (_____)

Unit Cost to Investigate	$_____
Unit Cost to Enforce	$_____
Unit Cost for Attorney Referral	$_____
Unit Cost for Litigation	$_____
Unit Costs x Volume = Violation Subtotal	$_____
TOTAL =	$_____

the simple categories listed on the form may be adequate. However, using a base estimate of a few thousand dollars must be with the knowledge that a complex issue requiring lots of community meetings and aggravation can be many times that amount.

The remainder of the form is devoted to the actual implemention costs of a regulatory response. Offending uses or structures can be counted in the case of remedial regulations. For prospective ordinances, anticipated events must be estimated. Where discretionary actions result from a regulation, two calculations are needed: an estimate of the permits to be issued and an estimate of the percentage of those permits subsequently requiring enforcement actions. Some guesswork is surely involved. However, it is critical to assessing the impact on the budget—and to the quality of the legislation itself—that some estimate of violations and transactions be a step in the process of drafting new legislation.

Costs and percentages will vary with the type of enforcement and specific local regulations, but at each step in the enforcement process the minority of cases are closed and few move forward. Conversely, the few cases that move through the process to litigation take up an extraordinary portion of the agency's enforcement budget. The relatively inexpensive act of investigating complaints, which must be done in any case, accounts for a third of the sample budget. More difficult administrative steps of enforcement and preparing a case for referral to litigation, which deal with about a quarter of the caseload, takes up another third. Finally, litigation, which is required in only about five percent of the cases, takes up the final third of the sample budget.

> ### Why Fines Don't Fund Code Enforcement
>
> Staff are often asked if the implementation of new legislation can be funded by the fines or forfeitures generated by enforcement. Looking at a maximum misdemeanor fine of $1,000, the idea of doing the public good with funds contributed by scofflaws is very appealing. In fact, enforcement loses money. Municipal-level courts, which are a division of county government, collect misdemeanor fines. Thus, the court's direct costs and county overhead have first call on all fines collected, and the percentage returned to the originating local agency is quite small. Taken into the city's general fund, as is generally the practice, this amount is not earmarked for return to the originating department.

Generalized Case Cost by Process Step
(for 100 cases investigated)

	Cases	Unit Cost	Budget
(HARDEST)			
Litigation	5	$ 5,000	$ 25,000
Referral to Attorney	10	$ 1,000	$ 10,000
Enforcement	25	$ 500	$ 12,500
Investigation/Inspection	100	$ 250	$ 25,000
(EASIEST)			

F. Special Permits as Stand–Alone Regulation

In a discretionary process the permit document which permits the use or development of a site will have to meet the enforcement test as if it were a regulation all its own. Additional responsibilities attach to enforceable discretionary processes which create both opportunities and vulnerabilities. The opportunities are well appreciated by city councils and other local legislators: discretionary permits allow a case-by-case consideration that defers decision making until the factors and potential impacts of an action are known.

The vulnerability of special permits, particularly from an enforcement standpoint, is that the same tailoring that allows their flexibility also opens them to challenge as discriminatory or arbitrary. Further, special discretionary permits often provide the opportunity for crafting conditions during the permit process by the applicant, the issuing department, and the final decision-making board or council. This can lead to conditions of approval which, while clear when the participants were around the table, are hopelessly ambiguous to the inspector in the field and absolutely incomprehensible to a city attorney or judge when litigated.

Regulatory Conditions of Approval. Conditions of approval are similar to contracts. A violation of a condition is a violation of a permit issued pursuant to the municipal code. As such, a condition must meet all the tests of legality and defensibility. Conditions must reflect 'shall' language, and must be both measurable and objective. To the extent possible, an agency should adopt a list of standard conditions which are attached to all discretionary permits, covering such issues as the recision criteria and process.

A violation of a condition is a violation of a permit issued pursuant to the municipal code. As such, a condition must meet all the tests of legality and defensibility.

Self-Enforcing Conditions. Just because a condition is a contractual regulation does not mean that a certain amount of self-enforcement can't be built into those conditions. Self-enforcing conditions include requiring performance of certain tasks prior to the issuance of a subsequent permission (perhaps the simplest example is inspection prior to issuing a business license or permit to occupy). Other self-enforcing conditions tie the commencement of the use permitted by a discretionary permit to another approval (for example, a use permit for a day care facility is not valid until the delivery of proof that state licenses have been issued).

Security. Another means by which a permit can be enforced on its own terms is through security agreements. Some agencies use completion bonding or irrevocable letters of credit as a combination of funding source and monetary penalty to insure certain performances by the applicant. These have been applied to the requirement to install and maintain landscaping.

Realistic Design. Similarly, the discretionary process should not become a vehicle for non-standard and unworkable design solutions. Most model ordinances and ministerial codes, which

Recognizing the Hopeless
Condition of Approval

A conditional use permit was issued requiring, among other things, that "Noise in the outdoor patio area will be monitored, and the applicant shall make all reasonable effort to avoid disruption to the neighborhood." While it may have satisfied the neighbors at the moment that the permission was approved, this condition is not likely to keep the area quiet. It certainly won't provide much guidance to the code enforcement officer, because it asks more questions than it answers. Who will do the monitoring? What is the criteria for the monitoring? What constitutes "all reasonable effort," and is that judgment left to the applicant alone? What is a "disruption," and is that judgment left to the neighbors alone?

The condition is subjective and unenforceable. If it had been written that "The permit shall be revoked if more than two complaints for noise are received by the issuing agency in any calendar month," it would certainly comprise an objective standard, but it would also be arbitrary and probably unfair to the applicant. Maybe a better and fairer condition for the permit might require monitoring by the issuing agency with a standard of audibility from a prescribed distance: "Noise generated on the patio at any time shall not be audible for a person of normal hearing acuity, from any point in excess of 100 feet from the patio." Such a condition is probably enforceable and defensible. Now the only problems will be the complaint calls at 11:00 PM on a Friday night and finding an inspector with normal hearing acuity to respond to the noise complaints from the neighbors!

may seem mundane to a forward-thinking city planner, have derived from a long history of trial and error which has balanced project performance against equity for builders of those projects. When these established standards are compromised in a discretionary process, enforcement or performance problems often result. Some examples include—

- ▓ **Access, Maneuvering, and Parking.** When a discretionary permit allows for 'tight' maneuvering and parking, residents and users often find ad hoc solutions. Turfed or hardscaped emergency accesses become favored as guest parking, and storage shows up in the inaccessible spaces in underground garages.

When these established standards are compromised in a discretionary process, enforcement or performance problems often result.

Unique structural designs are often proposed in a discretionary process.

■ **Landscaping**. Viable landscaped areas large enough to support vegetation must be created, which will not be 'bricked in' as time and inconvenience take their toll.

■ **Fill-ins and Lofts**. Unique structural designs are often proposed in a discretionary process. Conditions in discretionary permits must indicate limitations on use and reuse of structures by future owners so that mezzanines do not later become office lofts, thereby aggravating available parking.

■ **Maintenance Accessibility**. Authorities issuing permits must be cognizant of the maintenance issues which desired structures and uses present. If a landscape is to be maintained in perpetuity, the project design must provide access to the area. The maintenance provisions and modification requirements for lakes, fountains, and unique artwork or landscapes must be clearly specified.

G. Administrative Effect of Discretionary Legislation

The Subdivision Map Act specifies the means for issuing a particular discretionary approval, the subdivision of land. Due to its specificity of application, notice process, and findings, the Map Act has often been used as a model for the development of permit processes for special uses. A key difference between the Map Act and other discretionary provisions involves record keeping. Because the Map Act process creates new land parcels which enter the property tax rolls, all participants in the process have the luxury of county records. Further, the final map is its own reward for fulfilling the conditions of tentative approval. This model does not transfer to other discretionary processes, where record management is entirely the responsibility of the issuing agency. From the viewpoint of enforcement this is especially critical, because records are the basis for all regulatory control of property and the fulfillment of a performance agreement between a property owner and the issuing agency.

This record keeping includes—

■ The consolidation of files

■ Plan check of new structures constructed pursuant to a permit being issued

■ Progress inspections in the event of change orders in the field or conflict with requirements of other agencies

■ The ability to retrieve previously approved permits for the purpose of reviewing performance of conditions

■ Field inspection of structures, appurtenances, and special features

It is usually the intent of the agency that all of these elements of record keeping are to be cost-recoverable. This usually takes the form of an overhead cost—factored into the application fee to cover plan checks, field inspections during construction, and the management of the record system. For other actions, such as records access, investigation, and enforcement a direct service charge can be instituted. The burden of quality assurance and near-permanent record keeping, as well as the cost (though annually small on any given permit), must be tracked by the implementing department and should be understood when determining a regulatory response. Discretionary and special permits are particularly inefficient from an enforcement viewpoint, due to the need to research individual cases and to interpret the specific intent of special conditions. Such research and interpretation adds to the costs of enforcement.

Discretionary and special permits are particularly inefficient from an enforcement viewpoint, due to the need to research individual cases and to interpret the specific intent of special conditions.

H. Process Evaluation

Process evaluation, as discussed here, specifically relates to regulatory response. Since setting goals is the first step of regulatory response, evaluating the process by which those goals have been achieved forms a natural endpoint.

As the project matrix on page 34 indicates, the key participants in the process of formulating and carrying out the regulatory response are reconvened for the purpose of answering the following questions—

- Was the original goal of the response met?
- Were our estimations of case units and costs reasonable?
- When applied, did the regulation successfully provide the basis for enforcement and conformance?
- Were there unintended side effects from the regulation or its implementation?
- Did budget issues arise? Was the transfer of resources appropriate?
- What were the case success rates? What was the average time necessary to close an enforcement case? At the rate of closure, how long would it have taken to achieve increased percentages of compliance?
- What lessons can be applied to other programs or to the agency's general procedures and policies?

3 Managing Code Enforcement

The objective of this chapter is to identify and respond to the management issues confronting code enforcement programs of varying size in diverse environments.

Introduction

Regulatory Foundations

Local Regulatory Implementation

Managing Code Enforcement

Investigating Cases

Selection of Remedies

Administrative Remedies

Criminal Prosecution

Using Civil Injunctions

Defenses to CE Actions

Managing Code Enforcement

With the enactment of regulations comes the necessity to establish those organizations charged with the responsibility to carry out enforcement. Code enforcement organizations require unique management responses related to the service they perform.

Most agencies assign responsibility for the investigation of code enforcement cases to a specialized division or unit of building inspectors, zoning investigators, or code compliance officers, generically referred to as 'enforcement agents'. Some agencies accomplish their mission through one classification of code compliance officers that responds to citizen complaints of alleged building, zoning, noise, and litter violations. Other agencies employ a more specialized approach, vesting investigative authority in a variety of city departments.

The precise composition and organization will vary among jurisdictions, depending on the size of the agency, the number and types of code enforcement problems to be addressed, the needs assessment and policies which have been established, and of course the local agency's budget. Whatever code enforcement system is employed, the same fundamental management and investigation issues arise.

Because they already have a program and various policies and procedures in place, most agencies do not have the luxury of designing an enforcement program from scratch. Although the existing system may work well, enforcement agencies are coming under increasing pressure to do more things with less staff and resources, not a rarity for local government during the 1990s. The objective of this chapter, then, is to identify and respond to some of the management issues confronting code enforcement programs of varying size in diverse environments.

Because they already have a program and various policies and procedures in place, most agencies do not have the luxury of designing an enforcement program from scratch.

A. Organizational Structure: Generalists vs. Specialists

Smaller agencies provide a good illustration of the generalist model of organization for code enforcement. Here only a portion of a staff position may be assigned the enforcement responsibility for a number of regulatory areas. These often include zoning, litter, building, and basic permit requirements for health-regulated businesses. Smaller agencies can use the generalist approach effectively because the land area of the jurisdiction is contained, the case load is moderate, and typical code enforcement cases may be straightforward. When addressing a complex case that might involve expertise in the fire, building, or health codes, a smaller agency generally relies on personnel from those municipal divisions.

Smaller agencies can use the generalist approach effectively because the land area of the jurisdiction is contained, the case load is moderate, and typical code enforcement cases may be straightforward.

In contrast, the specialist model commonly used in larger jurisdictions divides enforcement authority into a number of units for specific types of problems. This model uses separate staff specialists for enforcement in the fields of zoning, building inspection, housing, litter, health, fire prevention, signs, planning permits, and environmentally sensitive resources. The specialist system is able to marshal the expertise of different inspectors. If multiple violations affecting several specialties are found to exist in a certain instance, specialists can be brought together on a particular issue or location.

In some situations, state and local ordinances demand certifications—for example, only a certified health inspector can enforce certain laws relating to food service establishments and the State Housing Law. Even though it has the advantage of expertise, the specialist approach can create confusion if activities of the various specialists are not coordinated effectively. Stories abound of different investigators arriving at different times, crawling over the same property to issue separate notices of violation, each with different compliance needs and separate deadlines.

B. Code Enforcement Coordination

Usually, agencies have certain aspects of both generalist and specialist models in their code enforcement programs, which underscores the need for effective coordination among the different units and divisions. Coordination must be under a recognized leader with the authority either to direct or coordinate staff assignments. Further, coordination must occur early in the process—at the initial complaint and disposition—and continue through completion of the code enforcement cycle.

Community-Oriented Policing

With the advent of community-oriented policing, internal coordination within the official city structure is becoming increasingly important. This method of crime prevention and community outreach attempts to establish relationships between the police department and the neighborhood through one-on-one interaction between officers and residents.

As more police departments employ the problem-solving principles associated with community-oriented policing, code enforcement can assist officers in ridding neighborhoods of eyesores that attract criminals.

Cooperative code enforcement might target a vacant, abandoned building operating as a haven for local drug dealers. In most communities, while they can be trained to identify possible violations, police officers are not equipped to do actual code enforcement and will need to rely on the expertise of a fire, building, zoning, or health inspector to achieve a neighborhood's objectives. To coordinate efforts, police and enforcement divisions have a strong impetus to develop written policies that clearly define their roles and how they work together.

Written policies concerning enforcement coordination should identify: (1) The rationale for selection of an enforcement unit which will serve as lead agent; and (2) how communication between units is to be handled.

Written policies should identify the rationale for selecting an enforcement unit to serve as lead agent and how communication between units is to be handled.

Coordination is especially necessary with elements of agencies not considered part of the traditional code compliance process, such as police and fire departments. In some instances, a case may call for the special statutory authority represented by these departments and their officers, while in others code compliance officers might represent a relatively inexpensive way to respond to community issues without draining the time of uniformed law enforcement services. Integrating code compliance specialists into overall law enforcement service delivery can be cost-effective. This approach has been used successfully by fire departments for years, but historically has been neglected by police departments.

C. Scope of Code Enforcement Services

Most local agencies respond to enforcement issues on a 'complaint-only' basis. While possibly satisfying the complainant, this method is not necessarily an effective use of limited resources.

Strategic Planning as an Enforcement Tool

The use of a strategic plan is relatively new to local government. Used extensively in private business as a means to assess market needs and design products, in the management of local government the strategic plan is designed to—

- Inventory issues
- Establish priorities
- Allocate resources
- Assign responsibility
- Set measurable goals
- Evaluate success

These steps make it possible to respond to the threats and opportunities that a code enforcement manager faces. To carry out its objectives, the strategic plan may allocate personnel and resources in a manner which crosses traditional departmental lines. In a larger agency some areas where a strategic plan may be useful include—

Assigning Team Responsibilities. Since two components of a strategic plan involve assigning responsibility for tasks and providing resources throughout the organization, the strategic plan is an excellent vehicle for the establishment of multi-departmental teams for code enforcement.

Geographic–Based Enforcement. The strategic plan might designate an area where a prescribed code enforcement effort is needed. This is often the case when identifying blighted neighborhoods within redevelopment areas, but is also applicable to areas where a sustained effort could keep the neighborhood from falling into blight.

Object–Based Enforcement. The strategic plan might also identify particular types of code compliance issues which are more broadly distributed throughout a community. This is commonly the case with sign abatement and the regulation of 'adult' businesses.

Establishing Priorities. The strategic plan can also be the vehicle for establishing priorities among competing community preservation needs. This is especially useful for balancing geographic– and category–based programs, which can have widely dissimilar characteristics.

Specialized and proactive code enforcement programs are more likely to develop the expertise and efficiency to respond to the objectives of an agency and its constituents.

Code enforcement programs which are specialized and proactive are more likely to develop the expertise and efficiency to respond to the issues and objectives which are the goal of an agency and its constituents.

When setting overall priorities, an agency can achieve a greater degree of efficiency by precisely targeting programs. They fall into two categories—

Geographic. Geographic targeting focuses enforcement resources on a specific area or district within a jurisdiction. The target area may have a high incidence of a particular type of violation or a higher density of violations than other neighborhoods. By targeting the area, enforcement agents become familiar with the neighborhood and the nature and nuances of its cases, allowing agencies to realize efficiencies of investigation and case management.

Object. Object targeting focuses enforcement resources on a particular issue, which might include sign abatement, mobile homes, or closely regulated businesses. Again, efficiency results from specialization and familiarity gained regarding the type of violation, the applicable regulations and the means for gaining compliance.

Accomplishing code enforcement efficiency in this manner is well suited to agencies with distinct goals for combating deterioration. These methods fit well into a program of strategic planning, where response to chronic problems can result in a greater overall degree of citizen satisfaction than simple one-on-one resolution of complaints.

D. Code Enforcement Budgeting

An agency budget clearly needs to provide for the enforcement of those policies, laws, and standards which are adopted as a part of the annual work program. This can be done by integrating code enforcement into ongoing activities or providing specialized enforcement in the context of an agency's strategic plan, discussed above. It also includes making enforcement a part of new public/ private partnership agreements and tapping volunteerism.

Integration. Integrating the recovery of code enforcement costs as part of the budget process should occur when issuing a permit or taking a discretionary action. Including code enforcement charges in the accounting system for permit processing should be as routine as any element of overhead commonly attached to such permits, with larger permits and development agreements containing their own ongoing maintenance/enforcement clauses.

Ongoing enforcement agreements are already becoming a part of the California Environmental Quality Act's mitigation monitoring process, where items such as wetlands restoration are subject to long-term review and management. In addition, projects funded from grants and programs should have reserve allocations to protect the investment through enforcement. Clearly, where allowed by law, redevelopment and block grant projects designed to save neighborhoods from deterioration are candi-

An agency budget clearly needs to provide for the enforcement of those policies, laws, and standards which are adopted as a part of the annual work program.

Project First Class
Evaluating the Efficiency of a Proactive Program

To paraphrase Will Rogers, in the 1980s the City of San Diego learned that it could enforce all of the municipal code in some of the places and some of the code in all of the places, but not all of the municipal code in all of the places. For this reason, beginning in 1984, the city established proactive code compliance teams to complement a neighborhood revitalization program. The first of these programs was called 'Project First Class', a zoning and building code violation sweep. This program used the careful identification of community issues, a limited regulatory response, and proactive code enforcement to provide spectacularly efficient neighborhood improvement. The program targeted glaring violations in an area comprising about five percent of the city, leading to the following comparison for the fiscal year of 1985/1986—

	Project First Class	City-wide Zoning
Closed Cases	1217	1318
Cases Closed through—		
Courtesy Contact	50%	10%
Notice/Litigation	50%	90%
Cases Closed per Staff Position Year*	405	188
Staff Hours per Case Closed	4.2	6.1

* Reflects the fact that city-wide zoning investigators had duties other than enforcement, which diluted field strength.

The table reflects a number of things about the program. First, the high rate of closing after a courtesy contact, signifying the initial interaction with the violator, is an indication that the proactive program allows investigators to develop an understanding of the violators and a familiarity with the target area—which lessens litigation and intransigence.

Second, the staff hours per case reflects the efficiency of working a target 'sweep' area as opposed responding to complaints at various addresses within a city. Coupled with the high courtesy contact closure rate, this efficiency is achieved without degrading the quality of customer contact and service. In many instances it reflects little more than less driving time to work on a number of cases in a concentrated area.

Finally, the cases per position year shows the efficiency of specialization and concentration with Project First Class. By contrast, the city-wide zoning investigator was not only required to respond to reactive code compliance cases, but also served rotations in other zoning functions, fractionalizing the time that could be spent to close a case.

Over time the successful evolution of proactive programs has led to the establishment of separate code enforcement units within the office of the city attorney and in various implementing city departments, culminating in the establishment in 1992 of a separate code enforcement department within the city itself.

Common Interest Development Laws

In California, a growing body of legislation deals with such 'common interest developments' as condominium projects and cooperative housing. Much of this legislation is contained within section 1350 *et seq.* of the State Civil Code, often referred to as the Davis–Stirling Act. Directed at all matters related to common interest development management, the Act includes a number of provisions clarifying the authority of the boards of such developments to enforce private covenants.

For example, recent amendments require mediation or alternative dispute resolution techniques (many of which are discussed in Chapter 6) prior to the assessment of penalties or the filing of litigation against a member by the association's board. In addition, the Community Associations Institute (CAI) has been established to organize, inform, and train both professional property managers and volunteer homeowner association board members. While the CAI is a national organization, California provides its primary membership base. Because of this, the CAI has a particular interest in the Davis–Stirling Act and other legislative initiatives dealing with common interest developments.

CAI = Community Associations Institute

Both the Davis–Stirling Act and the CAI are resources which can factor into the structuring of public/private partnerships involving common interest developments.

dates for a *situs* or target area enforcement funding reserves. But projects in areas not considered blighted should also contain provisions for ongoing enforcement and code management.

Public/Private Partnerships. The burgeoning number of planned unit developments taking the form of condominium projects and cooperatives has led to controls on land use being shared increasingly by private property managers and municipal agencies. In the past, private covenants and restrictions have been enforced solely by the manager on behalf of users and owners. As the scope of developments has grown, developers and managers of long-term projects have come to see the private enforcement of maintenance covenants as an important way to add value to future phases of development. This allows a public agency to avoid much of the enforcement cost in the early phases of a long-term project. Since maintaining the overall built environment is ultimately a public goal, however, partnerships should be considered for these private restrictions to provide for ongoing public stewardship.

Volunteer efforts have traditionally been directed towards issues of blight, such as graffiti and litter.

To prevent volunteers from crossing the boundary and becoming vigilantes, the agency should coordinate a training program and maintain an active presence.

Tapping Volunteerism. In neighborhoods where compliance is a substantial public issue, volunteerism is usually available as a powerful element of a code enforcement program. This form of community activism knows no social or economic stratification, and exists in some form almost everywhere. Incorporating volunteerism in the budgeting process accomplishes two positive objectives—

- It provides direct access between citizens with the most demonstrated interest and the municipal service provider, creating teamwork
- Citizen energy is channeled into carefully crafted programs to produce vivid results

Volunteer efforts have traditionally been directed towards issues of blight, such as graffiti and litter. But citizen involvement can be cost-effective when planning and implementing most programs of code compliance. By themselves, volunteers cannot constitute an enforcement program. To prevent volunteers from crossing the boundary and becoming vigilantes, the agency should coordinate a training program and maintain an active presence. Despite this expense, the use of volunteers is a worthwhile and probably necessary element of any enforcement program.

E. Training

Code enforcement agents come to their profession from many backgrounds. Some are from the construction trades, some from planning, and some from law enforcement. This diversity is healthy, but it demands that an enforcement agency have uniform training. An ongoing staff screening and training regimen should be composed of the following elements—

Training in the Objectives and Policies of the Agency. The first step in the training of most new employees is a general orientation to the mission, values, and culture of the organization, which could extend from something as basic as the location of the coffee machine to the overarching reason the agency exists. Clearly, it is important for managers and supervisors to learn the agency's objectives and values from the outset, so that the organization can be more effective.

Training in the Code to Be Enforced. The most simple and straightforward, training in the code itself is often the sole component of a program. A zoning investigator may learn how to measure dimensional standards such as height and floor area ratio. For building, fire code, and public health inspectors, the requirements of the various uniform codes and their practical application is the obvious training, and, in some cases, this includes certification requirements.

Training in Use of Enforcement Options. An agency resolves many of its cases by issuing informal notices and courtesy contacts. In those cases where voluntary compliance is not forthcoming, an agency can use a host of administrative and judicial remedies. Supervisors and field staff should be thoroughly familiar with agency policies about when to use and how to process various enforcement options. As part of this training, an agency also needs to stress collegial relations between agency staff and municipal attorneys, the city manager's staff, councilmembers and other city departments.

Training in the General Laws of Enforcement. An agency with field enforcement personnel not versed in basic constitutional and statutory provisions can accrue great liability. In California, many agencies take advantage of peace officer training programs (known by their Penal Code authority as PC 836 training) which provide non-police agency personnel with a basic background in the power of arrest and apprehension.

Training in Public/Customer Relations. Since code enforcement is, in large part, the process of achieving compliance through a transaction between an agency and a violator, public relations plays a large role in an agency's success. A complete training program will include public relations as a discrete, acknowledged element. Viewing this more as a merchandising problem, some agencies have gone so far as to seek the assistance of sales trainers for the purpose of improving compliance through customer relations.

F. Enforcement Discretion

Managing code enforcement agencies and departments is an administrative act, much of which lies outside the particular language of the regulation being implemented. Within a code enforcement operation, many elements of implementation are legally the province of the enforcement agency manager.

1. Determination of Significance

All code violations do not need to be corrected. If a 6'½" fence exists where 6'0" is the standard, it is unlikely that anyone would find the violation significant or worthy of the expenditure of an agency's resources—anyone, that is, except the complaining next door neighbor. In these instances, individual inspectors must be armed with the discrete and agency-endorsed authority to declare that, although a technical violation exists, the

---

Rotational Training

In a larger agency, creating opportunities for experience can improve the training performance of enforcement employees. For example, a rotational scheme could allow field personnel to staff public counters as a way to understand the code and its application from a difference perspective. A more extensive rotational program might be implemented through longer rotations, allowing employees to achieve certification in various building and code specialties. Rotational programs allow for renewal and a fresh perspective, and can serve as a valuable training component. In a large agency, a rotational program replicates the experience an employee gains in a small agency where a single position performs a number of roles in policy and implementation.

Priorities through Point Systems

A good way to translate the objectives of enforcement into case priorities is to produce a point system that attaches a relative score to an enforcement case. Such a system is a more accurate measure of an investigator's performance than the number of cases closed. A point system recognizes that some cases take more time and effort—and offer greater satisfaction of an agency's objectives—than the myriad number of small and easy cases which might otherwise make up a case load. With the completion of a sign abatement grace period in 1988, the City of San Diego established a 'top ten' list of the most notorious nonconforming signs and ranked the priority for conformance. The 'Sign Investigation Scoring Formula' was used to measure the relative significance of other non-listed signs as well.

Sign Investigation Scoring Formula

1. **Sign Visibility.** The sign is viewed or is notorious to what scale of audience?

Regional Significance	=	20 points
Community Significance	=	10 points
Neighborhood Significance	=	5 points
Not Significantly Significance	=	0 points

2. **Sign Surface.** What is the relationship of the sign's size to the provisions of the local code?

200% of Code or More	=	20 points
125-200% of Code	=	10 points
100-125% of Code	=	5 points
Observes Code for Size	=	0 points

3. **Number of Signs.** Does the number of signs on the site exceed the allowance of the local code?

Multiple Signs in Excess	=	20 points
Single Sign in Excess	=	10 points
Observes Code for Number	=	0 points

4. **Height of Sign(s).** Does the height of the sign exceed the allowance of the local code?

200% of Code or More	=	20 points
125-200% of Code	=	10 points
100-125% of Code	=	5 points
Observes Code for Size	=	0 points

5. **Location of Sign(s).** Does the location of the sign meet the local code criteria?

Off Site/Public Right-of-Way	=	20 points
On site, not observing code	=	10 points
Observes location criteria	=	0 points

For any given site, the total points from the five criteria are totaled. When comparing a number of sites, the one with the highest score, in all probability, is the site that deserves the most attention. San Diego's Sign Code Administration even tracked a 'most wanted' list of high-scoring offenders to which the highest priority was attached. When these clear and notorious 'landmark violations' were abated, the agency sent a clear message to the community that the program was achieving results.

violation does not meet a standard of significance. However, for accountability this determination must be documented. The aggregate experience of an agency's staff can lead to the establishment of general agency standards or policies. Ultimately, careful training and a policy of allowing agency staff some latitude in the field is preferable as long as the general parameters of an agency's mission and particular program objectives are being met. Adopting priorities can aid the determination of significance at the agency level.

Ultimately, careful training and a policy of allowing agency staff some latitude in the field is preferable as long as the general parameters of an agency's mission and particular program objectives are being met.

2. Substantial Compliance

Substantial compliance is the post-enforcement cousin of determination of significance. When first discovering a violation, the enforcement agent makes a complete list of all acts which must be undertaken to bring a property into conformance.

Satisfying Conformance

Early in the process, an agency must be able to define fully and specifically what constitutes an acceptable solution to an enforcement case. It is not enough to indicate that a violation exists and that the violator has the sole responsibility to come into compliance. A violator who asks, "What must I do?" must be given a precise answer. The question may require a list which not only contains the end result, but also the mandatory steps and alternatives where they exist.

This list becomes the goal. It can serve as the basis for cooperative efforts during the 'courtesy' phases of establishing a case, or may be the offer during settlement negotiations. In the worst case, the list may be the result sought through litigation. Early on, the list must be established and, with few exceptions, adhered to during the duration of the enforcement action. Conformance criteria for a case might look like this—

Violation: Fence 7' 0" high where zone allows maximum fence height of 6' 0".

Conformance: Either—
- Reduce height of fence to 6' 0", or
- Obtain variance for overheight fence.

Say that the violator chooses to reduce the height of the fence. Say, further, and that the fence is made of 10" blocks, of which the violator counter-proposes to remove one course, leading to a fence which is 6' 2" where a maximum of 6' 0" is allowed. The investigator now has the option of accepting the counter-proposal as substantial conformance or rejecting the offer.

This is an essential first step, which must be done without compromise before processing a significant violation. At some point, however, although each and every item on the list has not been completed, an agency official should have the power to determine that a violator has achieved substantial compliance. Such a determination should be documented and judged against the agency's objectives and priorities, and must derive from the particular relationship of the regulation to the circumstance. Substantial compliance is not something an agency could, or would want to, establish as specific, objective criteria. For example, if it routinely accepted a five percent margin of dimensional criteria as substantial compliance, an agency would be dangerously open to question by elected officials and the community.

G. Press Relations

Code enforcement is often portrayed poorly in the media. Sometimes it seems that code enforcement activities are only visible when the press perceives that an agency is insensitively enforcing its will on a weak business or a penniless family. Further, since the objective of most code enforcement actions is to create the absence of something—through the abatement of a violation—the process does little to provide a substantial focal point for positive press coverage.

Establishing a program of press relations by an enforcing department or an agency can do a lot to promote agency objectives.

Establishing a program of press relations by an enforcing department or an agency can do a lot to promote agency objectives. A press relations program must be incremental and ongoing, so that the media will portray a positive, fair, and accurate image of the agency's efforts. In practice, a positive press account can actually achieve compliance before enforcement simply by educating potential violators of requirements that affect them. Key junctures in the enforcement process should include producing press releases and occasionally press events which might announce—

- Adoption of new regulatory responses
- Institution of code enforcement programs or sweeps
- Closing of particularly significant violation cases
- Commencement of interagency cooperative initiatives

Cultivate an honest and forthright relationship with local beat writers. This will encourage the media to contact you when a story relating to a particular case or your agency's mission is being covered. This opportunity to respond with facts will allow the best possible interpretation of your intentions to emerge.

4 Investigating Code Enforcement Cases

An enforcement agency must collect sufficient facts either to confirm or deny the existence of a violation.

Introduction

Regulatory Foundations

Local Regulatory Implementation

Managing Code Enforcement

Investigating Cases

Selection of Remedies

Administrative Remedies

Criminal Prosecution

Using Civil Injunctions

Defenses to CE Actions

Investigating Code Enforcement Cases

Enabling ordinances for municipal regulation and enforcement are in place, the agency is identified by ordinance and policy, and the framework for management and training are clear. The stage is now set. However, enforcement of municipal regulations requires a 'code enforcement event' or an offending action or use. The event is generally signaled by a written or telephone complaint which vaguely describes a site or building that may violate a municipal regulation or some applicable state statutes. A possible violation may also become an enforcement case, either through routine or annual inspections or during the inspection of an adjacent complaint.

A. Overview

Collect the Facts. Initially, an enforcement agency must collect sufficient facts either to confirm or deny the existence of a violation. Enforcement agents must visit the property, talk to the neighbors, take photographs, and speak to the owner or person responsible. Here the enforcement agent serves both the complainant and the alleged violator. How an agent interacts with each person is critical to the credibility and effectiveness of the agency, and how an agent can inspect private property and collect evidence that may be used in subsequent enforcement actions is limited by the state or federal constitutional controls. Consequently, the agency must design and implement an approach to investigation that can be effective without impinging on constitutional rights.

Evaluate the Facts. After collecting facts, an enforcement agency must determine whether or not violations exist and, if so, what steps should be taken to bring about compliance. If there is insufficient evidence, when does investigation cease? How far

How an agent interacts with each person is critical to the credibility and effectiveness of the agency, and how an agent can inspect private property and collect evidence that may be used in subsequent enforcement actions is limited by the state or federal constitutional controls.

should the investigation go? When should a complainant be informed that no further action will be taken?

Compliance Is the Primary Objective. Facts are not blindly collected or evaluated without a purpose in mind. Penalties and costs can be assessed against a property owner, tenant, or other responsible person, but, unlike other violations of law, most municipal land use regulations are unique because of their continuous nature. The violations remain each day until the responsible person makes necessary corrections or the enforcement agency abates the violations. Until corrected, the violations continue. Depending on the cooperation of the responsible person or owner and the type of enforcement action, compliance may take some time, but, above all, the enforcement agency's mission is to obtain compliance.

B. Investigation Approaches

1. Collection of Information

At the moment a complaint is received or an agent discovers a possible violation, the building of a code enforcement case begins. Although at that precise moment a manila folder or computer file may not be opened to accept initial information, the first contact establishes a number of facts which will be crucial to the case throughout its life. From this moment on, the enforcement agency collects information about a particular matter. Probably the first entry in any case file will involve establishing that a matter which has the potential to be subjected to investigation has come to the attention of agency staff.

From the information gained by using the checklist, the first action will be to research agency records and code to determine if the complaint or alleged violation can be voided without field investigation. This can occur when agency records and codes indicate that the action is permissible, preempted, or simply not within the jurisdiction of the agency. This first level of research should respond to the following questions—

- **Is the property within** the area under the jurisdiction of the agency, and not subject to preemption?
  Sources: Maps depicting agency boundaries and preempted lands (in the case of a city, those lands owned by county, state, and federal agencies)

- **Is the alleged violation** of a type subject to the agency's authority?
  Sources: Descriptions of matters subject to the agency's legal jurisdiction as proscribed by operating regulations or the agency's charter

Above all, the enforcement agency's mission is to obtain compliance.

Preliminary Investigation Checklist

A checklist for the initiation of an investigation includes—

- Date, and possibly time, that the matter first comes to the agency's attention
- Whether the matter is observed directly by agency staff or reported by another party
- A description of the action or thing that may constitute a violation
- Location of the alleged violation
- The name of the property owner, resident, or other identifiable party who is believed to be responsible
- Whether the possible violation has ceased or is ongoing
- Other facts or allegations gained from complainant or direct observation of the violation to supplement this basic information

---

- **Do agency codes prohibit** the described construction or event at that specific location?
  Sources: Zoning district maps, hazard, and other regulatory maps

- **Has special permission** been granted to permit the described construct or event on that date?
  Sources: Agency permit records for regulated activities

- **Can agency records** confirm the identity of the owner, resident, or other agency?
  Sources: Utility, business license, and property ownership records;, and confirmation of location information

Only at this point can an allegation be established in the form of a reference to the particular site and its operating codes. The initial complaint and background research can then be combined to form the following declaration—

> On [date] it was [reported or observed] by [complainant or staff person] that a possible violation [citation of authority or section of code], in the form of [a particular construct or event], [has existed or currently exists] and is being carried out by [property owner, resident, or other identifiable entity] at [location] which is more particularly described as [distinguishing location reference].

When these facts have been established, investigation can proceed. Depending on the nature of the report, even if the record search does not indicate a cause for the allegation, either a cursory investigation of the site or a referral to another agency with more appropriate jurisdiction may often be warranted.

2. Customer Service

Code enforcement is a customer service business, serving both complainants and violators, and the staff of an agency must be responsive to their respective needs.

Code enforcement is a customer service business, serving both complainants and violators.

To a complainant, this means fairly appraising the status and prospects of the concern. Timeliness, accuracy, and a willingness to communicate is critical. Complainants should know when a case is being pursued and how it is expected to progress. Even if the period for bringing the case into conformance is lengthy, when a complainant is kept informed and progress is made as expected, a high degree of customer satisfaction can be achieved. Conversely, if long periods elapse with little communication or progress, complainants can become an enforcement official's worst enemy.

To a violator, customer service means understanding the reasons for the regulation and respectfully communicating what must be done to resolve the violation. Usually, it also means working with a violator to determine how his or her aims can conform to the regulatory scheme to the satisfaction of both the violator and the agency. In the end, only the violator can solve the problem efficiently. As such, the violator has particular service needs. This does not mean compromising standards or lengthening timelines without cause, but it does mean that the transaction should not start on a hostile note.

When dealing with a potential violator, the code enforcement process often begins with a courtesy notice or courtesy call. Referred to as 'nice guy' letters, they usually have a congenial tone and contain the specific allegation. ("Hey, friend, did you know that your chicken coop on the roof is against the law? Let's talk about ways to solve this problem that work for both of us.")

Some agencies also use a 'complaint received' card, which generally notifies a possible violator that a complaint has been received and that an investigator will call. This notice, which introduces the agency's interests and explains that an investigator will subsequently visit the site, gives a possible violator an opportunity to initiate contact before site inspection. Because it is sometimes mailed to a property owner or resident who can easily correct the situation, or who may not have a violation in the first place, a complaint received card may initiate a conversation which will save the agency a field investigation trip.

3. Disclosure of Complainant's Identity

Many complaints result from ill will between neighbors. Thus, the complaint may be a symptom, and not the problem. In these cases, the violator usually asks an agency to produce the name of the complainant. To prevent reprisals, most agencies attempt to keep this information confidential. However, the information is not privileged, and in most agencies is subject to disclosure under public records provisions. Where a violation does in fact exist, the best response is that, regardless of the reason the violation came to its attention, the agency itself is primarily interested in conformance.

Where a violation does in fact exist, the best response is that, regardless of the reason the violation came to its attention, the agency itself is primarily interested in conformance.

C. Field Investigations and Inspections

In order to confirm or deny the claim that a violation may exist, an agency's first investigative step is to inspect the property. Field inspections may require an enforcement agent to enter onto private property to inspect the interior of an apartment unit or business, or view the yards that surround the premises. If the property contains exterior violations (e.g., storage of inoperable vehicles and junk in the front or side yards), the enforcement agent can probably determine whether violations exist by viewing the property from public places such as the street, sidewalk, or alley.

When inspecting private property in the field, the agent steps into the domain of law enforcement. Although not police or peace officers, these public employees are governmental agents seeking to enforce applicable municipal regulations or ordinances. Thus, enforcement agents, like the police, must scrupulously adhere to the legal limitations and constitutional rules governing the search of private property. In some cases the agent will obtain a tenant's consent to inspect the property. If entry is refused, an agent may need to obtain an administrative inspection warrant. In other situations the courts have permitted the enforcement agents to inspect without a warrant.

Field inspections may require an enforcement agent to enter onto private property to inspect the interior of an apartment unit or business, or view the yards that surround the premises.

When inspecting private property in the field, the agent steps into the domain of law enforcement.

1. Agency Inspection Policies

Since inspection of private property is a sensitive area of the law, an enforcement agency should adopt rigorous, written policies governing inspection procedures and protocol. Some of these may include—

- How to request, arrange, and coordinate inspections with other enforcement agencies
- How an enforcement agent should conduct an inspection
- How to document violations during inspections through the use of photographs, notes, and detailed diagrams
- Protocol and demeanor during the inspection, including how to handle an irate property owner or tenant
- Alternative techniques when an owner or tenant refuses the inspection or access cannot be gained
- When and how to obtain an administrative inspection warrant

2. Overview of Constitutional Limitations

Many constitutional limitations that apply to police officers when they enter private property to search for evidence apply also to most code enforcement situations. Although not peace officers, when they inspect private property, enforcement inspectors must still adhere to the same fundamental legal limitations.

Although the Fourth Amendment's general principles have been interpreted and applied by the courts in volumes of case decisions, only those decisions relevant to the majority of code enforcement situations will be discussed in this section.

Basic Fourth Amendment Protections. The Fourth Amendment to the U.S. Constitution protects persons, houses, papers, and effects against unreasonable searches by government agents without a warrant. Where governmental agents violate the Fourth Amendment, the agency cannot use any of the evidence obtained as a result of the illegal search. Although the Fourth Amendment's general principles have been interpreted and applied by the courts in volumes of case decisions, only those decisions relevant to the majority of code enforcement situations will be discussed in this section.

Reasonable Expectation of Privacy Doctrine

The Fourth Amendment applies only to searches of places where the occupant has a reasonable expectation of privacy. Therefore, a court must evaluate the place where the search occurred and the surrounding facts to determine if it is a valid Fourth Amendment search. If the police or other government enforcement agents encounter a person at a place where a 'reasonable person' would have some notion of privacy, the courts have concluded that a search has occurred and generally a warrant must be obtained. If the court concludes that no expectation of privacy exists, then no search can occur which triggers the Fourth Amendment. Where the Fourth Amendment does not apply, enforcement agents can inspect places without a warrant.

Reasonable expectation of privacy is a complex constitutional doctrine which is subject to numerous court interpretations about whether a person in a particular situation or place has an objective and reasonable expectation of privacy. *See generally, Katz v. United States*, 389 U.S. 347, 353 (1967); *Smith v. Maryland*, 442 U.S. 736, 740 (1979) (use of pen register devise at telephone company's central office was not a search since no legitimate expectation of privacy exists in phone numbers dialed from a home telephone). For example, no reasonable expectation of privacy exists when garbage is left at the curb for collection; thus, garbage cans can be searched without a warrant. *California v. Greenwood*, 486 U.S. 35, 40 (1988).

Fourth Amendment Applies to Administrative Inspections. The Fourth Amendment's prohibition against unreasonable searches and seizures applies to administrative inspections by enforcement agents. The same public policy arguments prohibiting police officers from conducting unreasonable searches also apply to administrative inspections done by building and zoning inspectors.

In the context of code enforcement, a thorough understanding of the concept of a reasonable expectation of privacy and relevant case law is important for the agent when confronting situations not addressed in an agency's written policies or in a specific court decision.

One common situation is the inspection of areas between sidewalks and front yards adjacent to driveways in a basic subdivision single-family home. When walking down the sidewalk, an enforcement agent observes no fences blocking his or her view of the front and side yards. The garage is set back 30 feet. Does the owner have a reasonable expectation of privacy? Did the owner take reasonable efforts to secure his privacy? If no fences or gates prohibit visibility and the yards and driveway are open, the courts would likely conclude that an owner does not have a reasonable expectation of privacy. No reasonable expectation of privacy translates into no search, and the Fourth Amendment's warrant requirement would not apply.

This expectation is not the owner's personal expectation, but is an objective standard based on what society is prepared to recognize as reasonable. The court will examine this issue from the standpoint of common sense and practical judgment. It would not be reasonable for an owner to hold an expectation of privacy in a wide-open yard and driveway. Note, however, how this conclusion would change if the owner builds a six-foot-high fence and gate at each end of the property.

In the seminal case of *Camera v. Municipal Court*, 387 U.S. 523, 534 (1967), the U.S. Supreme Court for the first time applied the Fourth Amendment to administrative inspections conducted by housing inspectors. Here the tenant refused to allow housing inspectors inside his apartment for an annual inspection. Where tenants refuse entry, the court recommended that enforcement agencies petition a neutral judge for an administrative inspection warrant. The principles established in *Camera* were extended to administrative inspections of commercial uses and businesses in *See v. City of Seattle*, 387 U.S. 541, 545-546 (1967).

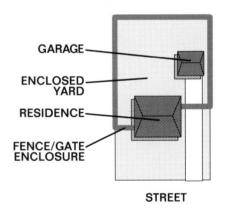

GARAGE

ENCLOSED YARD

RESIDENCE

FENCE/GATE ENCLOSURE

STREET

Inspection of Yards Surrounding Single-Family Homes

If the owners have taken steps to keep people out, such as with the construction of fences or posting of signs, inspection of enclosed yards in a single-family neighborhood either without consent or without an inspection warrant would likely violate the Fourth Amendment prohibition against unreasonable searches.

Numerous court decisions give the yards surrounding a single-family home special protection. As the inspector gets closer to the front door, the ability to inspect the yards without a warrant change dramatically.

3. Inspections without Inspection Warrants

Administrative inspections by enforcement inspectors may be done without a warrant. A warrant is not required when an occupant consents to the inspection or where no reasonable expectation of privacy exists in the place or situation. Some common code enforcement situations where inspection warrants are not required include violations that exist in plain view, open fields and yards, common areas of apartments, in certain highly-regulated businesses, and where the situation presents emergency or exigent circumstances.

A warrant is not required when an occupant consents to the inspection or where no reasonable expectation of privacy exists in the place or situation.

a. Consent. Voluntary consent is the most direct and legally permissible means for an enforcement inspector to enter private property. Before entering, an inspector should attempt to obtain the consent of the occupant or tenant, but not necessarily the consent of the owner. The Fourth Amendment affords greater protection to the person in the possession of the property than to the owner.

In an apartment building or house with a number of independent residents, consent is not so clear. Each resident has an expectation of privacy in certain rooms where they are permitted access. Common areas (for example, kitchens or living rooms) and the resident's bedroom are areas where all of the residents have access and some control. Thus, a resident can generally consent only to those rooms within his or her control.

As a general rule, an occupant may consent to an inspection. *People v. James*, 19 Cal. 3d 99, 106 (1977).

Who Can Give Consent?

A resident cannot consent to the search of another occupant's bedroom, unless the person giving consent has common authority over the place to be searched. *People v. Hamilton*, 168 Cal.App. 3d 1058, 1067 (1985). In searching a business, the lessor cannot consent to the search of leased premises unless the lessor has a right of entry. *U.S. v. Thriftmart, Inc.*, 429 F.2d 1006, 1010 (9th Cir. 1970); *U.S. v. Implink*, 728 F.2d 1228, 1232 (9th Cir. 1984) (landlady's consent was insufficient where she had a limited right to enter garage and co-occupant objected to the inspection).

b. Plain View. While consent is the most direct method, where the violations are in plain view, an enforcement inspector often can identify exterior code violations without needing an inspection warrant. An inspector can make observations from areas open to the public or open to public view where

An inspector can make observations from areas open to public view where no expectation of privacy exists.

no expectation of privacy exists. Common public places include streets, sidewalks, parks, and alleys. Places where an inspector has gained lawful access are also permissible—for example, a neighbor's backyard.

An enforcement inspector can make lawful observations of items stored in plain view from a neighbor's backyard where the neighbor gave the inspector access. *See Dillon v. Superior Court*, 7 Cal. 3d 305, 310 (1972) (police officer's observations from neighbor's yard did not violate Fourth Amendment). *See generally, Air Pollution Variance Board v. Western Alfalfa*, 416 U.S. 861 (1974) (state health inspectors can enter the yards of a business and lawfully observe discharges of smoke in violation of air pollution control standards; no Fourth Amendment search, since the plumes of smoke were visible to the general public).

Where the inspector does not obtain permission from the neighbor, it is a simple trespass. Therefore, the inspector's observations would violate the Fourth Amendment. *Phelan v. Superior Court*, 90 Cal.App. 3d 1005 (1979) (police officer's inadvertent trespass on owner's property in rural area violated Fourth Amendment).

Vacant Buildings. A common code enforcement situation is the inspection of a vacant and abandoned building. Inspections of vacant buildings do not require an inspection warrant. A fireman's warrantless inspection of a fire-gutted building, which was vacant and open to the public, did not violate the Fourth Amendment according to the court in *City and County of San Francisco v. City Investment Corp.*, 15 Cal.App. 3d 1031, 1038-40 (1971).

Apartment Buildings and Common Areas. Enforcement inspectors routinely inspect apartment buildings and enter common areas and courtyards without inspection warrants. A lawful search occurred when a city inspector followed a mailman through a locked security door into an apartment building's common area to enforce a business tax ordinance on vending machines. *Cowing v. City of Torrance*, 60 Cal.App. 3d 757, 762 (1976); *see also* 61 Op. Att'y Gen. 117 (1979).

Flashlights or Binoculars. Optical aids such as flashlights or binoculars do not affect the legality of observing violations in plain view if the violations could be seen in normal daylight hours or at close range.

In the case of *People v. Vermouth*, 42 Cal.App.3d 353, 361 (1974), the police officer's use of binoculars to confirm a report of marijuana plants on a sun deck did not invade the owner's reasonable expectation of privacy. *See also, People v. Capps*, 215 Cal.App.3d 1112, 1123 (1989) (police officer's use of flashlight to illuminate interior of handbag had no constitutional significance).

Aerial Surveillance. An aerial observation of a back yard without a warrant does not violate the Fourth Amendment. For example, in *People v. McKim*, 214 Cal.App.3d 766, 769-772 (1988) aerial surveillance by a helicopter at 400 feet above ground, without causing unnecessary noise, dust, or threat of injury, did not interfere with the defendant's rights of privacy at his home. Taking aerial photographs of an industrial plant from an aircraft lawfully in public air space is not a search, since the open areas which surround an industrial complex are not the same as the curtilage of a home. *Dow Chemical Co. v. U.S.*, 476 U.S. 277, 234-238 (1986); *see also Florida v. Riley*, 488 U.S. 445, 451-452 (1989) (no Fourth Amendment violation for aerial surveillance of residential back yard).

c. Residential Yards and Open Fields. Generally, most inspections of yards surrounding a residential house require an inspection warrant, because the courts have concluded that property owners' have a strong, reasonable expectation of privacy in the area surrounding their homes. This area is referred to as the curtilage.

> ### Curtilage
>
> "At common law, the curtilage is the area to which extends the intimate activity associated with the 'sanctity of a man's home and privacies of life', *Boyd v. United States*, 116 U.S. 616, 630 (1886), and therefore has been considered part of the home itself for Fourth Amendment purposes." *United States v. Oliver*, 466 U.S. 170, 180 (1984). A state health inspector may not enter an enclosed backyard absent the owner's consent or an administrative inspection warrant. *Vidaurri v. Superior Court*, 13 Cal. App. 3d 550, 552-53 (1970).
>
> A property owner's reasonable expectation of privacy was violated when a police officer squeezed between a garage and fence in an area covered with weeds and vines. *People v. Fly*, 34 Cal.App. 3d 665, 667 (1973); *People v. Freeman*, 219 Cal.App. 3d 894, 901 (1990).

See generally, U.S. v. Oliver, 466 U.S. 170, 179 (1984) (government intrusions into open fields are not searches as proscribed by the Fourth Amendment); *Betchart v. Department of Fish and Game*, 158 Cal.App. 3d 1104, 1107 (1984); *People v. Dumas*, 9 Cal. 3d 871, 882 (1973).

In contrast to residential yards, open fields may be inspected without a warrant, since the owner does not have a reasonable expectation of privacy in an area open to public view.

d.   Highly–Regulated Businesses. Warrantless inspections of certain highly-regulated businesses and industries are permissible where the search furthers an administrative policy or purpose designated by statute or ordinance. When warrantless inspection is authorized, an enforcement inspector must adhere to the statute's specialized procedures, which usually specify the time, place, and scope of the inspection, depending on the type of business. Some of these businesses and industries approved by the courts include—

Warrantless inspections of certain highly-regulated businesses and industries are permissible where the search furthers an administrative policy or purpose designated by statute or ordinance.

- **Liquor Industry.** A warrantless search of a bar for narcotics was approved as lawful pursuant to the inspection powers set forth in the Alcoholic Beverage Control Act. *People v. Paulson,* 216 Cal. App. 3d 1480, 1490 (1990).

- **Wholesale Fish Dealers.** Inspections of records and undersized fish without a warrant are necessary to enforce provision of the California Fish and Game Code that govern wholesale fish dealers. *People v. Harbor Hut Restaurant,* 147 Cal. App. 3d 1151, 1156 (1983).

- **Junkyards.** Inspections of junkyards without administrative inspection warrants were approved by the U.S. Supreme Court based on the closely regulated industry exception. *New York v. Burger,* 482 U.S. 691, 704 (1987) (warrantless search of junkyard held not to be a violation of the Fourth Amendment). *See also People v. Doty,* 165 Cal.App. 3d 1060, 1066 (1985) (warrantless inspection of junkyard open to the public is lawful if conducted during regular business hours).

- **Massage Parlors.** Inspection of a massage parlor without a warrant was permissible because the inspection adhered to the local ordinance's procedures designating massage parlors as closely regulated businesses. *Kim v. Dolch,* 173 Cal. App. 3d 736, 743 (1985).

- **Health Care Facilities.** The courts have approved the warrantless inspections of health care businesses depending on the type of health care establishment. Family day-care homes were not considered a closely regulated industry sufficient to justify warrantless inspection. *Rush v. Obledo,* 517 F.Supp. 905, 909 (1981); *compare, People v.*

Firstenberg, 92. Cal. App.3d 570, 577-581 (1979) (warrantless search of a skilled nursing facility is reasonable on the basis of pervasively–regulated industry exception).

▨ **Hazardous Materials Exception.** A warrant was required to inspect a facility storing hazardous waste material in the case of *Los Angeles Chemical Co. v. Superior Court*, 226 Cal.App.3d 703, 708 (1990). Although Health and Safety Code section 25185 authorized the inspection without a warrant of all businesses which store and transport hazardous chemicals, the court ruled that this law applies to all businesses and not to a particular industry; thus, section 25185 cannot support the pervasively-regulated business exception for warrantless searches.

e. **Exigent Circumstances.** Properties with immediate hazards can be inspected without a warrant. For example, in the celebrated decision of *Camera v. Municipal Court*, the court listed several emergency scenarios where a warrant would not be necessary; for example, the seizure of unwholesome food, health quarantine, and the destruction of diseased animals. *Camera*, 387 U.S. at 530.

> In *Michigan v. Clifford*, 464 U.S. 287, 293 (1984), the court concluded that entry into a building to fight a fire did not require an inspection warrant. Moreover, a warrant was not required where chemicals used to manufacture illicit drugs posed a threat to the public's health and safety. *People v. Duncan*, 42 Cal. 3d 91, 101 (1986).

Code Inspectors and the Constitution

As inspectors emulate more and more of the characteristics customarily associated with law enforcement officials, the courts will apply the strict constitutional requirements historically reserved for police. This is especially relevant where enforcement inspectors issue infraction or misdemeanor field citations.

4. Administrative Inspection Warrants

If a tenant or another person occupying the premises refuses permission to inspect the property for code violations, an enforcement inspector can obtain an administrative inspection warrant. Inspection warrant procedures are established in California Code of Civil Procedure sections 1822.50 through 1822.57. However, the requirements to obtain an administrative inspection warrant are somewhat less restrictive than those necessary to obtain a warrant for criminal search and seizure.

Gaining Compliance by Inspection Warrants

Inspection warrants can also be viewed as cost-effective enforcement remedies. Although warrants are primarily an investigative tool and not a true remedy, when the situation requires an inspection warrant, an agency may obtain immediate voluntary compliance. Administrative inspection warrants send a message to a reluctant owner or occupant that code violations are taken seriously by the enforcement agency and the court. The execution of an inspection warrant by itself may be sufficient to persuade the responsible person to cooperate and correct outstanding violations.

Two basic requirements must be met to obtain an inspection warrant: (1) refusal by the occupant to inspect; and (2) reasonable cause to suspect code violations or reasonable legislative or administrative standards.

Two basic requirements must be met to obtain an inspection warrant: (1) refusal by the occupant to inspect; and (2) reasonable cause to suspect code violations or reasonable legislative or administrative standards.

a. Refusal to Inspect. Because many different scenarios can arise when a tenant refuses entry, enforcement inspectors should follow written guidelines on how to respond and document the refusal. An inspector's response and recollection are critical when determining whether sufficient evidence exists to support a request for a warrant. Sufficient evidence would include an enforcement inspector's written statement of the conversation with the occupant and copies of any letters exchanged between the occupant/owner and the enforcement agency.

b. Reasonable Cause. Reasonable cause is the legal standard that judges apply when deciding whether or not to issue inspection warrants. Reasonable cause is different from probable cause, which is the legal standard for issuing a criminal search and seizure warrant. *See* Penal Code section 1524.

Reasonable cause is justified by the government's primary interest in preventing the development of conditions considered hazardous to the public's health and safety. Probable cause is justified by the government's interest in obtaining evidence of a crime. Compared to criminal investigations, administrative inspections are designed to obtain compliance with certain minimum standards developed in building, zoning, and similar regulations.

Reasonable cause can arise in two basic ways: (1) enactment of an ordinance or administrative policy which establishes areawide or annual inspections; or (2) evaluation of a particular location that is suspected of having code violations.

"Unlike the search pursuant to a criminal investigation, the inspection programs at issue here are aimed at securing city-wide compliance with minimum physical standards for private property. The primary governmental interest at stake is to prevent even the unintentional development of conditions which are hazardous to public health and safety." *Camera* 387 U.S. at 535. Inspection warrants required for federal OSHA inspections can be issued without the criminal standard of probable cause. *Marshall v. Barlow's Inc.*, 436 U.S. 307, 320-321 (1978).

Annual Inspections. Many municipalities use annual inspections to ensure compliance with building and housing codes as well as hazardous materials regulations. Annual inspections are also common for many closely-regulated businesses. Annual area inspections were approved by the U.S. Supreme Court in *Camera*.

Site-Specific Violations. Reasonable cause is also likely to arise where an enforcement inspector suspects code violations on properties that are not part of an annual or area inspection. In this situation, the inspector must support his or her suspicions with a written statement of specific facts that describe why a particular property or building may violate applicable land use regulations. The written statement must list the code sections being violated. The judge will then review this written statement to determine whether or not reasonable cause exists to issue the warrant.

> Statement of articulable facts must be sufficient to justify a reasonable belief that a condition of nonconformity exists in a place, dwelling, or structure. *See generally, Salwasser Manufacturing Co. v. Municipal Court*, 94 Cal.App. 223, 233 (1979).

Salwasser and Reasonable Cause

Reasonable cause is still the prevailing view in California. *See generally, People v. Wheeler*, 30 Cal.App. 3d 282, 298 (1973). However, the two reported *Salwasser* decisions appear to create some confusion about the applicability of reasonable cause. In the first *Salwasser* case (*Salwasser Manufacturing Co. v. Municipal Court*, 94 Cal.App. 223 (1979)), since the inspection resulted in a criminal prosecution for Cal-OSHA violations, the court did not apply the administrative inspection warrant standard of reasonable cause.

Ten years later in *Salwasser Manufacturing Co. v. Occupational Safety & Health Appeals Board*, 214 Cal.App. 3d 625, 629 (1989), the court distinguished the first *Salwasser* opinion. The second *Salwasser* decision involved an inspection warrant based on an employee complaint rather than on a routine inspection. Here the court applied the lesser standard of reasonable cause, since the primary purpose of Cal-OSHA inspections is to ensure safe and healthful working conditions and not the discovery of evidence of crimes.

Based on the two *Salwasser* decisions, unless the nature of the investigation is entirely focused on criminal prosecution, reasonable cause is still the appropriate standard for the issuance of administrative inspection warrants. Thus, inspectors cannot use the administrative inspection warrant process as a pretext to conduct a criminal investigation. In such a scenario, the courts would likely apply the higher standard of probable cause if the investigation evolves into a criminal investigation or if the investigation's design was criminal from the outset.

c. Inspection Warrant Statute and Ordinances.

Procedures for administrative inspection warrants are set forth in California Code of Civil Procedure sections 1822.50 through 1822.57. These statutes also codify the reasonable cause standard.

Local ordinances can also authorize routine or annual inspections. However, these ordinances cannot conflict with procedures established in the Code of Civil Procedure for administrative inspection warrants. Even when they are conducting inspections pursuant to a local inspection ordinance, enforcement inspectors must adhere to the state procedures.

One local ordinance authorized inspections by health officers to enforce occupancy permits for moored vessels used as residences. *Tellis v. Municipal Court*, 5 Cal. App. 3d 455, 457-58 (1970) (ordinance was a valid exercise of municipal police powers to permit inspections where health officers had a reasonable belief that a violation was present). Another local occupancy ordinance required routine inspections with a change of ownership, occupancy classification, or use. The court approved this occupancy ordinance as long as the inspections followed the requirements of the *Code of Civil Procedure. Currier v. City of Pasadena*, 48 Cal.App. 3d 810, 815 (1975). Municipalities can enact inspection ordinances for pervasively-regulated businesses. *Kim v. Dolch*, 173 Cal.App.3d 736, 744 (1985).

d. Inspection Warrant Practice and Procedure

Inspector's Declaration. Inspection warrants, as required by Code of Civil Procedure sections 1822.50 through 1822.57, must be supported by a written declaration. The declaration must describe the place, dwelling, or premises to be inspected, the purpose for the inspection, the occupant's refusal, and any evidence of suspected code violations. Evidence of code violations would be based primarily on the observations of the enforcement inspector. These may have been made from outside the premises—for example, from a neighbor's yard or from the street—and may also include statements from neighbors. These statements might describe, for example, a dramatic increase in foot traffic to a home suspected of operating a business in a residential zone.

Ex Parte Court Hearing. The written declaration and the proposed inspection warrant are then submitted to a judge at an *ex parte* hearing. The law does not require the enforcement agency to inform the responsible person or occupant in advance that a warrant will be requested. Any judge of the municipal or superior court can issue an administrative inspection warrant, and

Examples of an Inspector's Affidavit/ Declaration, an inspection notice, and a sample inspection warrant can be found in Appendix B.

some judges request the presence of the enforcement inspector. If the inspector submits an affidavit instead of a declaration, section 2012 of the Code of Civil Procedure requires the inspector to sign the affidavit in the presence of the judge. Note, however, that Code of Civil Procedure section 2015.5 permits written declarations as a general substitution for affidavits, and if a declaration is submitted, the inspector need not attend the *ex parte* hearing.

Who Should Attend an *Ex Parte* Hearing?

Whether or not the inspector attends the *ex parte* hearing before the judge to obtain an inspection warrant, as a general rule the municipal attorney should attend. The municipal attorney can answer any questions the judge may have about administrative inspection warrants and general code enforcement issues. Remember, many judges are not familiar with code enforcement cases.

See generally, People v. Wheeler, 30 Cal.App. 3d 282, 299 (1973) (administrative inspection warrants must sufficiently describe the addresses and structures in violation of building codes).

Scope of Inspection Warrant. If satisfied that reasonable cause does exist, the judge will issue an inspection warrant. Just like a criminal search warrant, the inspection warrant must specifically describe the premises, the purpose of the inspection, and any limitations imposed on the inspection. One important limitation is that Code of Civil Procedure section 1822.56 requires that 24-hour advance notice be given to the occupant. Waiver of this requirement or permission for forcible entry must be specified in the inspection warrant.

Forcible Entry and Waiver of 24–Hour Notice

Forcible entry without prior approval by the judge resulted in suppression of the evidence in *People v. Tillery*, 211 Cal.App. 3d 1569, 1581 (1989) (forcible execution of administrative warrant to inspect for building code violations was an unreasonable search under the Fourth Amendment; police officers should not have detained the tenant, but returned to court to amend the warrant to permit forcible entry). If an immediate threat to the public's health and safety is present or if an enforcement inspector makes numerous unsuccessful attempts to execute a previously issued inspection warrant, a judge may waive the 24-hour notice requirement or permit forcible entry. *See generally, People v. Lepeilbet*, 4 Cal.App. 4th 1208, 1215 (1992) (failure to provide 24-hour notice as required in the inspection warrant violated the Fourth Amendment, but evidence was not suppressed due to defendant's written consent).

Execution of Administrative Inspection Warrants and the Role of the Police

Asking for police help when executing inspection warrants is a good practice where the inspector believes the tenant or owner may impede or interfere with the inspection. In the case of *People v. Tillery*, 211 Cal.App.3d 1569, 1574 (1989), the police lawfully accompanied a building inspector because of the tenant's history of violent behavior and presence of pitbulls. "One of the purposes of the administrative inspection procedures is to avoid violent confrontations between owners and occupants of private residences and the administrative inspectors charged with the responsibility of enforcing building or other regulatory codes." Id. at 1578.

However, the courts are particularly watchful when the police enter private property. Remember the police are held to a higher legal standard to justify their inspections compared with building inspectors. Enforcement agents should avoid the appearance that administrative inspections warrants are being used by the police as means to circumvent this higher legal standard. If the occupant or tenant refuses to permit an inspection with a warrant, the police officer's only option is to arrest the individual—he or she cannot forcibly execute the inspection warrant unless the warrant expressly gives permission for forcible entry.

5 Selection of Code Enforcement Remedies

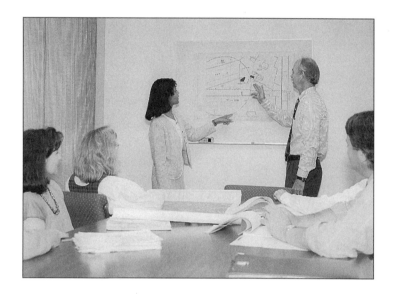

The agency's primary objective is to select the most appropriate remedy to gain timely and effective compliance.

Introduction

Regulatory Foundations

Local Regulatory Implementation

Managing Code Enforcement

Investigating Cases

Selection of Remedies

Administrative Remedies

Criminal Prosecution

Using Civil Injunctions

Defenses to CE Actions

Selection of Code Enforcement Remedies

Once inspection of the property reveals code violations, an enforcement agency notifies the responsible person to seek compliance. Generally, the responsible person is the property owner, but may also include the tenant, lessee, or occupant, depending on the violation.

Compliance can be obtained by using one or a combination of administrative and judicial remedies. In most cases an enforcement agency gains compliance merely by issuing a notice of violation. If the notice of violation does not persuade the responsible person to comply, the agency can schedule an office hearing, mediation, or initiate a formal administrative hearing. Instead of pursuing administrative remedies, the agency may pursue judicial action with assistance from the prosecutor or municipal attorney.

Evaluating remedies is the heart of code enforcement. Enforcement options are the basic legal tools and mechanisms that can be used by an agency to gain compliance. Given the significance of selecting the appropriate option, the remainder of the book is devoted to a thorough discussion of remedies, which can be classified into three broad categories—Administrative, Criminal Prosecution, and Civil Injunction. Each remedy has unique advantages and disadvantages, depending on the nature of the violation. The agency's primary objective is to select the most appropriate remedy to gain timely and effective compliance.

A. Enforcement Discretion

Selecting the appropriate remedy depends upon the particular facts and circumstances of the case. Enforcement agencies have broad discretion and flexibility, and, if an administrative remedy fails to bring about compliance, an agency may even file a criminal action. To avoid unnecessary delay, from the outset the agency

Evaluating remedies is the heart of code enforcement. Enforcement options are the basic legal tools and mechanisms that can be used by an agency to gain compliance.

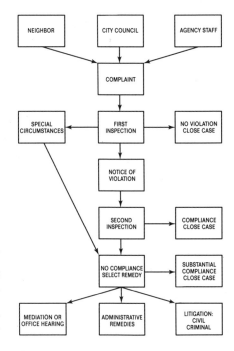

See generally, Riggs. v. City of Oxnard, 154 Cal.App. 3d 526, 530 (1984) (municipality is not always required to issue a criminal citation for a zoning violation, but may logically resolve a violation in other ways); *Fox v. Fresno,* 170 Cal.App. 3d 1238, 1241 (1985) (duties imposed on public entities by Health and Safety Code section 17980, to abate or take other appropriate action with regard to nuisances, are discretionary and not mandatory).

Once the agency is unable to gain compliance using an informal enforcement approach, the assistance of the municipal attorney or prosecutor may be necessary.

should attempt to select the most effective remedy. In addition, the agency should develop a close working relationship with the municipal attorney or prosecutor to help ensure the effective selection of enforcement options.

B. Case Evaluation Policies

The enforcement agency should develop written case evaluation policies to guide inspectors in selecting the most appropriate and effective action. These policies should establish—

- **Case Priorities.** How the agency will process violations with imminent health and safety hazards compared to overheight fences
- **Time Frames.** How long the agency will work with the responsible person before taking more significant enforcement action
- **Requirements for Submittal to Municipal Attorney.** Guidelines for submitting cases to the prosecutor or municipal attorney and the respective roles of enforcement inspector and attorney during subsequent enforcement action
- **Case-Specific Criteria.** Common characteristics and issues which must be evaluated in each case
- **Policy Evaluation Criteria.** The broader public policy considerations affected by the enforcement agency's enforcement action; whether the agency's internal policies (budget, number of inspectors, etc.) will be affected by its decision to proceed with enforcement action in a particular case

Since administrative and judicial enforcement actions often present complex legal issues, case evaluation policies should be jointly developed by the enforcement agency, along with the municipal attorney and prosecutor. Decisions made at this critical stage by both the enforcement agency and municipal attorney will have a dramatic impact on subsequent administrative or judicial actions.

1. Case Priorities

Evaluation of code enforcement cases will also depend on the type of violation and its relative significance. How an agency handles a dumpster overflowing with trash will be much different than finding a remedy for a commercial building with fire code violations posing a threat to the public's health, safety, and welfare. The development of written policies establishing priorities for typical cases is critical for any enforcement agency given limited resources.

Written guidelines also give front line inspectors a gauge of the amount of time and effort a particular type of enforcement case may require. Because each case will turn upon its own unique facts, these guidelines must be used with flexibility.

2. Substantial Compliance*

Written enforcement policies should also address the notion of substantial compliance, discussing when a case should be closed and whether it's possible to achieve total compliance. Compliance is ever-changing. A particular property may be in compliance one week and in violation another, depending on the changes to the facts and the law.

Given constant change, and recognizing that perfect compliance may not be achievable, an agency's mission should be to bring properties into compliance with the applicable and most significant code violations at a particular point. This is not to advocate that inspectors should ignore violations or not enforce the letter of the law, but only to inject a note of reality. Not every piece of property within a community can be brought into perfect compliance. Nor should it be the duty of an inspector to obtain perfect compliance.

Given constant change, and recognizing that perfect compliance may not be achievable, an agency's mission should be to bring properties into compliance with the applicable and most significant code violations at a particular point.

Substantial compliance permits an agency to close those cases that fundamentally satisfy the requirements: for example, where a property owner brings the property into compliance by mitigating the most serious and significant violations, but still has an outstanding minor violation, perhaps a fence one inch above the height limitations. The enforcement agency might bring this to the owner's attention with a notice of compliance listing those items that have been corrected and minor items which the owner should correct, but which the agency will not pursue (unless, of course, these minor violations become more serious at a later date).

Adopting policies which advocate substantial compliance gives an agency and front line inspectors sanity. Together with the agency's written guidelines on case priorities, the use of substantial compliance is critical for managing scarce resources. However, in cases where neighbors are using the enforcement system as a means to retaliate against each other, closing a case on the basis of substantial compliance could become a political nightmare. To avoid this possibility, an enforcement agency should develop a cohesive set of written policies that have been

---

* The discussion of Substantial Compliance is very similar to the concept discussed in Determination of Significance, Chapter 3, page 57.

approved by the city manager or city council, so that political pressure is not likely to prevail over the application of substantial compliance in a particular case.

3. The Roles and Relationships with Municipal Attorney and Prosecutor

Municipal attorneys generally encounter code enforcement when drafting ordinances and advising municipal departments, or when representing city or county enforcement departments at administrative or judicial proceedings targeting specific individuals or parcels for code violations. Most municipal attorneys devote a large portion of their practice to the research and writing of ordinances and advisory memoranda, while implementation and enforcement are often left for the city or county department with little guidance or support.

The important lesson for both the code enforcement agency and the municipal attorney is knowing the limits of their respective roles and how they interact. Code enforcement does not neatly fit the traditional practice of municipal law. While an enforcement agency needs expert legal advice, advocacy, and representation from a municipal attorney, potential conflicts can arise during the transition from the role of advisor to litigator.

Advisory Role. As advisor, the municipal attorney provides an enforcement agency with research and analysis of the legal implications of particular policies, rules, and regulations, but here the agency makes the call. This delineation of authority can become vague at the case evaluation phase of the process. Even though the enforcement agency may ultimately decide how to proceed with a specific code case, this decision should not be made without the advice of a municipal attorney. In the long run this preventative approach will save the agency time and money.

Litigation Role. However, once an enforcement agency refers a particular case for criminal or civil action or requests representation at an administrative hearing, the municipal attorney takes the lead. In this instance, the municipal attorney decides whether or not to accept the case, which is known as the doctrine of prosecutorial discretion. Similar to an enforcement department's decision to accept or close a case once substantial compliance is obtained, the municipal attorney in the role of litigator can decide not to take a case to court. This is partly based on the ethical obligation of a municipal attorney to seek the truth. If evidence is uncovered which could ruin the case, as litigator the municipal attorney must reveal this evidence to the court so that

The important lesson for both the code enforcement agency and the municipal attorney is knowing the limits of their respective roles and how they interact.

CEU = Code Enforcement Unit

Community Gardens: A Positive Lesson in Prosecutorial Discretion

At a vacant lot once occupied by a single-family home, a group of nearby residents, with the help of the neighborhood redevelopment corporation, established a community garden. After several harvests, a few adjacent neighbors and their landlord registered complaints about the smell of fertilizer, noise, and the traffic of gardeners who apparently lived outside the immediate neighborhood. Zoning Investigations determined that a community garden could not be a primary permitted use in a single-family zone. Gardens would be permitted as accessory uses, but this lot had no structures. It was merely a garden with a surrounding fence.

Mediation was the initial enforcement option. A long history of political conflicts between some of the parties prevented resolution by mediation. The case was next sent to the City Attorney's Code Enforcement Unit (CEU). Since no imminent health and safety hazards were present, the CEU conducted an office hearing with the redevelopment corporation leaders who leased the property. Under threat of potential criminal prosecution, the redevelopment corporation agreed to remove the garden and fence within 30 days. One week before the deadline, local newspapers and television news programs ran stories about the desperate plight of this community garden.

Apparently, the redevelopment corporation waited until the last week before informing the gardeners about the earlier 30-day deadline. With this lack of adequate notice and high media visibility, the CEU met with the gardeners and granted a temporary extension. Public momentum against removing the garden continued to build, the tenant in opposition had moved, and the

mayor's office received inquiries from five other community gardens in other parts of the city.

Given this scenario, should the City Attorney's CEU file a criminal complaint? Although immediate enforcement action did not appear to be a prudent use of prosecutorial resources, a violation of the zoning laws did exist. Finally, a workable solution was forged with a creative use of prosecutorial discretion by postponing enforcement action until the city council could change the zoning regulation. If the council were to amend the law to permit community gardens as primary uses sub-

ject to a simple discretionary permit process, no need would exist for an enforcement action.

The community garden activists presented examples to the mayor and council of zoning regulations that permitted community gardens from other cities throughout the country. Concurring, the council referred the drafting of the amendment to the planning department. Until the amendment could be enacted, the existing community gardens agreed to control their operations closely to minimize adverse impacts on their respective neighborhoods.

This example illustrates that prosecutorial discretion can be exercised in a constructive fashion by evaluating zoning laws and measuring their reasonableness against changing community conditions. When the single-family zone was enacted decades earlier, community gardens did not exist in the same fashion they do today. Faced with the choice of enforcing a zoning regulation that was out of step with the community and the mounting political realities, the deputy city attorney used prosecutorial discretion to forge a creative solution acceptable to all parties. (It has been rumored that a basket of zucchini was offered by the community gardeners to show their appreciation, but regretfully rejected by the deputy city attorney.)

justice can be done. This is in contrast to the role of a private attorney or a municipal attorney as advisor, where the ethical obligation is to serve the client as long as it is not illegal.

Over the years the sometimes conflicting pressures caused by the roles of advisor and litigator can create tension and frustration between a municipal attorney and the enforcement agency if the agency does not fully understand why the municipal attorney will not or cannot accept a case.

4. Case–Specific Criteria

Written policies for evaluating cases should include characteristics common to most code enforcement cases. Since both administrative and judicial enforcement actions often present complex legal issues, the enforcement agency, together with the municipal attorney and prosecutor, should develop these criteria. Applying these case-specific criteria in a systematic fashion can help the agency and municipal attorney evaluate the strengths and weaknesses of a particular case and select the most appropriate remedy. The general characteristics include—

Nature of the Violations. Do the code violations pose an imminent threat to the public's health and safety? If so, the situation may require summary abatement or a temporary restraining order as part of a civil judicial action. Is the code violation *de minimis*? In this situation, an enforcement agency may not have sufficient resources to pursue certain types of violations, such as overheight fences, or may use only informal enforcement actions to gain compliance.

Permit Status. Was a valid permit issued to the responsible person? This is a critical fact when evaluating possible enforcement actions. If a permit was issued in error, can the responsible person successfully assert the defense of estoppel?* Despite the issuance of a permit, did the responsible person comply with the permit's terms and conditions?

Responsible Person's Profile. Why doesn't the responsible person voluntarily comply? Is he or she merely defying the law? Does the responsible person have the physical or financial ability to comply? Will an office hearing persuade the person to comply, or will stronger administrative or judicial enforcement action be required?

Applying case-specific criteria in a systematic fashion can help the agency and municipal attorney evaluate the strengths and weaknesses of a particular case and select the most appropriate remedy.

UBC = Uniform Building Code

---

* Estoppel is often raised where a building permit issued in error violates relevant zoning laws. For a more thorough discussion of the estoppel defense, turn to Chapter Nine, pages 161-166.

Desert View Drive: A Nightmare for Both Prosecutor and Enforcement Agency

The case of Desert View Drive illustrates the relationship of the enforcement agency and municipal attorney during the evaluation of various enforcement options and possible consequences. On Desert View, several very expensive homes were sliding down the hillside. Based on a thorough investigation by the city's geologists and engineers, the building official took swift action and declared the homes unsafe per section 203 of the Uniform Building Code. The building official's order required the owners either to vacate their homes or install an early warning detection system in case the rate of fall dramatically increased, thus giving the occupants a few minutes to evacuate. With this administrative remedy, the four homeowners had the right to appeal and request a hearing on whether the properties were unsafe.

The property owners and their attorneys used the administrative hearing process to delay implementation of the building offi-

cial's order. Six months later, after the building department and municipal attorney invested hundreds of hours and thousands of dollars, two homeowners voluntarily vacated their homes, and two agreed to install the warning system. All four attorneys used the information gained during the numerous administrative hearings to file civil law suits against the city for contributing to or causing the failure of the slope.

Given the lessons learned from this case, the building department and the municipal attorney probably should have immediately filed a civil complaint against the homeowners, letting the court decide whether the properties were unsafe instead of using the administrative enforcement procedures in the UBC.

This case illustrates—

- The need to consult with the municipal attorney early in the case evaluation process, especially on complex cases that involve possible health and safety issues

- When a case is tied up in an administrative enforcement procedure, the municipal attorney may not be able to initiate legal action, causing serious delay and stalling effective enforcement action

Postscript. Despite California's record-breaking rains of 1993, the homes still remain on Desert View Drive. Interestingly, one of the homeowners failed to install the warning device, as promised in the administrative order. Since the administrative remedy did not obtain compliance, the building official referred the case to the city attorney's office for misdemeanor prosecution. A complaint was filed charging the owners with failure to obey the terms of an administrative order. The owner plead guilty, paid a $400 fine, and was ordered by the judge to install the warning system.

Sufficiency of Investigative Reports. Should this case go to court or to an administrative hearing, is there enough evidence to connect the responsible person to the violation? Are there any inherent weaknesses or defenses in the case?

Decision Maker's Attitude. Will a judge or administrative hearing officer compel the responsible person to comply? Is there any factor which might evoke sympathy towards the responsible person or against the enforcement agency?

Time. What is the quickest way to obtain compliance?

5. Public and Administrative Policy

An enforcement agency should always be mindful of the effect its actions may have on broader public policy issues and its own administrative policies. Although strict adherence to laws and regulations may initially be viewed as the primary objective, the agency should be sensitive to contemporary and controversial local land use issues, availability of housing stock, and the displacement of tenants. Enforcement actions also affect agency policies. The agency should carefully evaluate the selection of remedies to ensure that each case is consistent with established policies relating to budgetary resources, time lines, number of inspectors, court calendars, etc.

6 Using Administrative Remedies

Although not required by law, many agencies establish a practice of using administrative alternatives before filing a case in court.

Introduction

Regulatory Foundations

Local Regulatory Implementation

Managing Code Enforcement

Investigating Cases

Selection of Remedies

Administrative Remedies

Criminal Prosecution

Using Civil Injunctions

Defenses to CE Actions

Using Administrative Remedies

As an alternative or supplement to judicial action, enforcement agencies may use a variety of administrative remedies to gain compliance with state and municipal regulations.* Administrative remedies which do not use the criminal or civil courts may be employed early in the enforcement cycle when the responsible person refuses to comply after receiving notices of violation. Although not required by law, many agencies establish a practice of using administrative alternatives before filing a case in court.

Administrative remedies which do not use the criminal or civil courts may be employed early in the enforcement cycle when the responsible person refuses to comply after receiving notices of violation.

A. Overview

Administrative remedies can be classified as either informal or formal. *Informal* administrative remedies generally include Notices of Violation, Stop Work Orders, and Mediation and Office Hearings. *Formal* administrative remedies are similar to court proceedings, and in many respects are substitutes for court. Formal rules and requirements must be followed by the enforcement agency to ensure that the responsible person obtains adequate notice and a fair hearing. Formal administrative remedies include Permit Revocation, Summary Abatement, Administrative Abatement, and Administrative Enforcement Hearings.

B. Informal Enforcement Actions

1. Notices of Violation

Most enforcement agencies inform persons responsible for violations of the code by delivering a notice of violation. A notice of violation, which lists specific code sections and estab-

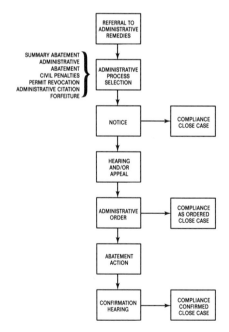

---

* Judicial actions, in the form of both criminal prosecution and civil injunction, are the subjects of Chapters Seven and Eight, respectively.

lishes deadlines for bringing the property into compliance, is in the nature of a warning. Unless mandated by ordinance, a notice of violation is issued by an agency based on enforcement policy. While appropriate in most cases, where an inspector confronts violations which pose imminent health and safety hazards, a notice of violation may be inadequate to compel compliance.

2. Stop Work Order

Another informal administrative remedy is the stop work order authorized by section 202(d) of the Uniform Building Code, 1991 edition, ICBO. Appropriate when an agency determines that current construction activity must cease immediately, a stop work order may be necessary because current construction work is inconsistent with the underlying building permit or zoning approval.

A stop work order may be appropriate to stop all current construction activity because the work is inconsistent with the underlying building permit.

3. Mediation and Office Hearings

Mediation and office hearings are increasingly being used by municipal enforcement agencies as effective and inexpensive informal methods to resolve code violations. Most agencies gain compliance merely by issuing the notice of violation or stop work order to the responsible person. However, in some cases the responsible person may not comply within the deadlines established by the agency, or in other cases the relevant building code or zoning regulation may be complex and subject to different interpretations. Office hearings and mediation may be appropriate to clarify code applications, establish new compliance deadlines, and inform the responsible person about the impending consequences should compliance not occur in a timely manner.

Office hearings and mediation may be appropriate to clarify code applications, establish new compliance deadlines, and inform the responsible person about the impending consequences should compliance not occur in a timely manner.

Office Hearings. Enforcement agencies often schedule an office hearing with the responsible person. Although generally conducted by agency staff, in some cases inviting the municipal attorney or prosecutor is helpful. Besides the enforcement agency, the responsible person may invite any experts (architect, engineer, attorney) to discuss the violations and explain why the deadline was not met. At the hearing the inspector and usually a supervisor discuss the nature of the violations and develop a list of corrective actions.

While the key to a successful office hearing is to establish specific, reasonable deadlines to bring the property into compliance, one of its shortcomings is the lack of any mechanism to compel attendance and guarantee compliance. This entire remedy rests upon the good faith of the violator.

When scheduling an office hearing, an agency must be wary that some owners and responsible persons use informal administrative remedies to delay compliance. To avoid this, an agency should conduct hearings shortly after signs of noncompliance, which sends the violator a message that progressively stronger enforcement measures will follow if compliance is not completed by the deadlines set in the notice of violation. To guarantee the integrity of the municipal enforcement program, deadlines and procedures established in the office hearing must be followed strictly, granting extensions only in the most unusual circumstances.

Mediation. Unlike office hearings, mediation uses a neutral third party, who is not a member of the enforcement agency's staff, to facilitate an objective discussion between the agency and the responsible person. In many cases the agency contracts with professionally-trained private mediators or uses volunteers. Since the mediators are neutral, there is a greater chance of success, with the responsible person more likely to participate and negotiate a written agreement to correct outstanding code violations.

The first step is for the enforcement agency to refer the case. Generally the mediators call the responsible person, explain the mediation process, and schedule a convenient date and time. The pool of mediators may includes citizens from the community who have completed extensive mediation training and conducted community mediations between private disputants.

Mediation differs slightly from other types of alternative dispute resolution such as arbitration. Not a hearing officer empowered to make administrative findings and render a decision, the mediator is a facilitator who will help the two parties develop an acceptable agreement. Therefore, enforcement inspectors who participate in mediations should appreciate the flexibility of the underlying code and develop various solutions or alternatives with the responsible person.

For example, pursuant to California Health and Safety Code section 17923 and Uniform Building Code sections 105 to 107, a building official has some discretion when approving alternative methods that comply with the spirit and intent of the code. In a mediation, this could be used as legal support for modifications to the building code.

Both sides in the mediation must be willing to thoroughly discuss and evaluate all potential options. At the end of the mediation session a written agreement is signed by all parties including the mediator. The agreement outlines specific

Center for Municipal Dispute Resolution (CMDR)

The City of San Diego and the University of San Diego Law School jointly operate a code compliance mediation program. The Center handles approximately 150 cases per year ranging from barking dogs to illegal storage of junk and debris in residentially-zoned neighborhoods. Between August 1988 and January 1994, the Center received more than 762 cases from various city departments, closed 658 cases, and conducted more than 525 mediations with a compliance rate exceeding 75%.

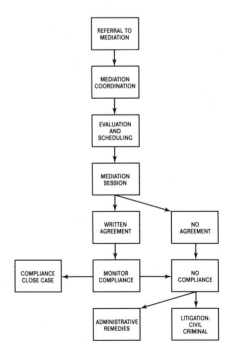

tasks and responsibilities for both parties to complete and establishes deadlines. (See Appendix A for an example of a mediation agreement.)

C. Formal Administrative Enforcement Actions

Where informal enforcement actions are either ineffective or inappropriate, an agency may use a variety of formal administrative enforcement actions as alternatives to judicial action or before a case is filed in court. Formal administrative actions can be classified into three general categories: (1) revocation of permits and certificates of occupancy; (2) summary and administrative abatement; and (3) administrative enforcement hearings.

1. Due Process: Notice and Hearing

When beginning any formal administrative enforcement action, the agency must guarantee the responsible person due process. Due process requires reasonable notice and an opportunity for a hearing before the agency can interfere with a person's significant property interest. Notice is essential so that a person can defend against the charges before government disturbs property interests or imposes a penalty, assessment, or possible forfeiture. *People v. Swink*, 150 Cal.App. 3d 1076, 1079 (1984). A hearing provides the person in violation with the chance to present arguments that challenge the assessment of a penalty or fine. *Ohio Bell Telephone Company v. Public Utility Commission*, 301 U.S. 292, 305 (1939).

2. Revocation of Permits and Certificates of Occupancy

Revocation of building permits and zoning approvals is a common administrative enforcement action. Section 303(c) of the Uniform Building Code, 1991 Edition, ICBO, authorizes the building official to revoke building permits whenever the permit was issued in error, based on incorrect information, or the permit violates other local ordinances. Zoning approvals (for example, use certificates, conditional use permits, planned residential development permits, etc.) may also be revoked as authorized by local ordinances.

Certificates of Occupancy may also be revoked by the building official pursuant to section 308(f) of the Uniform Building Code, 1991 edition, ICBO. Certificates of occupancy are required any time the property changes the existing occupancy classification. Government Code section 38780 authorizes the

Due process requires reasonable notice and an opportunity for a hearing before the agency can interfere with a person's significant property interest.

See generally, *Blinder, Robinson and Company v. Tom*, 181 Cal.App. 3d 283, 289 (1986) (a proceeding before an administrative officer or board is adequate due process if the basic requirement of notice and opportunity for hearing are met); *Horn v. County of Ventura*, 24 Cal. 3d 605, 615 (1979) (notice and hearing generally required in all quasi-adjudicatory land use decisions).

See generally, *O'Hagen v. Board of Zoning Adjustment*, 19 Cal.App. 3d 151, 158 (1971) (revocation of a conditional use permit must be based on compelling necessity); *Garavatti v. Fairfax Planning Commission*, 22 Cal.App. 3d 145, 148-149 (1971) (modification of conditional use permit and imposition of new conditions permissible); *City of San Marino v. Roman Catholic Archbishop*, 180 Cal.App. 2d 657, 669 (1960) (revocation of permits must meet basic due process requirements of notice, hearing, and written findings).

Currier v. City of Pasadena, 48 Cal. App. 3d 810, 815 (1975) (ordinance which requires certificate of occupancy is constitutional).

enactment of local ordinances that can prohibit the change of use, transfer, or sale of residential units until a new certificate of occupancy is issued by the building official.

3. Summary and Administrative Abatement

Instead of seeking a criminal prosecution or civil injunction, the enforcement agency may determine that summary or administrative abatement is appropriate. Abatement refers to procedures used to remove conditions that cause a public nuisance. In both administrative and summary abatement, the enforcement agency performs the corrective action and then assesses the abatement costs against the property. Instead of seeking a court order which compels the property owner or building manager to comply with the code, administrative abatement actions authorize municipal work crews or private contractors to enter the premises and perform the work. Consequently, abatement may be more appropriate for those situations where the responsible person cannot be found or where the property owner lacks the financial or physical ability to abate the public nuisance.

In both administrative and summary abatement, the enforcement agency performs the corrective action and then assesses the abatement costs against the property.

a. Summary Abatement. Government Code section 38772 authorizes municipalities to enact summary abatement ordinances. The agency uses summary abatement during emergencies where it must act without first obtaining a court order or formal administrative approval. In most enforcement cases the agency is well-advised to use either the court or administrative hearing process to obtain permission before abating the

Administrative abatement ordinances are commonly used to clean and secure vacant and abandoned buildings.

Dangers of Summary Abatement

"In an emergency situation involving the physical safety of the populace, the city could dispense with a due process hearing and demolish a building summarily." *Leppo v. City of Petaluma*, 20 Cal. App.3d 711, 718-719 (1971) (while the city may act summarily to abate a public nuisance in certain emergency situations, it is the city's burden to establish by a preponderance of the evidence that an emergency actually existed). Note the case of *Rose v. City of Coalinga*, 190 Cal.App.3d 1627, 1633-1635 (1987) where a city demolished a building which could have been repaired without affording the owners a due process hearing. The court ruled that an owner could sue the city for inverse condemnation since it destroyed the building in the absence of an emergency and for not affording the owner a hearing before demolition.

nuisance. Yet, summary abatement may be necessary in those emergency situations where the conditions are so severe that the tenants must be vacated or a building must be demolished without prior notice to the owner. Such a scenario could occur with sewage leaks, hazardous or toxic materials, or structural damages caused by earthquakes.

b. Administrative Abatement Procedures. Where the situation does not demand summary abatement, an agency can use administrative abatement procedures. In most cases this process does not require judicial intervention, but only a formal hearing before the agency can act to abate the public nuisance. Since a judge does not participate in the hearing, the agency must flawlessly follow the administrative abatement procedures to guarantee due process for the owner or responsible person.

Uniform Codes. Section 203 of the Uniform Building Code, 1991 edition, ICBO, provides administrative abatement procedures to repair, secure, and demolish unsafe buildings. The Uniform Code for the Abatement of Dangerous Buildings and the Uniform Housing Code also contain administrative abatement procedures. Most municipalities adopt one of these uniform codes and often enact their own variations.

State Housing Law. Substandard residential buildings may also be abated administratively in accordance with the rules and statutes provided in the State Housing Law. Substandard residential buildings may be repaired or demolished by the enforcement agency if the owner fails to correct the code violations within a reasonable time. *See generally,* California Code of Regulations, Chapter 1, Article 6, sections 50-70. Pursuant to California Health and Safety Code section 17958, however, it appears that local enforcement agencies have some flexibility to enact their own abatement procedures, as long as they substantially comply with statewide standards. *See generally,* 55 Op. Att'y Gen. 157 (1972).

Under the State Housing Law, administrative abatement proceedings against a substandard structure may demand demolition. Health and Safety Code section 17980(b) authorizes demolition by the enforcement agency, but only as a last resort and only if certain conditions exist. The preference for repair over demolition is expressed a number of times in section 17980. Subsection (b) allows the owner the option of choosing between repair and demolition. If the owner fails to take any action, section 17980(b)(3) provides, in part, that:

See *Bakersfield v. Miller,* 64 Cal.2d 93, 103 (1966) (administrative abatement by demolition is permissible against buildings that pose serious dangers to the public's health and safety).

HCD issued Information Bulletin 94-2 on January 3, 1994, declaring that all local abatement procedures for substandard residential dwellings must conform with California Code of Regulations, Title 25, Division 1, Chapter 1 §48. Apparently, HCD now wants municipalities to submit local abatement ordinances for its review. This Bulletin is currently under review by many municipal attorneys throughout the state.

In deciding whether to require vacation of the building or to repair as necessary, the enforcement agency shall give preference to the repair of the building, whenever it is economically feasible to do so, without having to repair more than 75 percent of the dwelling, as determined by the enforcement agency and shall give full consideration to the needs for housing as expressed in the local jurisdiction's housing element.

This provision suggests that full rehabilitation either will require repair of more than 75 percent of the physical structure, or that the expense of repair will exceed 75 percent of the value of the structure. The best way to handle this potential ambiguity is to make findings in the administrative proceeding on the economic feasibility of repair in all proposed cases of demolition.

In most situations, the feasibility of repair likely depends on the total cost of full rehabilitation to bring the building into compliance with the code. This means that a cost estimate will be required, preferably by qualified personnel in the local enforcement agency who have background and experience in construction and rehabilitation.

Due Process Hearing Requirements. Administrative abatement hearings must afford the owner due process. This includes: (1) adequate notice to the proper parties; (2) a reasonable opportunity to be heard; and (3) a chance to cross-examine the witnesses and controvert the evidence. Strict adherence to these ground rules is especially important where the enforcement agency seeks to demolish a building by administrative abatement. At the hearing, the agency must prove that the property is a public nuisance and that abatement by city crews is reasonable.

Enforcement agencies may present the case without the assistance of a municipal attorney. The enforcement supervisor and inspector testify about the conditions on the property and submit documentation proving that adequate notice was given to the owner or responsible person. The agency must also show that abatement by municipal work crews or private contractors is a reasonable solution.

Where the abatement case presents complex issues, or where the owner or responsible person hires an attorney to present his or her side of the case, an enforcement agency should be represented by the municipal attorney at the administrative abatement hearing.

Demolition Findings

Although the quotation from section 17980(b)(3) only relates to substandard residential housing, enforcement agencies may wish to consider a broader policy application to include any decision to demolish, rather than repair. Any time an agency determines that demolition is warranted, the decision should be based on specific findings in the administrative abatement proceedings that repair is not economically feasible.

See generally, Leppo v. City of Petaluma, 20 Cal.App. 3d 711, 718 (1971) (owners were not afforded a due process hearing either before a court or administrative body on the issue of whether the demolition of their building satisfied the criteria of a public nuisance and whether demotion was the only method to abate the nuisance). The enforcement agency has the burden of proof by a preponderance of the evidence. See generally, Armistead v. City of Los Angeles, 152 Cal.App. 2d 319, 324 (1957).

Administrative abatement is often effective where residential property is covered with debris, inoperable vehicles, trash, and junk.

Abatement costs are generally confirmed at a public hearing after the abatement. At this hearing, which is the final step before costs may be assessed against the property, the owners may claim that items of value were discarded or improperly included as part of the order. An inventory may help avoid disputes with the owner and possible litigation.

c. Abatement Practices

Scope and Terms of Abatement Order. Abatement orders must be specific. Precise directions in the abatement order will ensure the removal of the items or the correction of conditions which cause the public nuisance. Moreover, a well-written order will establish the parameters and conditions of the enforcement agency's powers during the abatement. For example, administrative abatement is often effective where residential property is covered with debris, inoperable vehicles, trash, and junk. The order should list items that can be removed and give instructions to the enforcement inspector about placement of items that can remain on the property in compliance with applicable zoning and building codes. The order should further explain how to dispose of the items which are removed.

Inventory. The inspector should prepare an inventory or list of those items which are thrown away. An inventory will provide proof of the items taken and their possible net worth in case the owner challenges the abatement costs. Abatement costs are generally confirmed at a public hearing after the abatement. At this hearing, which is the final step before costs may be assessed against the property, the owners may claim that items of value were discarded or improperly included as part of the order. An inventory may help avoid disputes with the owner and possible litigation.

Security. Although abatement is an administrative remedy, sometimes an owner may physically resist or obstruct the removal of his or her personal property. The presence of a police officer on the property during the early stages of the abatement should help to keep the peace.

Forcible Entry. Another implementation issue is whether the abatement order permits forcible entry. Government Code sections 38773 *et seq.* say nothing that would permit or prohibit forcible entry, when necessary, to execute an administrative abatement order. Since Government Code section 38773 empowers the enactment of local abatement ordinances, this statute together with the municipal police power could support a local ordinance permitting forcible entry when extraordinary circumstances are present. Alternatively, if an owner refuses access to the abatement crews, an enforcement agency could always petition the court.

d. Confirmation and Assessment of Abatement Costs.
After the abatement is complete, most local ordinances provide for a public hearing to confirm abatement costs, which is

The *Conner* Case: Forcible Entry and the Police

Forcible entry to implement an administrative abatement order was the issue in *Conner v. City of Santa Ana*, 897 F.2d 1487 (9th Circuit 1990). Here the court concluded that it was unreasonable for the police to scale a locked fence of an auto yard to get the vehicle registration numbers for the upcoming abatement hearing. After the hearing the police used forcible means to break down the gate to remove the inoperable vehicles.

Connor, however, can be viewed as a decision limited to abatement cases that only involve police, since they are held to a more exacting standard under the Fourth Amendment. *Connor* can be distinguished from situations where building inspectors enter property to demolish a structure pursuant to a valid administrative abatement order.

Conner has generated much discussion and controversy among enforcement agencies and municipal attorneys throughout the state. Where the administrative abatement does not involve police removal of property or vehicles, an enforcement agency probably does not need to obtain court permission before carrying out a valid administrative abatement order. In cases where police are removing inoperable vehicles (Abandoned Vehicle Abatement Statutes, Vehicle Code sections 22658 and 22660 through 22710), it may be prudent for the enforcement agency to obtain prior court approval.

Although some agencies have sought this approval through the administrative inspection warrant process, Civil Code section 1822.50, this statute merely provides for administrative inspections and not the authority to seize and remove personal property.

generally conducted before the same board or hearing officer that issued the order. At this hearing the validity of the underlying abatement order is not subject to review. The issues are limited to whether or not the costs for the abatement were reasonable. Thus, an enforcement agency must provide an itemized statement of the total costs, including the number of hours, hourly wages, dumping fees, etc. The owner may also challenge the enforcement agency's implementation of the abatement order, contending that the agency exceeded its authority by discarding property not listed in the order.

Once the costs are confirmed, Government Code section 38773.5 permits an enforcement agency to refer the total costs to the county auditor where they become a special tax

---

Inspection Warrants for Abatements

In the case of *Gleaves v. Waters*, 175 Cal.App.3d 413, 418-420 (1985), the court seems to suggest that administrative inspection warrants could be used when the enforcement agency must enter private residential property to abate a public nuisance. In *Gleaves*, the California Department of Food and Agriculture obtained the administrative authority to eradicate the Japanese Beetle, but did not obtain an inspection warrant to enter a private residential yard.

The court held, "that in the absence of consent or exigent circumstances, government officials engaged in the abatement of a public nuisance must have a warrant to enter any private property where such entry would invade a constitutional protected privacy interest. We do not mean to suggest or imply that the warrant requirement extends to all entries onto private property for nuisance abatement purposes, only those which infringe upon constitutionally recognized expectations of privacy." *Gleaves*, 175 Cal.App. 3d at 419. Another alternative is to file a civil action seeking abatement. However, this is a cumbersome process, which subverts the purpose of using administrative remedies to avoid the delays in our judicial system.

assessment against the property. If the owner fails to pay, the special assessment can become a municipal tax lien. If the owner fails to pay the lien, a county can foreclose. Revenue and Tax Code section 3691 gives the property owner five years to pay all municipal tax liens before a county can start foreclosure proceeding.

4. Administrative Enforcement Hearings

Some agencies use an administrative hearing process as a means to gain compliance with land use and other municipal regulations. Instead of bringing a judicial enforcement action, the agency can present evidence and testimony regarding the code violations to a board or hearing officer. Although not typically used for code violations that pose imminent health and safety hazards, an administrative hearing avoids the often backlogged court calendar and the strict rules of evidence. Also, in smaller municipalities an agency can present its own case in the administrative hearing without the cost of the municipal attorney.

Defiance of Administrative Enforcement Order

Where the responsible person is a business or commercial enterprise, an administrative order that assesses a sizeable civil penalty may be sufficient to persuade the owners or operators to comply with applicable building and zoning regulations. In some cases businesses attempt to avoid local regulations and permit requirements under the assumption that this will save time and money. Although the administrative assessment of an appropriate civil penalty may also create an economic disincentive to violate regulations in the future, the payment of a civil penalty is no guarantee of compliance.

In one administrative hearing, the City of San Diego obtained a $36,000 civil penalty against a business for converting a warehouse into a residential occupancy without any prior building, fire or zoning approvals. While they paid the civil penalty, the owners continued to operate the facility without proper permits. Only after months of extensive litigation did the operators finally obtain the proper zoning and building permits.

This example illustrates the interrelationship between administrative and judicial remedies. In cases as difficult as this one, the agency may have to pursue judicial action to gain compliance with a previously issued administrative order.

Although less costly and less formal than court, the administrative hearing process must still comply with the fundamentals of due process regarding advance notice and a fair hearing. The primary disadvantage is that an administrative order is not self-executing. Compare the execution of administrative orders to court orders. If a person ignores a court order, the enforcement agency can return to court and seek contempt. The judge can impose a fine, send the person to jail, and enlist the services of the marshall or police to enforce the order. These options are generally not available for administrative orders issued under local police powers. Thus, where the owner or responsible person ignores the order and fails to bring the property into compliance or fails to pay the assessed civil penalties, the only practical alternative in most code cases is to file a judicial action.

State and municipal enforcement agencies have created different types of administrative hearing procedures. The hearing authority may have the power to establish deadlines, issue a cease-and-desist order, assess civil penalties, and record notices or liens. Common administrative hearing powers in the code enforcement area include—

- **Code Enforcement Boards.** Appointed officials review cases to determine whether or not a particular parcel violates the codes and establish deadlines for compliance

- **Recording a Notice of Violation.** A formal hearing process permits the enforcement agency to record the notice of a violation against the property, but also permits an owner to appeal

- **Civil Penalties.** The statute or ordinance may permit the hearing officer or board to assess civil penalties for the violations

- **Franchise Tax Board (FTB) Deduction Denial Program.** A specialized remedy created by section 17980(d) of the California Health and Safety Code and sections 17274 and 24436.5 of the Revenue and Taxation Code which housing enforcement agencies can use to compel repairs of substandard residential dwellings

a. Code Enforcement Boards. Local ordinances may establish a special code enforcement board to conduct an administrative hearing. The board may be comprised of citizen appointments, or in smaller municipalities the city council may hear code enforcement cases.

Although less costly and less formal than court, the administrative hearing process must still comply with the fundamentals of due process regarding advance notice and a fair hearing.

See generally, Merco Construction Engineers, Inc. v. Los Angeles Unified School District, 274 Cal.App. 2d 154, 167 (1969) (statute must provide for notice of the time and place of hearing where the parties may present in a regular and orderly manner issues of law and fact).

FTB · Franchise Tax Board

Hearing Preparation. Enforcement agency staff typically prepare a packet for the hearing board to review before and at the hearing. The packet may include copies of notices of violation, reports, pictures, diagrams, a written case history, a staff report, and recommendations. The staff report should discuss the reasons for bringing the case before the enforcement board and summarize the different inspections, recommended corrections and repairs, status of pending permit applications, and current conversations or correspondence with the owner or responsible person.

Hearing. The enforcement inspector usually presents the case without the presence of the municipal attorney. The owner, tenant, or other responsible person has an opportunity to present a defense and cross-examine. After hearing the testimony and receiving all evidence, the public portion of the hearing will be closed, and the hearing body discusses the case and arrives at a decision.

Decision and Review. The administrative hearing body may decide to uphold the enforcement agency's notices of violation, establish a modified schedule for compliance, or overturn the agency's decision, requiring no action on the part of the owner. The local ordinance may also authorize the imposition of a civil penalty and assessment of investigation costs. Where it has discretion to impose penalties, a municipality must notify the violating party prior to imposing the penalty, giving the party an opportunity to be heard and present any facts or arguments on which the exercise of discretion may be predicated.

Some ordinances provide appeals from enforcement board decisions to the city council or board of supervisors. If the ordinance does not provide for further administrative review, the responsible person would need to file a court action seeking review by a writ of mandate.

b. Franchise Tax Board Income Tax Deduction Program. Pursuant to Revenue and Tax Code sections 17274 and 24436.5, the Franchise Tax Board may deny state income tax deductions (interest, taxes, depreciation, or amortization) to taxpayers who failed to bring substandard residential property into compliance with applicable housing codes. The statute requires the enforcement agency to notify FTB of an owner's noncompliance after the owner has been served with official notice and given a minimum of six months to correct the violations. As required by Health and Safety Code section 17980, the notice

Where it has discretion to impose penalties, a municipality must notify the violating party prior to imposing the penalty, giving the party an opportunity to be heard and present any facts or arguments on which the exercise of discretion may be predicated.

includes a statement informing the owner of the applicable provisions of the Revenue and Taxation Code.

If the owner fails to comply within the time period, the enforcement agency may notify FTB by preparing a notice of noncompliance as required by sections 17274(c) and 24436.5(c). This notice informs the taxpayer of the intent to notify FTB within ten days unless an administrative appeal is filed. If the owner does not appeal within ten days, or if the enforcement agency's position is upheld on appeal, the notice of noncompliance is mailed to FTB. No tax deductions will be allowed from the date of the notice of noncompliance until the violations have been corrected.

Once FTB receives the notice of noncompliance, the taxpayer's return is selected, and deductions for that residential rental property are denied. All state revenue that would have normally accrued to the property owner by way of the tax deductions is sent to the enforcement agency. There is often a substantial delay, several years in some cases, between referral to the FTB and receipt of funds. FTB remits revenues to the enforcement agency once a year, depending on the amount actually collected from the taxpayer.

Implementing an FTB Program

■ The enforcement agency can list the FTB provisions on its general notice of violation form in order to ensure that the six-month period starts to run as early as possible.

■ FTB staff encounter a common problem in processing the notices of noncompliance: ensuring that FTB can identify the correct taxpayer. Code enforcement agencies identify cases by property address, but FTB uses an individual's social security number. Thus, the enforcement agency should obtain the social security number of the owner to ensure proper processing of this administrative remedy.

■ The local enforcement agency must establish the administrative hearing procedures to process possible taxpayer appeals.

7 Pursuing Criminal Prosecution

Overall, the deterrent effect of criminal prosecution is one of the code enforcement official's most powerful tools.

Introduction

Regulatory Foundations

Local Regulatory Implementation

Managing Code Enforcement

Investigating Cases

Selection of Remedies

Administrative Remedies

Criminal Prosecution

Using Civil Injunctions

Defenses to CE Actions

Pursuing Criminal Prosecution

Criminal prosecution may be appropriate when administrative remedies fail to persuade the responsible person to comply or the case includes more serious violations which demand more immediate action. In some cases the enforcement agency will encounter a recalcitrant owner who refuses to comply even after a formal administrative hearing and the assessment of civil penalties. Remember that an administrative action does not need to precede the filing of a court action, either criminal or civil; in certain cases where the responsible person will not voluntarily comply, immediately filing a court action would save the enforcement agency valuable time. Overall, the deterrent effect of criminal prosecution is one of the code enforcement officials' most powerful tools.

An administrative action does not need to precede the filing of a court action. Where the responsible person will not voluntarily comply, immediately filing a court action will save an enforcement agency valuable time.

A. Why Pursue Criminal Prosecution?

The enforcement agency together with the prosecutor must consider several factors when evaluating whether criminal prosecution is appropriate—

- Type of Criminal Enforcement Program
- Comparative Advantages of Criminal Prosecution to Civil Injunction
- Potential for Criminal Stigma
- Prosecutorial Discretion
- Judicial Attitude towards Code Cases

1. Criminal Enforcement Programs

Municipalities employ a variety of criminal enforcement programs. Many cities authorize their code compliance officers to issue infraction field citations, similar to traffic tickets. The maximum fine for the first offense is $250 as established by Penal

Code section 19.8. In cases where owners have converted garages without building permits or continue to store inoperable vehicles and junk in residential neighborhoods, an infraction citation usually can persuade an owner or tenant to comply. In other cases, where the violations are more serious and likely to repeat, the owner may dismiss a $250 fine as a mere 'cost of doing business'.

Instead of issuing infractions, enforcement agencies have the option to escalate violations of their local municipal ordinances to misdemeanors. Misdemeanor prosecution increases the maximum fine to $1,000, plus the possibility of six months in jail, per Penal Code section 19. Misdemeanor prosecution is more appropriate where the violation is likely to continue, such as a business operating within a residential zone. Unlike an infraction, the court can impose summary probation on the violator for a maximum period of three years as authorized by Penal Code section 1203a. If the person again violates a similar municipal regulation during the three-year term of probation, the court can revoke probation and impose additional fines without restarting the entire criminal process.

Misdemeanor prosecutions do require representation by either the city or district attorney. Because jail time can be assessed against the responsible person, the prosecutor must present the case. The United States Constitution guarantees a right to a jury trial when any length of jail time can be assessed by the judge.

2. Criminal Prosecution vs. Civil Injunction

The prime advantage of criminal prosecution compared to a civil injunction is the relatively short time required to obtain a court order to compel compliance.

The prime advantage of criminal prosecution compared to a civil injunction is the relatively short time required to obtain a court order to compel compliance. In many code cases a judge can impose a sentence compelling compliance within one to four months. The time will vary depending on whether the case goes to trial. However most code enforcement cases do not go to trial because relatively few factual defenses are available to the responsible person. Consequently, criminal code cases are usually resolved within six weeks as part of settlement negotiations.

Compared to civil proceedings, criminal prosecution has a higher burden of proof. 'Beyond a reasonable doubt' is the criminal standard, while 'Preponderance of the evidence' is the civil standard. Despite this difference, in most code cases the burden of proof is not a major factor, since the evidence is generally straightforward with few defenses against the facts.

Where the case involves an imminent hazard to health and safety, a preliminary injunction or a temporary restraining order may prove more expeditious than criminal prosecution. A restraining order can be issued immediately. In a criminal action the violation continues until the responsible person enters a plea, which could be several months after a complaint is filed.

3. Criminal Stigma

Some city and district attorneys are reluctant to prosecute citizens for mere municipal code violations because misdemeanor convictions might impose the stigma of a criminal record on ordinary citizens. However, unlike other criminal prosecutions, most code enforcement agencies give the owner or responsible person several months to comply voluntarily. When either or both fail or refuse to comply, criminal prosecution may be the only effective alternative.

4. Prosecutorial Discretion

The city or district attorney may legally choose not to file a criminal enforcement action. A prosecutor has an ethical obligation to evaluate carefully whether or not the evidence meets the standards for filing a criminal complaint. This same ethical obligation applies to the filing of civil enforcement actions and should be extended to administrative actions as well. Whether the prosector files the complaint or the code compliance officer issues a field citation, this same ethical standard applies.

In deciding whether to file a criminal enforcement action the city or district attorneys must determine whether a reasonable probability of obtaining a conviction exists. If there is insufficient evidence or if a judge or jury is unlikely to convict because of sympathy for the owner's circumstances, the prosecutor is ethically required not to file the action. This evaluation is often referred to as prosecutorial discretion. Although irrefutable evidence of the code violation may exist, some judges and juries may be reluctant to convict a 75-year-old owner who isn't financially or physically able to remove all the junk and debris stored on his or her property. This is not to say that courts will ignore obvious violations of local codes, but the prosecutor must consider this possibility when determining whether a criminal prosecution would be appropriate.

In deciding whether to file a criminal enforcement action the city or district attorneys must determine whether a reasonable probability of obtaining a conviction exists.

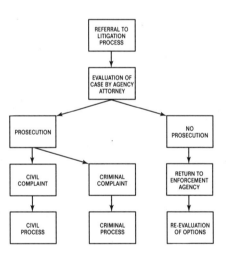

5. Judicial Attitude towards Code Cases

Judicial attitude about code enforcement and other regulatory offenses is another factor which a prosecutor must weigh before filing a criminal enforcement action. Where judges are not receptive to code cases, the likelihood of successful prosecution is diminished, and a prosecutor may decide not to proceed with a criminal action.

Some judges question whether code cases should be criminal offenses when compared with typical criminal prosecutions, such as robbery, prostitution, and driving under the influence. However, many judges understand that a connection may exist between serious crimes and code enforcement violations such as substandard apartments, dilapidated buildings, and inoperable vehicles (*see* 'Broken Window Theory' on page 8). Recognizing that an enforcement agency does not use criminal prosecution lightly, some judges appreciate the influence a single case may have on an entire neighborhood. These judges are aware that, unlike typical criminal violations, land use violations are continuous in nature and that a violation will remain until the responsible person is convicted and a sentence is imposed.

B. Criminal Enforcement Authority

Government Code section 36900 provides that a violation of a city ordinance can be prosecuted as a misdemeanor unless the ordinance specifically designates the violation as an infraction. This statute empowers the local city attorney to prosecute these violations in the name of the People of the State of California or to enforce such ordinances by civil action. Government Code section 25132 establishes similar authority for counties.

1. Municipal Code Enforcement Provision*

Most municipalities enact a general enforcement provision that applies to all violations of the municipal code. This traditional approach designates that violations of the municipal code can be enforced by filing a criminal or civil action and establishes the maximum fines and penalties that can be assessed for each violation.

Another variation is to include a general enforcement provision at the beginning of each chapter in the municipal code, an approach similar to that adopted by the Uniform Building Code and the Uniform Fire Code. The introductory sections spell out enforcement responsibilities and powers, and clearly express that all violations of a chapter are intended to be enforced by criminal or civil actions.

General Penalty Provision

The courts have approved this basic approach where the municipal code contains a general penalty ordinance that applies for all code violations. In *Benane v. International Harvester Co.,* 142 Cal. App.2d Supp. 874, 880 (1956), the case involved enforcement of Elections Code section 5699 which allowed waiver of wages for employees that took time off to vote. The court concluded that workers could be prosecuted because section 5699 fell within the scope of the general enforcement provision section 11501 which declared that all violations could be prosecuted by fine and/or imprisonment.

---

* Although this discussion about general enforcement provisions is within the chapter on criminal prosecution, the scope of such an enforcement ordinance applies to civil and administrative remedies as well. Appendix B contains examples of general enforcement ordinances.

a. Public Nuisance Basis. Traditionally municipal enforcement provisions declare all violations to be public nuisances, based on the municipal power to abate a public nuisance. However, since the courts have recognized that municipalities can enact and enforce regulations as part of their inherent police power, regardless of whether a particular violation reaches the level of a public nuisance, declaring that any violation of the municipal code is a public nuisance may be unnecessary.

b. Infractions vs. Misdemeanors. The municipal code enforcement provision must also designate criminal violations as misdemeanors, infractions, or a combination of both. Municipalities have experimented with each offense with varying degrees of effectiveness. While compliance with the municipal code is the universal goal of any enforcement action, each category has its own advantages and disadvantages.

Penal Code section 17(a) defines misdemeanors. The maximum penalty for a misdemeanor is imprisonment in the county jail not to exceed six months and/or a maximum fine of $1,000 as authorized by Penal Code section 19.

Penal Code sections 19.6 and 19.8 establish the maximum penalties ($250 fine) and the procedural limitations for infractions: no imprisonment, no jury trial, no public defender. All provisions of law relating to misdemeanors also apply to infractions, including the powers of peace officers, court jurisdiction, and burden of proof per Penal Code section 19.7.

c. Hybrid Penalty Ordinances. Some municipalities have adopted a hybrid system. Using a sliding scale, first-time violations are treated as infractions. Any subsequent convictions or repeat violations become misdemeanors. The violator is charged with a misdemeanor after three convictions. *See* Government Code section 36900(b).

Under this sliding-scale system, an enforcement agency must investigate and prepare reports for each incident until the requisite number of infractions escalates the offense to a misdemeanor, which will likely result in several more trips to the courthouse. Consequently, enforcement inspectors must keep accurate records regarding the number of prior convictions. The problem is that this system fails to penalize and deter a serious first-time violator and requires detailed record keeping.

Another type of hybrid ordinance vests discretion with the local prosecuting attorney. With this approach all violations are designated misdemeanors, but the prosecutor is authorized to

> The police power is consistently discussed by the courts as the legal basis for the enactment and enforcement of municipal ordinances. *City of Bakersfield v. Miller*, 64 Cal.2d 93, 101 (1966) (all violations of local building codes may not amount to a public nuisance); *Sullivan v. City of Los Angeles*, 116 Cal.App. 2d 807, 810 (1953) (building regulations are within the scope of the municipal police powers); *Schroeder v. Municipal Court*, 73 Cal. App. 3d 841, 848 (1977) (zoning regulations are also valid exercise of police power).

exercise discretion to reduce any violation to an infraction. Therefore, the serious, first-time offender is confronted with the full deterrence of a misdemeanor; but, where mitigating circumstances are present, the prosecutor can make a motion at arraignment to reduce the charge to an infraction. This hybrid ordinance formalizes a prosecutor's inherent discretion to negotiate and resolve cases. Similar discretionary authority is found in Penal Code section 17(d). Penal Code section 17(d) allows the prosecutor to file a complaint charging the offense as an infraction, unless the defendant at the time of arraignment elects to have the case proceed as a misdemeanor, or, with the consent of the defendant, the court determines that this offense is an infraction and conducts the case with that assumption.

A municipality may discover an illegal dwelling unit or garage conversion several years after the owner actually built the structure without proper permits. Because the owner is guilty of maintaining an illegal dwelling unit, the enforcement agency could prosecute at the time the violation is first discovered.

> "[A] provision declaring each day a violation continues [to be] a separate offense is designed to make enforcement of a zoning ordinance more facile and more effective. Indeed, it is argued that if the provision is not included, the result in many cases is that a chronic violator will simply 'buy a license' with a small fine, charge it to the 'cost of doing business' and continue to violate the zoning ordinance." [citations omitted]. *People v. Djekich*, 229 Cal.App. 3d 1213, 1221-1222 (1991).

d. Continous Violations. Another common clause found in the general enforcement provision is the expression that a separate crime can be charged for each day a violation continues. The language of most municipal land use ordinances also reflects this continuous nature. Uniform Building Code section 205 makes it unlawful for "any person, firm or corporation to erect, construct, enlarge, alter, repair, move, improve, remove, convert or demolish, equip, use, occupy or *maintain* any building or structure or cause or permit the same to be done in violation of this code" [Emphasis added]. For example, a municipality may discover an illegal dwelling unit or garage conversion several years after the owner actually built the structure without proper permits. Because the owner is guilty of maintaining an illegal dwelling unit, the enforcement agency could prosecute at the time the violation is first discovered. In the municipal code enforcement provision and any municipal regulation, 'maintain' is a critical term.

Continuous Violation Cases

Code enforcement violations were found to be continuous in nature in *Dapper v. Municipal Court*, 276 Cal. 2d 816, 818 (1969), cert. denied, 399 U.S. 910 (penalty provision designating that continuous code violations do not violate constitutional protection against double jeopardy). *See also, City of Fontana v. Atkinson*, 212 Cal.App. 2d 499, 509 (1963) (zoning violations recognized as continuous offenses). *See generally, People v. Curry*, 69 Cal.App. 501, 504 (1924) (where the crime charged is continuous in nature, a prosecution is not barred if the crime is continued within the statutory period).

2. Language of Municipal Regulation

The language used in each municipal zoning or building regulation has a significant effect on its enforcement, especially in criminal prosecutions. Municipal agencies can adopt a format similar to the Penal Code where each ordinance declares that, "It is unlawful to...". Since it is clear from this language that criminal prosecutions were intended by the legislative body, judges usually subscribe to this format. Unfortunately, many municipal code regulations would need to be rewritten to conform to this style. Similar language such as "No person shall maintain..." or "Every person shall obtain a permit..." also sets forth prohibited conduct or establishes an affirmative duty which can be punished as a crime. While not as direct, these expressions can be read together with the general penalty provision to support a prosecution.

Each ordinance in the municipal code need not refer to the general municipal code enforcement provision. Municipal ordinances and codes are not treated any differently than the Penal Code. Penal Code section 19 designates the maximum penalties for misdemeanors and infractions, but it is not necessary for these penalties to be repeated in each of the crimes listed in the Penal Code before the court imposes a sentence.

3. Prosecution of Code Enforcement Statutes

Violations of some state land use statutes can be enforced by misdemeanor and prosecution.

a. State Housing Law. The State Housing Law establishes the minimum habitability standards for residential buildings (single-family and apartments). It is unlawful to maintain a substandard building as defined in Health and Safety Code section 17920.3. Anyone who violates the State Housing Law or the State Building Standards Code or any rule or regulation promulgated pursuant to the State Housing Law can be charged with a misdemeanor per Health and Safety Code section 17995. Conviction carries the usual maximum penalty of a $1,000 fine and/or imprisonment, not to exceed six months.

Section 17995.1 increases the penalty for a person who is convicted for maintaining a substandard dwelling for a second or subsequent time in five years. The maximum fine then becomes $5,000 and can include imprisonment, not to exceed six months. Section 17995.3 increases the penalty for a repeat offender to include the penalty of imprisonment of not less than six months, and not more than one year, if the person satisfies additional criteria outlined in the statute.

The courts have approved this basic format as enforceable. *Richter v. Lightston*, 161 Cal. 260, 264 (1911) (valid ordinance which prohibited issuance of a business license despite its failure to affix a penalty for violations); *See also, Alichoff v. Los Angeles Gas & Electric Corp.*, 84 Cal.App. 33, 39 (1927). Where there is ambiguity as to whether a particular statute or ordinance was intended to be enforced by criminal prosecution, the courts will look to the statute's plain language and legislative intent. *People v. Crutcher*, 262 Cal.App. 2d 750 (1968) (Election Code sections 11703-11704 did not suggest any penal enforcement).

b.   Public Nuisance. A property in violation of local regulations may also constitute a public nuisance and, under certain circumstances, could be prosecuted as a misdemeanor. The definition of a public nuisance for purposes of criminal prosecution (Penal Code section 370) is the same definition found in sections 3479 and 3480 of the Civil Code.

Penal Code section 372 provides that any person who maintains or willfully fails to remove any public nuisance is guilty of a misdemeanor. To maintain a public nuisance after notice to abate from a health officer, district attorney, or city attorney is also a misdemeanor according to Penal Code section 373a. In addition, section 373a makes the continued existence of a public nuisance a separate misdemeanor for each day after notice is given.

c.   Subdivision Map Act. Municipalities control the development of subdivisions within their boundaries through the powers provided in the Subdivision Map Act (Government Code section 66410 *et seq.*). Primarily procedural, the Map Act establishes time frames and procedures that property owners must follow in designing and improving subdivisions. According to Government Code sections 66499.30 through 66499.36 the Map Act can be enforced by criminal prosecution with penalties for violations that exceed those for misdemeanors.

C. Basic Criminal Procedure

Criminal prosecution starts with the filing of a complaint. This can take the form of a field citation issued by an enforcement agency or a complaint written and filed by a prosecutor. All complaints must comply with the constitutional requirements of due process: the charge must be sufficiently specific to inform the defendant about the nature of the crime.

Once a complaint is filed, the defendant's first court appearance is at the arraignment. Here the defendant can plead guilty, not guilty, or no contest. Depending upon the plea and the circumstances of the case, a trial date may be set by the court; or, if the defendant is represented by counsel, the next court appearance may be in the trial setting department where negotiations about settlement may take place. If the case is not settled at that time, a trial date is set. At trial, if the violation charged was a misdemeanor, the defendant has a constitutional right to a jury trial.

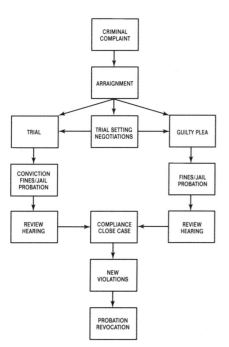

1.   Drafting a Criminal Code Enforcement Complaint

Several different approaches can be used to write a criminal complaint in a code enforcement case. For example, a zoning inspector's report may indicate that on November 1 an owner's residential property contained ten inoperable vehicles, automobile parts, and assorted junk, and that a subsequent reinspection on December 1 revealed identical violations. Sufficient circumstantial evidence exists to charge the owner with a criminal violation or count for each day in the entire month of November. While this strategy can easily be applied to exterior code violations such as improper storage or an illegal structure, zoning violations involving nonpermitted uses must be corroborated by the direct observations of a neighbor or an enforcement agent.

California Criminal Law—Procedures and Practice (1986) published by the California Continuing Education of the Bar (CEB) is a good resource for criminal procedure issues. *See also California Criminal Law* by Witkin & Epstein (2d edition, 1988).

Inspection Dates

As a general guideline, select the dates for the complaint that correspond to actual inspections. This approach will focus the judge or jury on a short span of time. Also, no circumstantial evidence or inference is necessary. The dates in the complaint will match the dates the inspectors were present on the property and witnessed the violations. Moreover, a conviction for only one day is all that is necessary to place the violator on misdemeanor probation. (*See* pages 129-132 for a thorough discussion of probation.)

2. Identification of Proper Defendants and Strict Criminal Liability

In drafting a code enforcement criminal complaint, another requirement is to identify the persons responsible for the violation. In most cases, the prosecutor can charge the tenant, property owner, or both. Where the owner resides at the property, the choice is simple.

California law generally requires that every crime or public offense must have both a violation or criminal act and criminal intent as established in Penal Code section 20. An exception to this rule is the doctrine of criminal liability without fault or strict liability. Based on this doctrine, where local ordinances or statutes protect the public's health, safety, and welfare, proof of intent is not required.

Strict criminal liability applies to most regulatory offenses and other violations of the police power. The courts have applied strict criminal liability to the misbranding of motor oils, *People v. Travers*, 52 Cal.App. 3d 111, 114 (1975); misbranding of drugs, *People v. Stewart*, 47 Cal. 2d 167, 172 (1956); misbranding the weight of produce, *People v. Beggs*, 69 Cal.App. 2d Supp. 819, 822 (1945); and unsanitary conditions in nursing homes, *People v. Balmer*, 196 Cal.App. 2d Supp. 874, 877-878 (1961).

Where property owners have been placed on notice about a violation, they may be compelled to make their property safe regardless of who caused the condition. *People v. Greene*, 264 Cal. App. 2d 774, 778 (1968) (landowner can be criminally charged for the condition of his or her property, and a municipality can demand affirmative acts to remedy the condition of the premises).

Strict Criminal Liability in Code Cases

In *People v. Bachrach*, 114 Cal.App. 3d Supp. 8, 12 (1980), the court approved the use of strict liability in upholding a conviction for violations of various provisions of the uniform building and fire codes.

"[W]hether the context be civil or criminal, liability and the duty to take affirmative action flow not from the landowner's active responsibility for a condition of his land that causes widespread harm to others or his knowledge of or intent to cause such harm but rather, and quite simply, from his very possession and control of the land in question. [citation omitted]. This principle that the private right to control land carries with it certain strictly enforceable public responsibilities is, as we have seen, a venerable idea; and it is one that grows progressively more vital in the law as the interdependencies in our society become more apparent and the threat to the integrity of our environment more ominous." *Leslie Salt Co. v. San Francisco Bay Conservation Comm.*, 153 Cal.App. 3d 605, 622 (1984) (property owner held responsible for violations of state environmental protection statutes even though some person, without the owner's permission or knowledge, dumped illegal materials on his property). *See also People v. Chevron Chemical Co.*, 143 Cal. App.3d 50, 53-54 (1983) where Chevron was held criminally liable under Fish and Game Code section 5650 for discharging fertilizer waste and storm water runoff into a bay despite the lack of criminal intent.

3. Field Citation vs. Arrest Warrant

A criminal action can be initiated either by a field citation or a criminal complaint.

A criminal action can be initiated either by a field citation or a criminal complaint. A code compliance officer can issue a field citation, or the prosecutor can file a complaint and either mail a courtesy notice or notify warrant or execute an arrest warrant.

Field Citation. Whenever the enforcement agent has reasonable cause to believe that a misdemeanor was committed in his or her presence, Penal Code section 836.5 establishes the authority for public officers and employees to arrest a person without a warrant. Essentially, this statute permits the enforcement agent to issue a criminal citation in the field. The local legislative body must have enacted an ordinance granting the authority to arrest for municipal code violations which are either misdemeanors or infractions.

In most situations, the enforcement agent issues field citations as a substitute for a physical arrest. Unless the violator demands to be taken before a judge, a field citation may be issued to the violator based on his or her written promise to appear. Consult Penal Code sections 836.5(c), 853.6 and 853.5. A copy of this citation becomes the criminal complaint per Penal Code section 853.9.

Criminal Complaint. Instead of issuing a field citation, a prosecutor can file a criminal complaint. *See* Penal Code sections 948 (form of complaint) and 949 (authority to file complaints in municipal court). This method can be employed when the property owner or tenant cannot be located to sign a field citation. While an inspector may observe the violation, since no individual was seen performing the illegal act, a citation cannot be issued because the offense is not considered to be committed within the inspector's presence.

> ### Citation Training
>
> The effectiveness of any citation program depends on the training and skill of the enforcement agent. While not subject to the mandatory peace officer standards and training (POST) requirement, code compliance officers could benefit from a POST-certified powers of arrest course, which provides basic training for properly issuing misdemeanor field citations.

POST = police officer standards and training

> ### Zoning Violations and Notice of Pending Action
>
> When the prosecutor files a criminal complaint for zoning or planning code violations, a notice of pending action should be filed in the county recorder's office to prevent the owner from transferring the property to another person without first correcting the outstanding violations. Government Code section 65908 permits the enforcement agency to file a notice of pending action in the county recorder's office at the time the enforcement action is initiated.
>
> Recording this document puts prospective purchasers of the property on notice that this property is subject of a current enforcement action involving zoning or planning violations. Once the action is completed, the enforcement agency must file a withdrawal of the notice with the county recorder.

Arrest Warrant. Once a complaint is filed, the prosecutor may immediately file a declaration in support of an arrest warrant pursuant to Penal Code section 1427. This declaration discusses the facts surrounding the violation and reasons for filing the complaint. The judge reviews the declaration and, if the facts are sufficient, will issue the warrant. Penal Code section 816 authorizes a peace officer or any public officer or employee to execute the arrest warrant. The form of the warrant is discussed in Penal Code section 814. After the arrest, the defendant must be taken before a judge without unnecessary delay according to Penal Code section 825.

Notify Warrant. Instead of a request for an arrest warrant, prosecutors in some municipalities mail code violators official courtesy notices, called 'notify warrants', which list the municipal code violations and establish the court appearance date for arraignment. In this situation a complaint will have already been filed and signed by the prosecutor. Since most zoning and building code violators typically are not criminals, the notify warrant is usually successful in securing their appearance in court.

Since most zoning and building code violators typically are not criminals, the notify warrant is usually successful in securing their appearance in court.

4. Failure to Appear and Warrants for Arrest

If a violator fails to appear for the scheduled arraignment date, a prosecutor can easily obtain an arrest warrant. If a misdemeanor field citation was issued and signed by the violator, Penal Code section 853.8 instructs the court to automatically issue and deliver a warrant for the violator's arrest within twenty days after failure to appear. This can also be charged as a new and separate misdemeanor offense per Penal Code section 853.7. If no citation was issued or the violator did not sign a written promise to appear, a prosecutor will need to file a written declaration to obtain an arrest warrant pursuant to Penal Code section 1427.

Arresting Code Violators

Recognize that a judge issuing a warrant does not guarantee that police officers, sheriffs, or marshals will arrest the violator. Given the overcrowding in many metropolitan correctional facilities, most law enforcement agencies give priority to felons and serious misdemeanants before executing arrest warrants for zoning and building code violators. Meet with local law enforcement officials responsible for the execution of arrest warrants to discuss your municipality's concerns about arresting serious code violators.

5. Corporate Defendants

When the defendant is a corporation, Penal Code sections 1390 through 1397 establish special procedures for filing a criminal complaint. A date for arraignment is scheduled by presenting a summons for the judge's signature. The summons must be served on a designated agent or officer of the corporation at least five days before the scheduled appearance in arraignment court. After the summons has been served, if a representative of the corporation fails to appear, the court enters a plea of not guilty and another court date is set, per Penal Code section 1427.

In addition to filing against the corporation, a prosecutor can also file a criminal action against officers of the corporation as individuals. Commonly referred to as 'piercing the corporate veil', this doctrine allows a court to disregard the corporate entity and hold the individuals within the controlling corporation responsible where the corporation is used by those individuals or by another corporation to commit fraud, circumvent statutes, or perpetrate other wrongful or inequitable acts.

The doctrine referred to as 'piercing the corporate veil' allows a court to disregard the corporate entity and hold the individuals within the controlling corporation responsible.

Field Citations and Corporations

Field citations cannot be issued against a corporation. Thus, when deciding to take criminal action against property owned by a corporation the enforcement agency will have to seek the assistance of the city or district attorney to draft a summons, as required by Penal Code sections 1390-1397.

> In order to disregard the corporate entity, the evidence must show that persons, such as corporate officers, dominate or control the corporation's affairs, and that in this particular case justice and equity can best be achieved by disregarding the corporate entity. *See generally, People v. Conway*, 42 Cal.App. 3d 875, 884-886 (1974) (president of car dealership found criminally liable for grand theft based on acts of subordinates done in the normal course of business).

D. Due Process Analysis of Criminal Complaint

Whether the criminal enforcement action is initiated by a citation or complaint, the language of the complaint and the ordinance itself must satisfy the threshold constitutional standards of the due process clause. The Fifth Amendment to the U.S. Constitution requires the government to enact fair and reasonable procedures before people can be jailed or deprived of property. In the context of criminal charges due process demands that adequate notice be given to the accused. Thus, the enforcement agency and prosecutor must ensure that the ordinance and the language used in the criminal complaint is specific.

Criminal statutes or ordinances which either forbid or require an act must not be drafted in terms so vague that "men of common intelligence must necessarily guess at its meaning and differ as to its application . . . ." *People v. McCaughan*, 49 Cal. 2d 409, 414

(1957), quoting *Connally v. General Construction Co.*, 269 U.S. 385, 391 (1925). Due process requires that a person accused of committing a crime be advised of the charges so that he or she has an opportunity to prepare and present a defense and avoid surprises at trial. *Byrd v. Municipal Court*, 125 Cal.App. 3d 1054, 1057 (1981).

Zoning Prosecutions and Due Process

Within the context of code enforcement, the courts have approved criminal prosecutions of zoning ordinances against claims that the ordinances were vague and violated the due process clause. In *Sechrist v. Municipal Court*, 64 Cal.App. 3d 737, 743-744 (1976), the court approved the criminal enforcement of zoning laws and upheld the specific ordinance against a due process challenge. Sechrist was charged with the unlawful storage of junk and inoperable motor vehicles on his property in a single-family residential zone. The court noted that zoning laws are written differently than other criminal laws. Unlike criminal statutes which inform the accused of prohibited conduct, in a zoning ordinance permitted uses are listed while all other uses not listed are deemed prohibited.

Despite this difference, the court approved the use of criminal prosecution by concluding that due process does not mandate a specific list of prohibited uses within a given zone. *See also, People v. Tollman*, 110 Cal.App.3d Supp 6, 9-10 (1980) (conviction affirmed for violations of a zoning ordinance prohibiting parking of commercial vehicles on public streets in single-family residential neighborhoods); in contrast, review the case of *In re Scarpetti*, 124 Cal.App. 3d 434, 439-442 (1981) (zoning ordinance was unconstitutionally vague where storage of large commercial trucks could be viewed as a valid accessory use in a rural residential zone—conviction reversed by the court).

Demurrer

In code cases it is fairly common for the defendant's attorney to file a motion challenging the specificity of the criminal or civil complaint or municipal ordinance. This motion is called a demurrer. As a precaution, a prosecutor should take special care to use language in the complaint that is based on the review of applicable court cases which have interpreted due process challenges to municipal police power ordinances.

Evaluation of trial-worthiness begins when a prosecutor determines whether or not sufficient evidence exists to file a complaint.

When determining whether an ordinance or statute is sufficient for criminal prosecution, a court will apply a standard of "reasonable certainty, not mathematical exactitude." *Solander v. Municipal Court*, 45 Cal.App. 3d 664, 667 (1975) (Health and Safety Code provisions required restaurants to provide hot and cold water in their kitchens—criminal conviction was affirmed); *see also, People v. Ngyuyen*, 161 Cal.App. 3d 687, 691-695 (1984) (definition of gill net sufficient to affirm conviction for Fish and Game Code violations).

E. Strategies for Proving a Code Enforcement Case

Evaluation of trial-worthiness begins when a prosecutor determines whether or not sufficient evidence exists to file a complaint. Once a complaint is filed, the prosecutor must work closely with the enforcement agency to prepare for trial. Although most code enforcement criminal cases do not go to trial, advance preparation can facilitate negotiations and a possible settlement. Many of the following comments and suggestions apply equally to civil trials and administrative enforcement hearings.

1. Case Preparation

Trial veterans usually advise new attorneys to prepare their case thoroughly, weeks before a court hearing or trial. Always the key to a successful prosecution, early preparation is particularly important when prosecuting a code enforcement case.

Always the key to a successful prosecution, early preparation is particularly important when prosecuting a code enforcement case.

Code Cases Present Novel Issues. For many judges or commissioners, the issues presented in a code case are novel, and a prosecutor must anticipate potential evidentiary issues and provide pre-trial briefs so that the merits of the case can be evaluated effectively. Common evidentiary issues may include admissibility of maps and documents, proving the underlying zone, and qualifying the inspector as an expert witness.

Code Cases Are Unique to Juries. Where the case involves a misdemeanor violation, a jury may be the trier of fact. A prosecutor should appreciate the possibility that some citizens will question the wisdom of prosecuting zoning and building code violations. Development of a profile describing the positive and negative characteristics of the ideal juror will help the prosecutor prepare questions for jury selection.

In addition, since many judges read jury instructions at the beginning of the trial, the prosecutor should write the jury instructions well in advance. While general criminal jury instructions for misdemeanors can be found in California Jury Instruction-Criminal (CALJIC) (5th edition, 1988), the actual elements of the local zoning or building code must be translated to match the complaint.

CALJIC = California Jury Instruction–Criminal

Code Cases May Rely on Inexperienced Witnesses. Many enforcement agents, zoning investigators, and building inspectors have little experience testifying in court. Several weeks before the trial the prosecutor should meet with these witnesses to discuss their testimony and coordinate the preparation of diagrams, exhibits, photographs, and other documents that may be entered into evidence.

Many enforcement agents, zoning investigators, and building inspectors have little experience testifying in court.

Code Cases Often Require Trial Briefs. Early trial preparation helps to focus on the presentation of evidence. Since the judge and the defense attorney are probably unfamiliar with code enforcement cases, a prosecutor must be prepared to submit trial briefs on a variety of evidentiary issues unique to code cases such as strict liability, continuous offenses, and the actual elements of zoning or building code violations.

2. Jury Selection

> Jury selection is conducted under the supervision of the trial court and its scope is primarily left to the sound discretion of that court. *People v. Banner*, 3 Cal.App.4th 1315 (1992); *see also, U.S. v. Powell*, 932 F.2d 1337 (9th Cir. 1991). The trial court's discretion must be exercised in a manner consistent with the right of counsel to reveal the full extent of juror bias. *People v. Martinez*, 228 Cal.App. 3d 1456 (1991). (Citation)

Jury trials for code enforcement cases are not common. Where the code violations are charged as misdemeanors, a defendant has a constitutional right to a trial by jury. If a defendant chooses to exercise this right, a prosecutor is thrust into the midst of jury selection. Although the judge usually controls jury selection in a misdemeanor trial, a prosecutor should prepare a list of potential questions for the judge to review prior to the start of jury selection. These questions should be designed to elicit an honest response from a prospective juror. The prosecutor should then compare these responses to the key characteristics of an ideal juror.

One effect of Proposition 115, The Crime Victim's Bill of Rights, approved by California voters in 1990 was to reform procedures for jury selection. Code of Civil Procedure section 223 now provides that the court shall examine all prospective jurors in a criminal case. Upon a showing of good cause, the court may permit the parties to pose supplemental questions, or the court can ask additional questions which have been submitted by the prosecutor or defense attorney.

3. Evidentiary Issues

Because code enforcement cases invariably involve the introduction into evidence of numerous documents, a prosecutor should carefully consult the Evidence Code regarding the rules for admission of business records, public documents, and their authentication. Code cases often raise evidentiary issues involving the best evidence rule and hearsay doctrine. Whether a zoning or building inspector is qualified to testify as an expert is another evidentiary issue which must be addressed.

a.   Documentary Evidence, Letters, and Correspondence. Code enforcement cases usually involve the introduction of numerous letters and correspondence. Evidence Code section 641 establishes a presumption that a letter correctly addressed and properly mailed will have been received in the

The Persuasive Power of Diagrams and Photographs

Given the unique nature of many code cases, whenever possible the prosecutor should use diagrams, maps, photographs, and enlargements during any court presentation. A clear color photograph which shows a side yard filled with junk is often the most powerful piece of evidence in a code case. Enlarging several key photographs for the hearing can also persuasively affect the judge, hearing officer, or jury. If possible, the inspector should photograph each violation and mount an enlargement on a separate sheet of paper with the code violation listed below.

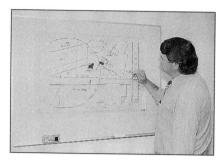

As a general rule, diagrams and pictures of the property in violation can be used as illustrations in opening statements. *People v. Green*, 47 Cal.App. 2d 209, 215 (1956).

ordinary course of mail, while Evidence Code section 644 provides that a book purporting to be printed or published by a public authority is presumed to have been printed or published.

b. How to Prove the Zone. Where the code case involves a zoning violation, a prosecutor must prove the underlying zone. The quickest and most obvious solution is a stipulation from defense counsel. If that's not possible, several methods will allow the zone to be introduced as evidence—

Certified Maps. A prosecutor may introduce a copy of an engineering map, certified as true and accurate by the custodian of city records, which portrays the zones. *See* Evidence Code section 1280 (hearsay exception for official records); Evidence Code section 1506 (best evidence exception for certified copies of official writings); and Evidence Code section 1530 (presumption of authenticity for certified or attested official writings).

Testimony of Enforcement Agent. Another approach is to ask the zoning investigator to testify about his or her familiarity with the location of the property and the zoning classifications applicable to the area. If the court qualifies this zoning investigator as an expert in this area, the testimony would be admissible. An expert is entitled to use hearsay, in this case the zoning maps, to form an expert opinion per Evidence Code section 801.

Judicial Notice. Evidence Code section 452 permits a judge to take judicial notice to prove the existence of a zone. While required to take judicial notice of municipal ordinances under Evidence Code section 452(b) when requested by one of the parties to the case, the court is not required to do so if the party fails to provide the court with the ordinance in question. *Salinero v. Pon,* 124 Cal.App. 3d 120, 131-133 (1981) (municipal courts must take judicial notice of city or county ordinances because these courts were formed to hear these cases). *See also, People v. Cowles,* 142 Cal.App. 2d Supp. 865, 867 (1965).

Some code cases hinge on whether the person charged with the violation owns or controls the property, and thus whether he or she is obligated to correct the violation.

c. Property Ownership. Another evidentiary issue for a prosecutor to prove is ownership of the property. A stipulation saves the court and the prosecutor from having to prove an indisputable fact. Yet, some code cases hinge on whether the person charged with the violation owns or controls the property, and thus whether he or she is obligated to correct the violation.

Presumption of Ownership. Evidence Code section 638 establishes a presumption of ownership when a person exercises acts of ownership over the property. Testimony of a neighbor or tenant who observed activities or conversations which led either or both to believe the defendant was the property owner may be sufficient to raise this presumption. Introducing utility and tax bills or lease and rental agreements into evidence would also serve to raise this presumption. The defendant may offer rebuttal evidence, since presumption of ownership merely affects the burden of producing evidence and not the burden of proof, per Evidence Code section 630.

After the introduction of sufficient evidence to establish ownership and the essential elements of the offense, the owner's statements or admissions may be used to collaborate ownership. *See* Evidence Code section 1220 (hearsay exceptions for a defendant's admissions).

Defendant's Statements

As a general rule of evidence, the defendant's statements alone are not admissible into evidence until the prosecutor has introduced other types of evidence which connect the defendant to the violation. This is called the 'corpus delicti rule', where some evidence exists of the corpus or elements of the offense. In a code enforcement case, ownership of the property is an essential element in prosecuting the owner for zoning and building code violations. The amount of evidence necessary to satisfy the corpus delicti rule is minimal. Showing that a crime was committed by someone is sufficient. *People v. Mehaffey,* 32 Cal. 2d 534, 545 (1948); *People v. Garcia,* 149 Cal.App. 3d Supp. 50, 53 (1983).

Certified Grant Deed. A certified copy of the grant deed from the county recorder's office is often the best method to prove ownership. Evidence Code section 1330 establishes an exception for documents affecting an interest in real or personal property (testimony from the custodian of records is irrelevant. *See* Evidence Code section 1280). The certified copy is simply offered into evidence.

Evidence Code sections 1400 and 1401 permit only the admission of authentic documents or copies. Evidence Code section 1530 responds to this burden by authenticating a copy of an official record by certification. A copy of the official record is considered *prima facie* evidence, per Evidence Code section 1600. Evidence Code section 1507 establishes an exception for recorded public records under the best evidence rule.

d. Permits and Licenses. Many code prosecutions involve the defendant's failure to obtain proper building permits or municipal licenses. In these cases, either the enforcement agent or a clerk from the agency responsible for keeping permit records must testify about the results of the search for applicable permits at this address. Evidence Code sections 1272 and 1284 provide hearsay exceptions for a clerk's testimony that a diligent search of those public records failed to reveal a permit for a particular property or person.

Another approach is to inform the judge that the prosecutor does not have the burden to show that no permit exists. The court should request information from the defendant about whether proper permits were obtained.

e. Statements and Admissions of the Defendant— The *Miranda* Rule. Statements made by the defendant in a criminal action can be valuable evidence to collaborate the prosecutor's enforcement case. The defendant's statements or admissions, however, can only be used in a criminal proceeding if they satisfy elaborate requirements that apply to questioning in the field. This is often referred to as the *Miranda* rule.

The *Miranda* rule holds that a person's statements made to police officers during a formal interrogation cannot be used against that person at a later criminal proceeding unless the police officers gave that person the *Miranda* warnings before they started their questioning. If a judge determines that *Miranda* warnings should have been given, but were not, those statements cannot be used as evidence in the pending criminal proceeding. Note that *Miranda* only applies to criminal proceedings.

The unresolved issue is whether or not *Miranda* warnings are required in code enforcement situations. Unfortunately, no court cases directly resolve this issue. *Miranda* compris-

Many code prosecutions involve the defendant's failure to obtain proper building permits or municipal licenses.

The defendant has the burden to prove that he or she possesses the necessary license or permit. *People v. Flores*, 62 Cal. App. 3d Supp. 19, 22-23 (1976). Flores was prosecuted for violating Penal Code section 654.1 (soliciting a person to pay for transportation without possessing a valid license or permit to act as a carrier). The prosecution rested its case without presenting any evidence that the defendant was not in possession of a valid license or permit. The court affirmed the conviction, since the defendant knew whether a valid license or permit had been obtained. The defendant could easily have provided this fact, which, if true, would have been a complete defense to the charge. *See also, People v. Yoshimura*, 91 Cal.3d 609, 625-629 (1979) (permit to possess explosives).

The Miranda *rule holds that a person's statements made to police officers during a formal interrogation cannot be used against that person at a later criminal proceeding unless the police officers gave that person the* Miranda *warnings before they started their questioning.*

es questioning by law enforcement officers after a person has been taken into custody or otherwise deprived of his freedom in any significant way. A brief analysis of *Miranda* and a comparison with common code enforcement situations should provide some guidance in this uncertain area.

The first element of *Miranda* is questioning. The courts have concluded that *Miranda* warnings do not have to be given where the person makes voluntary statements not in response to questions. The second element is whether zoning and building inspectors could be considered law enforcement officers. Although they are government agents designed to enforce land use regulations, they are not peace officers. In a similar situation, the courts have concluded that *Miranda* does not apply to a private security guard in the arrest of shoplifters, *In re Deborah C.*, 30 Cal.3d 125, 130-34 (1981), or private citizens, *In re Eric J.*, 25 Cal.App. 3d 522, 527 (1979). In each of these situations, the person was a nongovernmental employee not acting in concert with law enforcement officials. The courts, however, have applied *Miranda* to state prison correctional officers and county probation officers. *People v. Claxton*, 129 Cal.App. 3d 638, 670 (1982).

A conservative interpretation of these cases concludes that zoning and building inspectors could be viewed as law enforcement officers for purposes of *Miranda*. Although not peace officers, zoning and building inspectors are government employees empowered with the enforcement of local ordinances which can be prosecuted as criminal violations.

The third element is the surroundings where the questioning takes place. *Miranda* applies only to formal situations where the person has been taken into custody or its equivalent in the field. The courts evaluate whether the person's liberty has been deprived in any significant way.

Two court cases somewhat closer to code enforcement situations involved statements to a social worker and statements made to police enforcing regulations of auto dismantlers. The court found that *Miranda* did not apply to a noncustodial setting where the defendant knows that his or her statements will be reported to a state agency for possible prosecution. *People v. Battagglia*, 156 Cal.App. 3d 1058, 1064-65 (1984) (defendant's statements to a licensed social worker). Statements to police regarding a license to dismantle automobiles were appropriate without *Miranda* warnings. *People v. Shope*, 128 Cal.App. 3d 816 (1992).

Application of *Miranda* to Code Enforcement. Since case law is scarce in the code enforcement field, as a general guideline enforcement agents should give *Miranda* warnings when (1) working side by side with police officers, and (2) confronting similar situations where the courts have required the police to issue the warnings. For example, a code compliance officer or building inspector asking questions of the owner at his or her property does not appear to be a custodial interrogation or even a detention. The owner is free to go at any time and thereby is not coerced into answering questions. Thus, *Miranda* is probably not necessary. Where the enforcement agent issues a criminal field citation (misdemeanor or infraction), however, *Miranda* warnings should be given regardless of the location.

Since case law is scarce in the code enforcement field, as a general guideline enforcement agents should give Miranda *warnings when working side by side with police officers, and when confronting similar situations where the courts have required the police to issue the warnings.*

> ### *Miranda* and FDA Inspectors
>
> A case that has some similarities to code enforcement situations involved a routine search of a food warehouse by FDA inspectors. In *U.S. v. Thriftimart, Inc.*, 429 F.2d 1006 (9th Cir., 1970), the court in a short footnote dismissed the need for *Miranda* warnings. "Such warnings were unnecessary since appellants were not in custody." *Thriftimart*, 429 F.2d at 1010, n.6).
>
> Therefore, a typical inspection conducted on private property should not raise a *Miranda* issue even if the inspector poses questions to the owner or tenant. It should be noted, however, that the court in *United States v. Thriftimart, Inc.*, did not state that *Miranda* was inapplicable to code enforcement officers. In the unlikely event that an owner or code enforcement violator is significantly detained or taken into custody by the inspector, *United States v. Thriftimart, Inc.*, would suggest that a *Miranda* warning is required. This further supports the practice of giving *Miranda* warnings where the inspector issues a field citation.

FDA = Federal Food and Drug Administration

F. Sentencing and Terms of Probation

Conviction as a result of either trial or settlement requires the judge to impose a sentence for the code violations. The sentence may include a fine and time in jail, depending on the severity of the violations. In code enforcement cases, despite the imposition of a fine, ordering compliance as part of the sentence is more important, and this is accomplished when the judge imposes terms of probation.

Probation for misdemeanors is informal and can last for three years. This is the prime advantage of misdemeanor prosecution. Formal probation, which suspends the imposition or execution of a sentence under the close supervision of a probation officer, is rarely imposed for misdemeanor violations.

As a general rule, because the statutes are silent regarding the time limit for probation, enforcement of misdemeanor probationary conditions may not be available for infractions. Penal Code section 1203a delineates a maximum period of three years for the enforcement of a conditional sentence or informal misdemeanor probation. Some municipal court judges refuse to impose probationary conditions which apply to future criminal conduct when the violation is a mere infraction. While Penal Code sections 1203a and 1203b expressly empower the court to grant a conditional sentence in infraction cases, no time period for future enforcement of the conditions is mentioned. Therefore, a conditional sentence may only relate to the criminal acts charged in the complaint, and the municipality has no protection against future violations.

Because the statutes are silent regarding the time limit for probation, enforcement of misdemeanor probationary conditions may not be available for infractions.

Benefits and Burdens of Misdemeanors

An enforcement agency must weigh the deterrent effect of misdemeanor prosecutions against the procedural burdens. For infractions a defendant has no constitutional right to a jury trial or court-appointed counsel. The municipality must decide whether adequate staff is available to conduct misdemeanor prosecutions. In many situations, the extra amount of staff and time may be well worth the extra effort to establish misdemeanor probationary terms to prevent future code violations.

1. Multiple Violations

In most criminal convictions the defendant can only be sentenced once for the same violation according to Penal Code section 654. This section is designed to prevent multiple punishments of fine or jail for the same course of conduct. In code enforcement cases, however, the courts have approved an exception where the municipal code declares that each and every day is deemed a separate violation. *See generally, People v. Djekich*, 229 Cal.App.3d 1213, 1221-1222 (1991).

2. Probationary Terms

The terms of informal probation or a conditional sentence are in the nature of a contract, with courts having broad authority to draft the terms of probation to fit the case. Probationary conditions must reasonably relate to either the crime for which the defendant was convicted or the possibility of future criminality. *See generally, People v. Lent*, 15 Cal.3d 481, 486 (1975) and *In re Young*, 121 Cal.App. 711, 714 (1932).

3. Scope of Probationary Terms

In the context of code enforcement, the terms of probation must be tailored to fit the facts of the case. For example, where an owner is convicted of failing to obtain proper permits, a judge could require the owner to obtain the permits in addition to the payment of a fine. Another important term of probation is to establish subsequent review hearings so that the court can monitor an owner's progress in obtaining permits. This is especially important in the case of complex construction where the permit process may take six months or longer. (Examples of possible probationary conditions are found in Appendix A).

> Note that some statutes provide enhanced penalties and terms of probation. Penal Code section 1203.1i authorizes the judge to order the owner of substandard properties to live in his or her slum as a sentencing option. *People v. Avol*, 192 Cal.App. 3d Supp. 1, 8 (1987) (upheld condition that required defendant to live for 30 days in apartment units which he owned and had failed to maintain in compliance with the county health code).

Terms of Probation Can Be Severe

As a condition of probation, a judge may compel a defendant to give up certain rights and privileges, even constitutional rights, which everyday citizens can exercise. *People v. Mason*, 5 Cal. App. 3d 759, 764 (1971) (upheld condition that required submission to warrantless search by probation officer at any time); *People v. Keefer*, 35 Cal.App. 3d 156, 168 (1973) (upheld condition that defendant not engage in furnace or heating business as a result of a conviction for fraud arising from this business); *People v. Lewis*, 77 Cal.App. 3d 455, 463 (1978) (upheld condition that defendant not work in bars or drive a cab since those conditions were reasonably related to potential criminality based on conviction for pimping).

4. Probation Revocation

A judge will most likely place a defendant convicted of a misdemeanor municipal code violation on three years' informal probation, subject to certain specified conditions, including—

- Payment of a fine
- Cessation of the unlawful use within 30 days
- Requirement that appropriate plans and permit applications be filed with the building inspection department within 45 days or remove the illegal structure
- An order not to violate the same or similar laws

Where the defendant fails to comply with the terms and conditions of probation within the three-year period, a prosecutor can file a motion to revoke probation. Probation revocation illustrates another advantage of misdemeanor prosecution. Since the revocation procedures are expedited, a new criminal complaint does not have to be filed. Thus, if an owner is on misdemeanor probation, the enforcement agency does not have to start at the beginning of the criminal process.

a. Probation Revocation Procedure. The enforcement agent must prepare a declaration in support of revocation. The declaration describes the current violations on the property and the defendant's failure to comply with probationary conditions. After obtaining a hearing date, a prosecutor serves the defendant with an order to show cause why probation should not be revoked.

At the revocation hearing, a defendant can either admit the violation or request an evidentiary hearing. Where the defendant admits the violation, the judge can summarily revoke probation, send the defendant to jail, and impose a fine. The judge can also modify the terms of probation and require the defendant to accept stricter probationary terms. *See generally,* Penal Code section 1203a.

b. Evidentiary Hearing. Should the defendant elect an evidentiary hearing, many procedures and constitutional rights normally afforded a defendant in a criminal proceeding do not apply. The basic procedures during a probation revocation hearing include the following—

- Notice consistent with due process clause
- A hearing before revocation
- Written notice discussing the alleged violations
- Disclosure of evidence or opportunity to be heard in person and present witnesses and evidence
- Right to confront witnesses
- A neutral and detached judge or hearing body

Revocation of probation generally takes about 20 days depending on the calendar of the municipal court. Therefore, probation revocation of a misdemeanor code violation provides a municipality with adequate protection against future violations during the three-year time period.

In the case of *People v. Vickers*, 8 Cal. App. 3d 451, 461 (1972) the California Supreme Court concluded that these basic probation revocation procedures satisfy the constitutional requirements of affording a defendant due process. The prosecution need only prove by a preponderance of the evidence the grounds for revocation, *People v. Rodriguez*, 51 Cal.App. 3d 437, 441 (1990); hearsay evidence is admissible in a probation revocation hearing, *People v. Brown*, 215 Cal.App. 3d 452, 454 (1989) and *People v. Burden*, 105 Cal.App. 3d 917, 921 (1980); no Fifth Amendment violation if defendant testifies at revocation hearing before trial on new charges, *People v. Jasper*, 33 Cal.App. 3d 931, 934 (1983); the court may enlarge the probationary period at any time before it expires, *People v. Williams*, 24 Cal. 2d 848, 850-51 (1938).

Using Civil Injunctions

Civil injunctions are ideal for imminent threats to health and safety—destruction of sensitive habitat, toxic waste dumping, substandard buildings, vacant structures, or sewer line breaks.

Introduction

Regulatory Foundations

Local Regulatory Implementation

Managing Code Enforcement

Investigating Cases

Selection of Remedies

Administrative Remedies

Criminal Prosecution

Using Civil Injunctions

Defenses to CE Actions

Using Civil Injunctions

A civil action is another enforcement method that can be used to address violations of land use regulations. On behalf of the enforcement agency, a municipal attorney requests an injunction requiring the responsible person to correct outstanding violations and thereafter maintain the property in compliance with local or state laws. As part of this civil action, the court may impose civil penalties and order the owner to reimburse the enforcement agency for its investigation costs. Specialized statutes provide for other civil law remedies, such as the appointment of a receiver for substantially substandard residential properties.

Civil injunctions can be used to enforce local zoning and building codes, including the basic cases where the owner fails to obtain proper permits for a room addition. The municipal attorney need only prove the existence of the code violations by using the enforcement agent's written declarations. Live testimony is not required to obtain an injunction.

Civil injunctions are ideal for those properties that pose imminent threats to the public's health and safety, such as destruction of environmentally sensitive habitat, dumping of toxic waste, substandard buildings, vacant structures, or sewer line breaks on private property.

If the violation continues to destroy sensitive habitat or the owner defies a stop work order by continuing to build without permits, the municipal attorney can request the court to issue a temporary restraining order. Unlike criminal prosecution, the municipal attorney can request the court to issue either temporary restraining orders or preliminary injunctions that can compel compliance while the civil action is pending. This differs from a criminal action, where a conviction must occur before a court can order compliance. Thus, an enforcement agency can obtain

If the violation continues to destroy sensitive habitat or the owner defies a stop work order by continuing to build without permits, the municipal attorney can request the court to issue a temporary restraining order.

preliminary court orders within several days or weeks after the civil complaint is filed, depending upon the severity of the health and safety violations. Once the preliminary injunction is issued requiring the owner to abate the immediate hazards, most code enforcement civil cases settle without a trial.

A further advantage is that, once obtained, a permanent injunction can be recorded against the violating property and can remain in effect forever. Final civil judgments can last well beyond the maximum period of three years for misdemeanor probation.

Advantages of Using Civil Injunctions

"Mindful the emphasis in zoning enforcement is upon prevention, rather than punishment and the attainment of conforming uses [citation omitted], injunctive relief 'is probably the most efficient way for a local government unit to deal with continuing zoning violations. [citations]. Compared to injunctive relief, repeated prosecution for a violation of a zoning ordinance, seeking imposition of a fine or jail term, is an inadequate method of attaining the goal of a zoning ordinance—compliance. The purpose of use restrictions is not punishment but the attainment of conforming uses. An injunction ordering compliance with use restrictions is peculiarly suited to this end." *People v. Djekich*, 229 Cal.App.3d 1213, 1222 (1991) quoting *City of Minneapolis v. F and R, Inc.*, 300 N.W.2d 2, 4 (Minn. 1980).

A. Cause of Action

A cause of action is a legal theory approved by the courts that forms the basis of the civil enforcement action of land use regulations. The complaint may allege one or more of five legal theories, depending upon the facts and circumstances of the case.

1. Local Ordinances

The most common cause of action, which derives from the municipal police power, is to allege violations of municipal ordinances and regulations. The courts have approved the use of civil actions as a means to correct violations of valid building, zoning, or other local land use regulations.

Where a city seeks to enforce a valid zoning, building, or fire ordinance by injunction, the court's inquiry is limited to whether a violation exists. No proof of a public nuisance is nec-

Where the personal welfare and property rights of a large number of inhabitants would be detrimentally affected by a violation of a police or sanitary regulation—whether or not the ordinance provides other means of enforcement—the city or town may itself appeal to a court of equity, by means of a forceful writ of injunction, to restrain the violation or cause its wrongful effect to be removed. *See City of Stockton v. Frisbie & Latta*, 93 Cal.App. 277, 289-90 (1928) (zoning); *See also, City of San Mateo v. Hardy*, 64 Cal.App. 2d 794, 796 (1944) (zoning and building codes); *San Francisco v. City Investment Corp.*, 15 Cal.App. 3d 1031, 1041 (1971) (fire code).

essary. *City and County of San Francisco v. Burton,* 201 Cal.App. 2d 749, 756-57 (1962).

2. General Public Nuisance

Another cause of action, which is a separate legal basis from violations of municipal police power, is to allege the maintenance of a public nuisance. In many code enforcement cases, the facts indicate that both violations of local regulations and the condition of the property are serious enough to be declared a public nuisance. In such a situation the municipal attorney should allege both causes of action so that a judge can issue an injunction on either legal theory.

Section 731 of the Code of Civil Procedure authorizes the district attorney or the city attorney to bring a civil action in the name of the People of the State of California to abate public nuisances. Any activity that creates a public nuisance may be enjoined by the court. A particular condition may be considered a public nuisance if it meets the common law or general statutory definition, which is found in Civil Code section 3479. Section 3480 defines public nuisance.

Specified conditions may also be declared to be a public nuisance by a local legislative body or by the state legislature. California Government Code section 38771 authorizes a city to declare by ordinance what constitutes a public nuisance. Where defined by statute or ordinance, a public nuisance is considered a 'nuisance per se'. In such a situation, the function of the court is to determine whether in fact a statutory violation exists, without any independent assessment of the danger caused by the violation.

3. State Housing Law

A civil enforcement action may be based on a violation of the State Housing Law (Health and Safety Code sections 17910 through 17995). The State Housing Law also provides for other remedies in addition to an injunction.

After declaring a building substandard, as defined in Health and Safety Code section 17920.3, and if there is no correction within the period specified, the enforcement agency may file a civil action against the owner or other responsible person. In this lawsuit the municipality may ask the court to take any of the following actions—

- Enjoin the violation (Health and Safety Code section 17980)

Public Nuisance Cases

■ Under the statutory definition found in the Civil Code, the courts have concluded that a number of common property violations and conditions, including substandard buildings and housing code violations, amount to a public nuisance, *City of Bakersfield v. Miller,* 64 Cal. 2d 93 (1966). Likewise, conditions on property causing a fire hazard have also been recognized as a public nuisance. *Vedder v. Imperial County,* 36 Cal.App. 3d 654, 661 (1974); *San Diego County v. Carlstrom,* 196 Cal.App. 2d 485, 489-491 (1961); and *People v. Oliver,* 86 Cal.App. 2d 885, 890 (1948).

■ The right of a municipality to declare certain conditions public nuisances has been upheld as constitutional. *City of Bakersfield v. Miller,* 64 Cal.2d 93, 100 (1966).

■ Civil enforcement actions based on a public nuisance per se affect the burden of proof. The actual condition of the property is the only proof required to establish a public nuisance, and no proof of a harmful effect is necessary where the conditions violate a law that was declared a public nuisance. *See McClatchy v. Lagina Lands Ltd.,* 32 Cal.App. 718, 725 (1917). Furthermore, alleging irreparable injury is not necessary to obtain an injunction against a nuisance. *See L.A. Brick etc. Co. v. City of Los Angeles,* 60 Cal.App. 2d 478, 486 (1943). Once the existence of a public nuisance, as defined by the local or state ordinance, has been demonstrated, the only remaining issue is whether the ordinance is valid.

■ Enter a preliminary injunction (section 17981)

■ Enter an order permitting the enforcement agency to abate any public nuisance violations (section 17982)

California Health and Safety Code sections 17980.6 and 17980.7 authorize the following additional remedies where a building can be classified as 'substantially substandard'—

Civil Penalties and State Income Tax Deductions. If the substandard building is in such a state of disrepair that the health and safety of the residents or the public is substantially endangered, a court may assess civil penalties in the event of repeat violations and may negate the owner's state income tax deductions for interest, taxes, depreciation, or amortization if the building is rented. Health and Safety Code sections 17980.6 and 17980.7(a) and (b).

Receiver. If an owner fails to comply with a court order or notice to correct the violations, the court may appoint a receiver to repair the violations. Health and Safety Code section 17980.7(c).

Cost Recovery. If the court finds that the conditions "substantially affect the health and safety of residents," upon entry of any order or judgment, the court *must* award the enforcement agency all of its expenses for inspection, investigation, enforcement activities, attorney hours, and costs of prosecution. Health and Safety Code sections 17980.6 and 17980.7(d)(1).

Relocation. In the event that repairs are undertaken as a result of a court order and the condition of the premises or the rehabilitation "significantly affect the safe and sanitary use of the premises by any lawful tenant," the court must order the owner to pay the tenant moving and storage costs and relocation compensation, as well as first offer the tenant the right to re-occupy the premises after repairs are complete. Health and Safety Code section 17980.7(d)(3).

4. Unfair Business Practices

Injunctive relief may also be available under the Unfair Business Practices Act, Business and Professions Code sections 17000 through 17208. Under this statute, the municipal attorney may file a civil enforcement action seeking an injunction and civil penalties against any individual or entity engaging in unfair business practices, per Business and Professions Code sections 17200 and 17206. The maximum civil penalty is $2,500 per day per violation.

Unfair Business Prosecutions by Small Cities

The city attorney, in a city with fewer than 750,000 residents, can either refer the case to the district attorney or have the district attorney deputize the city attorney—with the possibility of an agreement by which a portion of any civil penalties recovered are shared with the city to offset the cost of developing the case. Alternatively, it may be possible for a city attorney, in a jurisdiction of insufficient population to enter into an agreement with the local district attorney, to be 'cross-deputized' as a district attorney for a particular case. This can usually be accomplished simply by an exchange of letters.

Section 17206(b) sets forth criteria for the court to consider in assessing the civil penalty. These include, but are not limited to, "the nature and seriousness of the misconduct, the number of violations, the persistence of the misconduct, the length of time over which the misconduct occurred, the willfulness of the defendant's misconduct, and the defendant's assets, liabilities, and net worth."

Unfair business practices are broadly defined so as to encompass "anything that can properly be called a business practice and that at the same time is forbidden by the law." *Barquis v. Merchant's Collection Agency*, 7 Cal. 3d 94, 112-3 (1972). Thus, a cause of action for an unfair business practice merely requires proof of code violations that were made in the context of a business enterprise. In 1992 the legislature expanded the definition of unfair business practices to also include unfair business 'act'. Now the municipal attorney need only prove a single instance of unfair or fraudulent business conduct. *See* Business and Professions Code section 17203.

Code Violations Can Be Acts of Unfair Business Practices. Given this broad definition, violations of local land use regulations can be alleged as acts of unfair business practice as long as they are part of a 'business practice'. In the context of renting substandard residential property, an owner's long-term and ongoing pattern of failure and refusal to comply with the building and housing laws could constitute an unlawful business practice.

Procedural Requirements. An action under the Unfair Business Practices Act may be brought by the state attorney general, or the district attorney, or county counsel authorized by the district attorney, or the city attorney of any city with a popula-

Unfair business practices are broadly defined so as to encompass "anything that can properly be called a business practice and that at the same time is forbidden by the law."

In *People v. McKale*, 25 Cal. 3d 626, 634 (1979), violations of the Mobile Home Parks Act, Title 25 of the California Code of Regulations, were found to be unfair business practices. In *Stoiber v. Honeychuck*, 101 Cal.App. 3d 903, 927 (1980), the court suggested that an unfair business practices action might be appropriate to enjoin a landlord's maintenance of substandard, uninhabitable rental properties despite the technical deficiencies in this lawsuit's pleadings. In *People v. Thomas Shelton Powers, M.D., Inc.*, 2 Cal. App.4th 330, (1992), the court required restitution and disgorgement of excess profits against a developer who violated resale provisions of a municipal subdivision ordinance. Violations of the local subdivision code were found to be unlawful businesses practices.

tion exceeding 750,000 or, with the consent of the district attorney, or by a city prosecutor in any city or city or county having a full-time prosecutor. *See* Business and Professions Code section 17204.

5. Drug and Red Light Abatement

Drug and Red Light Abatement statutes have unique procedures for the abatement of repeated and continuous criminal activities which cause a public nuisance on private property. Although these statutes may appear unrelated to land use, an enforcement agency may encounter properties which attract large numbers of prostitutes or drug dealers. Thus, a civil enforcement action relying on these statutes may be an effective means to abate both the criminal activities and code violations.

Red Light Abatement Law. Sections 11225 through 11235 of the Penal Code constitute the Red Light Abatement Act. Section 11225 declares that every building or place used for the purpose of illegal gambling, lewdness, assignation, or prostitution, and every building or place used as a bathhouse which encourages or permits conduct which could lead to the transmission of AIDS, is a public nuisance. This public nuisance may be enjoined and abated, and damages may also be recovered. Section 11226 allows a city or district attorney to maintain a civil injunction to abate and enjoin the nuisance. Section 11229 provides for punishment by contempt. The fines can become an enforceable lien against the property in violation, per section 11233.

If the existence of a public nuisance is established, a court may order that all items used to maintain the nuisance be removed and the building be closed, per section 11230. In lieu of closure, the court may order the person responsible for the public nuisance to pay damages in an amount not to exceed the fair market rental value of the building for one year, per Penal Code section 11230.

Drug Abatement. Sections 11570 through 11587 of the Health and Safety Code constitute the Drug Abatement Act. Health and Safety Code section 11570 declares that every building or place used for the purpose of unlawfully selling, serving, storing, keeping, manufacturing, or giving away any controlled substance, and every building or place wherein those acts take place, is a public nuisance which may be enjoined, abated, and prevented. Damages may be recovered, and civil penalties may be assessed.

Section 11571 allows a city or district attorney to maintain a civil enforcement action to prevent and abate this public nuisance. A temporary restraining order is also possible under Health and Safety Code section 11573.

Property owner was found liable under the Drug Abatement Act for criminal drug activities created by their lack of property management. *Lew v. Superior Court*, 20 Cal.App.4th 866, 871 (1993). In *Lew* a group of neighbors took the property owner to small claims court alleging violations of the Drug Abatement Act where the owner allowed his rental property to be used by drug dealers, prostitutes, and their customers. The neighbors claimed damages and emotional distress from living next door to this drug house. The appellate court affirmed the award of damages to the neighbors on the basis that Health and Safety Code section 11570 created a presumption of a public nuisance per se. "Liability was imposed in this case on a theory of active fault on part of petitioners in the management of their property." *Id.* 873.

Section 11579 provides that, if a nuisance is established, an order shall be entered as part of the judgment, and that a plaintiff's costs are an enforceable lien against the property in violation.

Drug Abatement Case Law

Many of the provisions in the Drug Abatement Act were patterned after the Red Light Abatement Act. To date, only one recent court decision has interpreted the scope of the Drug Abatement Act. Given the similar statutory language found in the Red Light Abatement Act, citations to reported decisions that interpret the Red Light powers is acceptable when discussing the Drug Abatement Act.

6. California Coastal Act

Civil enforcement actions can be filed by any person to restrain violations of the California Coastal Act or a cease-and-desist order issued by the Coastal Commission. *See generally*, Public Resources Code section 30803. Section 30820 also provides for civil liability and the imposition of civil penalties against any person who undertakes a development in violation of the Coastal Act or a Coastal Development Permit. A minimum civil penalty of $500 or a maximum penalty of $30,000 may be imposed for such violations. If the enforcement agency can prove the person intentionally and knowingly violated the Coastal Act, the civil penalties increase to a minimum penalty of $1,000 and a maximum penalty of $15,000 per day for each day the violation exists. Section 30826 of the Public Resources Code also provides the additional remedy of site restoration where the development occurred without a coastal development permit.

B. Civil Procedure and Remedies

1. Civil Procedure Overview

A civil action starts when a municipal attorney files the complaint in superior court. After jurisdiction over the defendants is obtained by proper service of the civil summons and complaint, the municipal attorney is confronted with a variety of options and civil remedies.

Lis pendens. Pursuant to Code of Civil Procedure section 409, where the litigation affects real property, the plaintiff may record a notice of pending action or *lis pendens* with the county recorder's office. A *lis pendens* serves to notify interested

Civil enforcement actions can be filed by any person to restrain violations of the California Coastal Act or a cease-and-desist order issued by the Coastal Commission.

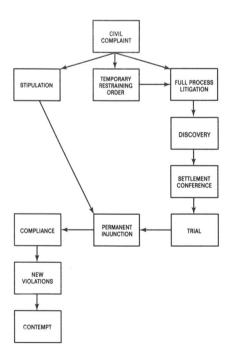

TRO = Temporary Restraining Order

parties that a current civil action affecting this parcel of real property has been filed and is pending. Some of the statutes discussed previously provide specific sections which authorize or even mandate the filing of a *lis pendens*. For example, per California Health and Safety Code section 17985, in an action brought pursuant to the State Housing Law the municipality is required to record a notice of pending action in the county recorder's office at the commencement of the action.

Lis Pendens and Code Properties for Sale

As a general rule of civil litigation practice, a *lis pendens* should always be recorded simultaneously with the filing of a civil complaint. The benefit of filing and recording a *lis pendens* is that potential buyers of the property will be advised of the civil action brought by the enforcement agency. This will likely prevent the current owner from selling or transferring the property either to avoid liability or the expense of correcting the violations.

Should the owner sell or transfer the property after the *lis pendens* is recorded, the new owners are presumed by law to know about the pending civil enforcement action and could be required to make the necessary corrections.

Temporary Restraining Order (TRO) and Preliminary Injunctions. In those code enforcement cases with imminent health and safety hazards, the evidence is sufficient for provisional relief by obtaining either a TRO or preliminary injunction. To obtain a TRO or preliminary injunction, the municipal attorney must schedule a motion date and file declarations signed by the enforcement agents. Since live testimony is usually not permitted for either a TRO or preliminary injunction, the success or failure of a civil enforcement case rests upon the organization and content of the declarations. The municipal attorney must carefully review these declarations to ensure that sufficient facts are present to prove the violations and assist in preparing the terms of the potential orders the court may issue.

Discovery and Settlement. Depending on the outcome of the request for provisional relief, a municipal attorney may need to develop a discovery plan. However, in most code enforcement cases discovery is not necessary. First, the evidence to support the injunction is gathered by the enforcement agency, with little need for information from the property owner or person responsible for the code violations. Second, few valid defenses to the graphic photographs of a substandard building or dilapidated property are possible. Depending upon the nature of the case, discovery might be helpful to clarify any ambiguities regarding ownership or business identity.

Permanent Injunction and Contempt. Although provisional relief may order an owner to abate the imminent health and safety violations, the municipal attorney should obtain a permanent injunction to prevent future violations. After the issuance of a preliminary injunction, many owners are willing to sign a stipulated final judgment for a permanent injunction (*See* Code of Civil Procedure section 664.6), making it possible for most code enforcement cases to end without a long and tedious discovery battle. Should these violations recur several months or years later, a contempt action could be filed for violations of the permanent injunction instead of starting with a new civil enforcement action.

2. Injunctive Relief

Injunctive relief is available as one of the remedies under any of the civil causes of action discussed above. The injunction itself may take the form of a court order prohibiting the maintenance of code violations (prohibitory injunction) or requiring the responsible person to remedy those conditions (mandatory injunction). Since courts are often reluctant to issue a mandatory preliminary injunction, the order should be phrased in such a way that it 'prohibits' the maintenance of conditions that violate land use regulations or constitute a public nuisance.

Prohibitory v. Mandatory Injunctions. A prohibitory injunction does not become mandatory merely because the owner is required to perform affirmative acts.

Temporary Restraining Order. Where code violations must be corrected immediately, as in the case of substandard housing or illegal grading, a temporary restraining order may be available *(See* Code of Civil Procedure section 527 and California Rules of Court section 379).

TROs are typically issued by a judge after an informal hearing in the judge's chambers, often referred to as an *ex parte* hearing. Although neither formal, written notification nor the presence of the responsible person is required, the municipal attorney must attempt to notify the responsible person informally prior to the hearing, per Code of Civil Procedure section 527.

Generally a temporary restraining order will be issued if it satisfies the same standards as a preliminary injunction, al-

In the case of *People v. Mobile Magic Sales*, 96 Cal.App. 3d 1, 13 (1979), the injunction prohibited certain unlawful acts and required retail dealers to remove mobile home models displayed in violation of Vehicle Code section 11709(c). The court noted that, although the order required an affirmative act (the removal of the models), this was incidental to the injunction's prohibitory objective to restrain further violation of a valid statute. In the context of a public nuisance, the court may issue both prohibitory and mandatory injunctions. *County of San Diego v. Carlstrom*, 196 Cal.App. 2d, 485, 493 (1961); *City and County of San Francisco v. City Investment Corp.*, 15 Cal.App. 3d 1031, 1042 (1971).

Where code violations must be corrected immediately, as in the case of substandard housing or illegal grading, a temporary restraining order may be available.

though additional evidence will be necessary to justify the need for immediate relief prior to the formal hearing on the preliminary injunction.

Preliminary Injunction. If no imminent threat to the public's safety is present, the municipal attorney may request the court to issue a preliminary injunction to prohibit the illegal activity until a decision on the merits of the case is made at trial. A preliminary injunction requires a formal court hearing, based on written declarations or affidavits submitted to the judge establishing the need for provisional relief. The responsible person is provided with notice of the hearing and has the opportunity to respond by filing briefs in opposition to the request for the preliminary injunction.

A hearing on a preliminary injunction is set by formal motion or by the issuance of an order to show cause at the time the court issues a TRO. In either case, the preliminary injunction hearing will not occur until several weeks after the lawsuit is filed.

Traditional Balancing Test. In most injunction cases the judge usually considers two factors when deciding whether to issue a TRO or preliminary injunction: whether the plaintiff is likely to prevail on the merits at trial; and whether the plaintiff will suffer more harm if the injunction is denied than the defendant will suffer if the injunction is issued.

The Public Agency Rebuttable Presumption. Where a governmental entity seeks to enjoin violations of a statute or ordinance which expressly provides for injunctive relief, the traditional balancing test does *not* apply. Instead, the governmental entity need only prove a 'reasonable probability' that its arguments will prevail at trial. This reasonable probability gives rise to the rebuttable presumption that the potential harm to the public outweighs the potential harm to the defendant. Once this is raised, in order to avoid a preliminary injunction, the responsible person must prove that the injunction will inflict grave and irreparable harm. Only then does the court balance the two traditional factors.

The *IT Corporation* test applies when a governmental entity seeks to enjoin violations of a statute or ordinance which expressly provides for injunctive relief. Thus, a municipal attorney can benefit from this rebuttable presumption only where the statutes and local ordinances expressly provide for injunctions. Examples include—

- The State Housing Law provides for injunctive relief (Health and Safety Code section 17980) and for temporary relief pending judgment (Health and Safety Code section 17981)

Where a governmental entity seeks to enjoin violations of a statute or ordinance which expressly provides for injunctive relief, the traditional balancing test does not apply. Instead, the governmental entity need only prove a 'reasonable probability' that its arguments will prevail at trial.

The rebuttable presumption in favor of public agencies requesting a preliminary injunction was created in the case of *IT Corporation v. County of Imperial*, 35 Cal. 3d 63 (1983). Here the court approved the issuance of a preliminary injunction that required cleanup of hazardous materials. The municipal attorney should stress the *IT Corporation* case in any pleadings, since most judges encounter cases that apply the traditional test.

Applying the *IT Corporation* Test

In many code enforcement cases a municipal attorney can easily satisfy the reasonable probability standard by referring to the enforcement agent's declarations documenting inspections of the property and observations of multiple violations. Moreover, the responsible person often has difficulty showing grave and irreparable injury. Frequently, the only harm alleged will be the cost of bringing the property up to code. However, a municipal attorney can argue that this injury was self-inflicted as a result of failing to maintain the property in the past. Far from causing irreparable injury, it can be argued that correction of the substandard conditions will benefit the responsible person by increasing the value of the property.

In *City of Los Altos v. Barnes*, 3 Cal.App.4th 1193, 1198-1199 (1992) the court affirmed the issuance of a preliminary injunction against a homeowner from carrying on a home occupation at her residence in violation of local zoning ordinances. Several of *Barnes'* employees worked at her home as part of her business of operating a recreational family camp. The trial court, applying the *IT Corporation* standard, concluded it was reasonably probable that the city would prevail at trial and the homeowner would not suffer grave or irreparable harm.

- The Civil Code provides for injunctive relief as authorized by section 3491 for a public nuisance
- The Unfair Business Practices Act permits injunctive relief in sections 17203 and 17204 of the Business and Professions Code

Permanent Injunction. A permanent injunction or final judgment enjoining any recurrence of illegal activity is only issued after a trial on the merits of the case, or after the parties to the lawsuit agree that a permanent injunction may be issued. In most jurisdictions, obtaining a trial date may take a year or longer from the date a lawsuit is filed.

As a practical matter, once a court issues a preliminary injunction, it is unlikely that the municipal attorney will need to bring the case to trial for purposes of obtaining a permanent injunction. Some owners and their defense attorneys recognize the futility of challenging the propriety of injunctive relief after a court has ordered correction pending trial by issuing a preliminary injunction. A responsible person will frequently agree to sign a formal stipulation permitting the issuance of a permanent

As a practical matter, once a court issues a preliminary injunction, it is unlikely that the municipal attorney will need to bring the case to trial for purposes of obtaining a permanent injunction.

Compare this picture after abatement with its earlier condition on page 100.

Authority for this approach can be found in Government Code section 38773 which provides that a local legislative body can enact ordinances to abate public nuisances and either assess the costs against the property (section 38773.5) or file a code enforcement lien (section 38773.1). *See* Appendix A for an example of such a local ordinance.

injunction, rather than expend the time and the substantial cost involved in a trial.

3. Judicial Abatement by a Municipality

The objective of a civil enforcement action is to obtain an injunction compelling the responsible person to correct the violations or abate the public nuisances that exist on the property. Where the responsible person does not have the financial or physical ability to abide by the terms of the injunction, or merely defies the court order, the municipal attorney should routinely include alternatives in the initial terms of the injunction. One option is for the municipality to correct the violations. The injunction could be phrased to compel the responsible person to abate violations within 30 days, or alternatively, to permit the municipality to hire work crews to perform the corrections and then assess costs incurred against the property.

Government Code sections 25845.5 (applicable to counties) and 38773.7 (applicable to cities) authorize the adoption of an ordinance providing that a court, after entering a second or subsequent judgment in a two-year period for conditions that were abated as a nuisance, may order the property owner to pay three times the costs of abatement. Please note, however, that this provision for treble damages expressly excludes substandard conditions from being abated pursuant to the State Housing Law.

Implementing Judicial Abatement Orders

The same practical guidelines on how the enforcement agency should implement an administrative abatement order also apply where a court orders abatement as part of a civil or criminal judicial action. Please consult Chapter Six, Administrative Remedies, pages 97-102. Although a confirmation of cost hearing is not mandated in a judicial abatement action, the municipal attorney should request the court to schedule a subsequent court hearing to review the abatement costs. The municipal attorney should also prepare a draft order which the judge can sign to confirm the abatement costs. This order will make it easier to refer to the county who will place the abatement costs as a special tax assessment against the property pursuant to Government Code section 38773.5.

4. Civil Contempt: Enforcement of Injunctions

After a court has ordered corrections of the conditions either through a preliminary or a permanent injunction, the responsible person may still fail to comply or violations may arise sometime in the future. Holding the party in contempt is the usual legal process by which the responsible person is punished for failure to comply with a civil order.

Basis of Civil Contempt. The violation by a party bound by, and aware of, a valid court order to do, or to refrain from doing, an act is considered civil contempt. The punishment for contempt may be a fine not to exceed $1,000, or imprisonment not to exceed five days, or both for each act of contempt (Code of Civil Procedure section 1218).

Code of Civil Procedure section 1219(a) also provides that "when the contempt consists of the omission to perform an act which is yet in the power of the person to perform, he or she may be imprisoned until he or she has performed it, and in that case the act must be specified in the warrant of commitment."

Contempt Procedures. The procedure to initiate contempt proceedings first requires that an affidavit be filed or a declaration be issued showing the facts constituting a willful violation of the order, in most cases a permanent injunction but it could be for any civil order. The party bound by the contempt order must have been properly served, and must have the ability to comply with that order (Code of Civil Procedure section 1211). These declarations constitute the complaint for the contempt action.

Upon filing an affidavit or declaration, the judge usually issues an *ex parte* order to show cause, which requires the violator to be present at a hearing. Except in unusual circumstances, the order to show cause, with all supporting declarations, must then be personally served on the party charged with contempt. At the hearing, the party charged with contempt may present his or her defense, either by way of declaration or affidavit or witnesses (Code of Civil Procedure section 1217).

Defenses to Contempt. A variety of defenses can be made to a charge of contempt, including—

- Invalid Order (such as lack of specificity of the terms in the injunction so that punishment for a violation would constitute a deprivation of due process)
- No Notice or Knowledge of Order (no service of order, or not present in court when ordered)
- Inability to Comply (financial or otherwise)

These defenses may be avoided if the municipal attorney carefully drafts the injunction, ensures that the order is served on all responsible parties, and undertakes a pre-litigation financial assessment of a defendant's ability to carry out needed repairs.

Holding the party in contempt is the usual legal process by which the responsible person is punished for failure to comply with a civil order.

State Housing Law. Contempt actions can be brought for State Housing Law violations. Health and Safety Code section 17980.7(d) requires that, where judgment is entered upon a finding that the condition of a building substantially endangers residents, the court shall punish any failure to comply with the abatement order by civil contempt.

In addition, section 17995.2 of the Health and Safety Code provides that any person found in contempt of a court order or injunction issued under the State Housing Law for a second or subsequent time within a five-year period is guilty of a misdemeanor, punishable by a maximum fine of $5,000, or imprisonment for up to six months, or both. Under Health and Safety Code section 17995.4, a second or subsequent contempt of an injunction or court order, where the violations are extensive and a variety of other findings are made, increases the misdemeanor imprisonment from a minimum of six months to a maximum of one year.

Unfair Business Practice. The Unfair Business Practices Act also provides for contempt proceedings to enforce injunctions, apart from general civil contempt. Business and Professions Code section 17535.5 allows for the recovery of a civil penalty of up to $6,000 per violation. Each day of continuing conduct is considered a separate and distinct violation. The penalty is recoverable in a civil action brought in the name of the People of the State of California by the attorney general, or any district attorney, county counsel, or city attorney. The penalty recovered is distributed as set forth in section 17535.5(c).

Contempt Action via Criminal Prosecution (Penal Code section 166.4). If the defendant fails to comply with the requirements enumerated in a preliminary or permanent injunction, a criminal contempt action may be brought against the defendant as punishment for his or her failure to comply. Penal Code section 166.4 provides that a person who willfully disobeys any process or order lawfully issued by any court is guilty of a misdemeanor. A misdemeanor is punishable by imprisonment in the county jail not to exceed six months, or by fine not to exceed one thousand dollars ($1,000), or by both (Penal Code section 19).

C. Other Civil Remedies

Although compliance is the primary objective, a judge can impose other remedies along with the civil injunction—including civil penalties, assessment of investigation costs and attorney fees, recovery of nuisance abatement costs, and the imposition of liens to collect the costs and penalties.

If the defendant fails to comply with the requirements enumerated in a preliminary or permanent injunction, a criminal contempt action may be brought against the defendant as punishment for his or her failure to comply.

1. State Statutes: Cost Recovery, Civil Penalties

State Housing Law. Where a residential building is declared substantially substandard, an enforcement agency may recover its expenses for inspection, investigation, enforcement activities, attorney hours, and the costs of prosecution. *See* Health and Safety Code section 17980.6 and 17980.7. In addition, the court may order the responsible person to pay penalties in the event of repeat violations and may prohibit claims on the person's state income tax applications for any deductions for interest, taxes, depreciation, or amortization related to substantially substandard rental property for a maximum period of two years (Health and Safety Code sections 17980.6 and 17980.7).

Where the enforcement agency is unsuccessful in its civil enforcement action, Health and Safety Code section 17984 protects the agency from paying the costs and attorney fees for the responsible person.

Unfair Business Practices. Civil penalties (maximum of $2,500 for each violation) can be assessed for acts of unfair business practices, per Business and Professions Code section 17206. If the action is brought by a district attorney, the penalties recovered are paid to the county treasurer. If brought by a city attorney, half of the recovered penalties are paid to the county and half to the city treasurer.

Drug and Red Light Abatement. Enforcement agencies can recover the costs of investigation and attorneys fees in drug and red light abatement actions pursuant to Civil Code section 3496.

Nuisance Abatement Cost Recovery. Where the enforcement agency obtains a civil injunction ordering municipal work crews or their contractor to abate the public nuisances on the property, the judicial abatement order should also permit the recovery of all abatement costs. The judge can issue this order based on inherent equitable powers to abate a public nuisance and any applicable local ordinances enacted pursuant to Government Code section 38773 (local legislative bodies can adopt ordinances to summarily abate public nuisances and assess the expenses against the property). The enforcement agency's ability to recover abatement costs are significantly increased where the municipality has an ordinance in place allowing for recovery by civil judicial actions.

This local abatement ordinance can also permit the court to assess treble abatement costs against a responsible person where the enforcement agency has obtained a second or subsequent civil or criminal abatement judgment within any two-year period per Government Code section 38773.7.

Where the enforcement agency obtains a civil injunction ordering municipal work crews or their contractor to abate the public nuisances on the property, the judicial abatement order should also permit the recovery of all abatement costs.

Local Nuisance Abatement Laws

A municipality has the power to enact an ordinance to recover summary abatement costs incurred to abate a fire. In *City of Los Angeles v. Shpegel-Dimsey, Inc.*, 198 Cal.App. 3d 1009, 1018 (1988), the fire department notified the owner about fire code violations that existed at his commercial property. A fire broke out, and the city filed a civil action to recover the fire suppression costs incurred on the legal theory of public nuisance abatement. Although the fire code violations did create a public nuisance, Los Angeles could not recover because a local cost-recovery ordinance was not in place. The court, however, seemed to indicate that, if a local cost recovery ordinance had been in place, Los Angeles could have recovered its nuisance abatement costs.

2. Litigation Cost-Recovery Ordinances

The enforcement agency's ability to recover its litigation and related enforcement costs in a civil enforcement action is primarily based on state statutes. However, a few municipalities have enacted local ordinances permitting the recovery of enforcement costs and imposing civil penalties as part of a civil judicial action. Because no cases to date have directly approved or denied these novel municipal ordinances, a careful legal analysis is necessary if they are to survive future legal challenge.

As a general rule, a municipality cannot recover damages or seek compensation for services that protect the public's health and safety.

As a general rule, a municipality cannot recover damages or seek compensation for services that protect the public's health and safety. The legal grounds that would justify an injunction to abate a public nuisance do not necessarily support a municipality's claim for damages. Public nuisances cause specific harm to the community at large, and thus the municipality does not incur specified damages.

Despite this legal obstacle to the collection of damages, a public nuisance could exist that created special injuries to the interests of a municipality (for example, the city owns adjacent property to a smelting plant) apart from its interest to protect the general public welfare. In this scenario where the city incurs a special injury, recovery of damages might be possible per Civil Code section 3493. It is also equally clear that a municipality cannot recover tort damages (e.g., abatement expenses) by reason of a public nuisance. *County of San Luis Obispo v. Abalone Alliance*, 178 Cal.App. 3d 848, 859 (1986); *Torrance Redevelopment Agency v. Solvent Coating Co.*, 763 F. Supp. 1060, 1065 (C.D. Cal. 1991).

Consequently, when drafting cost recovery ordinances, the municipal attorney must be careful to distinguish between litigation and enforcement costs as opposed to damages for general municipal services which protect the public's health and safety.

3. Municipal Civil Penalties Ordinance

The imposition of civil penalties for municipal code violations is another remedy available as part of an enforcement action. Although municipalities have the power to assess civil penalties, a local ordinance must be in place. Government Code section 36901 authorizes municipalities to impose fines, penalties, and forfeitures to enforce municipal code violations, but the fine or penalty cannot exceed $1,000. Government Code section 36900(a) authorizes both criminal and civil enforcement actions. Both statutes appear to support a municipal ordinance which establishes a civil penalty for municipal code violations.

Despite the limitation expressed in section 36901, some charter cities have enacted municipal civil penalty ordinances which exceed the Government Code's maximum civil penalty of $1,000. These local ordinances rely on both the police power and the municipal affairs doctrine. Sections 36901 and 36900(a) of the Government Code are general laws of the state which apply where no different punishment is prescribed by other state laws. Yet, local ordinances enacted by charter municipalities are also considered laws of the state. A local civil penalty ordinance could be viewed as an extension of the charter cities' municipal affairs which can then exceed the general Government Code provisions.

> A charter municipality has the authority to provide different penalties if they do not exceed the maximum limits set by its charter. *County of Los Angeles v. City of Los Angeles,* 219 Cal.App. 2d 838, 844 (1963). Any fine or penalty imposed by the municipal ordinance must not be considered by the court to be so excessive as to violate Article 1, section 17 of the California Constitution. *See generally, Hale v. Morgan,* 22 Cal. 3d 388, 404 (1978).

The enforcement of local ordinances by assessing civil penalties could be viewed as inherent to the municipal police powers doctrine. These local civil penalty ordinances would be justified pursuant to the municipal police power where it could be argued that civil penalty ordinances in excess of $1,000 do not conflict with state law, but are merely a complementary enforcement approach. Regardless of the penalty amount, a municipal ordinance must be in place which declares that any person who violates a municipal ordinance is subject to a maximum civil penalty per violation.

4. Code Enforcement Liens

Liens can be assessed against the property in violation or against the responsible person to recover costs and civil penalties incurred as part of a civil enforcement action. Civil Code section 2881 creates liens by either contract or enactment of a law.

State Law Liens. A number of state statutes permit the assessment of liens to recover costs and civil penalties incurred as part of an administrative abatement or civil enforcement action.

- **Code Enforcement Judgment Liens.** Government Code section 38773.1 authorizes municipalities to enact ordinances to recover abatement costs by recording a judgment lien

- **Weed and Rubbish Abatement Liens.** Government Code sections 39501 and 39502 authorize the assessment of liens to recover costs to abate weeds and rubbish that pose fire and health hazards

- **Forest Fire Abatement Liens.** Public Resources Code sections 4178 and 4179 authorize the assessment of liens to recover fire abatement costs incurred by the California Department of Forestry

Municipal Code Enforcement Liens. Civil Code section 2881 does not vest exclusive authority to create liens with the state legislature. Municipalities can enact local ordinances that create liens to recover abatement costs, investigation and inspection fees, and civil penalties.

Municipalities can enact local ordinances that create liens to recover abatement costs, investigation and inspection fees, and civil penalties.

Enforcement and Recovery of Code Enforcement Liens. General principles of due process require that an owner be given adequate notice of the lien and the opportunity to contest its validity and amount before a municipality records the lien against the property. Since most code enforcement liens established by state statute or municipal ordinance would be equivalent to judgment liens, the municipal attorney would need to undertake further civil litigation to foreclose pursuant to Civil Code section 697.310.

Enforcing a Lien

Recording a judgment lien is merely the first step and is significantly easier than trying to enforce and collect. Consult the Rutter Group's series on Enforcement of Judgments for more information on how to execute a code enforcement lien. Rutter Group's *California Practice Guide on Enforcing Judgments and Debts* by Schwartz and Ahart (1988).

5. Receivership

Another civil law remedy which can imposed as part of a civil judicial action is the appointment of a receiver. California Health and Safety Code section 17980.7(c) authorizes the appointment of a receiver to repair violations on properties that have been declared substantially substandard under the State Housing Law.

Code of Civil Procedure section 564 permits the court to appoint a receiver under the different circumstances listed in the statute. The appointment of a receiver rests within the discretion of the judge and should only be used as a drastic remedy.

Code Enforcement Receiver

A receiver can be appointed pursuant to Civil Procedure section 564 to remedy building and other code violations. In *City and County of San Francisco v. Daley*, 16 Cal.App.4th 734, 742-745 (1993), exceptional circumstances were present to justify the appointment of the receiver. The owner and her children avoided numerous attempts by the city to inspect the property and thwarted repeated efforts to remedy the situation during the three years between the filing of the civil complaint and the court hearing to appoint the receiver. Moreover, no less drastic remedy was likely to gain compliance given the owner's son had already been jailed for five days for contempt.

Defenses to Code Enforcement Actions

*Defenses to enforcement actions should
not be thought of as obstacles, but as
rules which establish a balance between
governmental power and the property
and personal rights of the regulated.*

Introduction

Regulatory
Foundations

Local Regulatory
Implementation

Managing Code
Enforcement

Investigating
Cases

Selection of
Remedies

Administrative
Remedies

Criminal
Prosecution

Using Civil
Injunctions

Defenses to
CE Actions

Defenses to Code Enforcement Actions

Although this book has emphasized legal authority and enforcement techniques from the perspective of the local enforcement agency, code enforcement is limited by the U.S. and California Constitutions and other legal doctrines. Instead of strictly enforcing every law or regulation, an agency should carefully evaluate the merits of each case. Because the agency, like the prosecutor, has an ethical responsibility to exercise its discretion in a reasonable and just manner, defenses to code enforcement actions should not be thought of as obstacles, but as rules which establish a balance between governmental power and the property and personal rights of the regulated. Equal attention and respect should be given to these legal limitations as is given to the regulations themselves.

A. The Rights of the Regulated

Property owners or other responsible persons often raise these legal limitations as possible defenses to enforcement actions. Compared to most judicial or administrative actions, few effective defenses can absolve property owners from being declared legally responsible for violations on their properties.* Yet, if the courts declared an ordinance unconstitutional, or if the facts supported the defense of laches or estoppel, an enforcement action could be defeated in its entirety. Where the owner has developed a nonconforming right to use the property in a manner contrary to current zoning regulations, a valid nonconforming rights defense could also prevent an agency from going forward with further action.

Compared to most judicial or administrative actions, few effective defenses can absolve property owners from being declared legally responsible for violations on their properties.

---

* Some courts have gone as far as to hold property owners responsible for code violations regardless of intent. Recall the discussion of strict liability in Chapter 7.

Depending upon the circumstances of the case, other legal limitations may only partially protect the rights of the property owner. Bankruptcy, for example, does not absolve legal responsibility, but could negate any civil penalties assessed.

This chapter focuses only on legal defenses, not on factual issues—for instance, the identity of the property owner or whether sufficient information shows that a particular person caused the violation. Not every possible legal defense is presented in this chapter, but only those most likely to be raised in code enforcement cases. The property owner or responsible person may have other legal claims against the agency or municipality for possible damages related to an enforcement action. This chapter will not discuss civil liability claims that an owner could assert against an agency, including denial of civil rights pursuant to 42 U.S.C. section 1983.

Not every possible legal defense is presented in this chapter, but only those most likely to be raised in code enforcement cases.

B. Invalid Ordinances and Regulations

One of the primary defenses is to attack the underlying ordinance or regulation. Although municipalities have broad constitutional authority to enact land use regulations, this power is not absolute. A responsible person or owner could challenge a zoning or building regulation, claiming that it exceeds the police powers of the municipality. The validity of a municipal regulation can be challenged in two ways. The ordinance could be viewed as invalid as written or invalid in its application. This first method questions a municipality's authority to adopt the regulation, while the second recognizes its validity, but declares that the ordinance was used in an illegal or invalid manner. Both approaches could defeat a pending enforcement action.

Validity of Ordinance in Administrative Hearings

The constitutionality of a land use regulation cannot be raised or decided in administrative proceedings. Only a judge, and not an administrative hearing officer, has the authority to declare land use regulations invalid. *Hand v. Board of Examiners*, 66 Cal.App.3d 605, 617-620 (1977) (administrative agency's declaration that statute is unconstitutional violates separation of powers).

1. Invalid as Written

To challenge the validity of a land use regulation, an owner could assert several different legal theories.

Preemption. One is to claim that state law is superior to the local law. This is the legal doctrine of preemption. *See generally, Galvan v. Superior Court*, 70 Cal. 2d 851, (1970) (local ordinance which required the registration of firearms was not preempted by state law). For further legal analysis surrounding preemption within the land use context, *see Public Needs and Private Dollars*, by Abbott, Moe, and Hanson, Chapter III, pages 52-59.

Interference with Constitutional Rights. Another is to claim that a land use regulation infringes on constitutional rights. For example, a court could invalidate a local ordinance where it interfered with a 'fundamental right' or the rights of a 'suspect class'. A fundamental right is one given great protection by our courts, such as freedom of speech. Race, national origin, or ethnicity are examples of the determinants of a suspect class. Where the ordinance affects a fundamental right or a suspect class, the courts apply a more stringent legal evaluation of the ordinance, called the 'strict scrutiny' test. As a general rule, application of the strict scrutiny test reduces the probability that an ordinance will be found constitutional. For example, in *City of Whittier v. Walnut Properties, Inc.*, 149 Cal.App.3d 633, 640 (1983), the original zoning dispersal ordinance had the effect of prohibiting operation of any adult business within city limits; such a total ban violated the First Amendment; *see also, Elysium v. County of Los Angeles*, 232 Cal.App 3d 408, 426 (1991) (zoning ordinance's definition of nudist camp violated California's Constitutional provision protecting rights of privacy).

Lack of Legitimate Government Purpose/Insufficient Legislative Findings. The owner could question the connection between the regulation and the actual land use issue or problem the regulation was designed to resolve. As the exercise of the police power must be reasonably related to a legitimate governmental purpose, the owner could challenge the justification for government action. Although not widely accepted by today's courts, this challenge could still be asserted in the proper case. Another more plausible attack could focus on the findings the legislative body made when enacting the regulation. If the findings proved to be inadequate, a judge could invalidate the municipal regulation. *See generally, Consolidated Rock Products Company v. City of Los Angeles*, 57 Cal. 2d 515, 522 (1962) (the legislative body's justification for the regulations must be supported by a reasonable basis in fact) and *Carlin v. City of Palm Springs*, 14 Cal.App. 3d 706, 711-712 (1971) (if the ordinance does not have any reasonable tendency to promote the public's general welfare,

A court could invalidate a local ordinance where it interfered with a 'fundamental right' or the rights of a 'suspect class'. A fundamental right is one given great protection by our courts, such as freedom of speech. Race, national origin, or ethnicity are examples of the determinants of a suspect class.

it is an arbitrary exercise of the police powers; ordinance must be reasonable in object and not arbitrary in operation).

Due Process Doctrines of Vagueness and Overbreadth. Challenging an ordinance on the grounds of a lack of due process is a common occurrence, and these challenges can be based on the concept of vagueness or overbreadth. The U.S. and California Constitutions require that ordinances and regulations be written to provide adequate notice about the types of conduct or uses prohibited by the regulation. In other words, citizens have a right to understand the laws which are being enforced against them. Overbreadth is where the scope of the regulation is so broad that it prohibits activities which are permitted by law. Both vagueness and overbreadth are premised on the same basic notion of equity and fairness. *See generally, People v. Trantham*, 161 Cal.App 3d Supp. 1, 7 (1984) (due process protects a person's liberty and property interests against unreasonable government action; statute that makes no distinction between harmful and innocent conduct is void for overbreadth) and *Mann v. Mack* 155 Cal. App.3d 666, 676 (1984) (if a noise ordinance, viewed in the context of common use and understanding, informs a person of ordinary intelligence of the nature of the prohibited conduct, the ordinance is not void for vagueness).

2. Invalid as Applied

The second approach is to claim that a valid ordinance was illegally enforced by the municipality or applied beyond its scope.* Unlawful application of a regulation is used by many owners of adult entertainment businesses to attack zoning ordinances which require that adult businesses be located separately from other adult businesses, schools, parks, churches, and residential zones at specified distances throughout a city. Business owners may claim that zoning dispersal ordinances allegedly prevent them from relocating within the city. Thus, the application of these zoning ordinances amounts to a total ban on the development of new adult businesses. Because this would violate the First Amendment, an enforcement agency is prohibited from applying the dispersal ordinance in such a way as to impose a total ban. *City of National City v. Wiener*, 3 Cal.4th 832, 847-849 (1992) (local zoning dispersal ordinance found valid in its application by providing alternative locations for adult entertainment establishments).

The U.S. and California Constitutions require that ordinances and regulations be written to provide adequate notice about the types of conduct or uses prohibited by the regulation. In other words, citizens have a right to understand the laws which are being enforced against them.

"[I]f the law on its face survives an equal protection challenge, our inquiry does not end until we decide whether the law must still be condemned as applied." *Supervisors v. LAFCO*, 3 Cal.4th 903, 913 (1992)

---

* Discriminatory or selective enforcement is a claim that a regulatory enforcement agency has unlawfully singled out a property owner for enforcement action (this is treated as a separate defense on page 167).

3. Procedural Due Process

An owner could claim that the administrative procedures used to apply a particular municipal land use regulation failed to afford due process. When a judicial enforcement action is used, such a due process claim is rarely successful as the criminal and civil courts have elaborate procedures which judges carefully apply. In administrative hearings, however, unless the enforcement agency, municipal attorney, and hearing officer are equally rigorous, this particular constitutional challenge by an owner could be successful.

> Due process requires adequate notice and opportunity for a fair hearing, before government disturbs a citizen's property interests. (*People v. Swink*, 150 Cal.App. 3d. 1076, 1079 (1984))

C. Laches and Estoppel

Laches and Estoppel, premised on general notions of fairness and equity, are two defenses which can apply to civil and administrative enforcement actions.* Laches applies where the enforcement agency's delay in taking action is excessive or unreasonable.

Estoppel prevents enforcement actions where the property owner reasonably relies on the representations made by the municipality or enforcement agency. Both focus on the actions or inactions of an enforcement agency that would make it unjust for the agency to proceed any further. Consequently, both defenses can defeat the entire enforcement action.

1. Laches

Laches occurs when the court rules that an agency's delay in filing an enforcement action is unreasonable, making the agency's request for a civil injunction invalid. If laches applies, the court can dismiss the civil enforcement action. To determine whether the delay was unreasonable, courts must decide whether the enforcement agency merely acquiesced in filing the action, causing the property owner or defendant to suffer a certain degree of prejudice or harm from this delay.

Where the violation amounts to a public nuisance or poses a threat to the public's health and safety, the owner may have difficulty showing that the delay in enforcement caused some amount of detriment. In most instances, no lapse of time can legalize a public nuisance, nor may the maintenance of a public nuisance be defended on the ground of laches.

> *City of Turlock v. Bristow*, 103 Cal. App. 750, 756 (1930) (laches could not defeat city's enforcement action to abate public nuisance caused by pollution); *Martin v. Fehl*, 145 Cal.App. 3d 228, 241 (1983) (whether laches applies depends on the facts of each case). The defense of laches may bar relief even though the statute of limitations has expired on the particular legal action. *Rouse v. Underwood*, 242 Cal.App. 2d 316, 323-324 (1966).

---

* Laches and Estoppel may also be available in criminal actions, as indicated in the case of *People v. Sapse*, 104 Cal.App. 3d Supp. 1, 13 (1980).

Laches in the Context of Code Enforcement

Laches has been applied by the courts as a proper defense to code enforcement actions. In *City and County of San Francisco v. Pacello*, 85 Cal.App. 3d, 637 644-645 (1978), the appellate court dis-  missed a civil enforcement action based on laches. Seeking an injunction against the use of a building that contained two dwelling units in violation of zoning laws, San Francisco filed a lawsuit against the current owners of the property. The previous owners had converted the building into two dwelling units without proper building permits and in violation of the single-family zone which permitted only one dwelling unit.

Although San Francisco had issued notices against the previous owners and taken administrative action before the Zoning Board of Appeals, in this case the laches defense applied because the city delayed enforcement action for eight years. Between the time the complaint was filed and the decision of the Board of Zoning Appeals, the Pacello family had subsequently purchased and used the property for a number of years, relying on the rental income derived from the second dwelling unit.

Another case applying laches to code enforcement is *Frabotta v. Alencastre*, 182 Cal.App. 2d 679, 684-685 (1960). This was a civil action between two private parties. One party sought an injunction to keep an easement open, while the other asserted the defense of laches because filing the action was delayed. The court did not agree, ruling that laches should not apply when the parties have attempted to negotiate the conflict for more than one year.

This case presents a convincing argument against laches where an enforcement agency issues a notice of violation to the owner and attempts to negotiate compliance for a period of one year without seeking the court's immediate assistance.

The Legacy of *Pacello*

The lesson to be learned from *Pacello* is that judicial enforcement actions must begin within a reasonable period of time after previous administrative enforcement actions have been unsuccessful in gaining compliance. Note that *Pacello* might have been decided differently if the original owner still owned the property or if the second owner had not suffered any prejudice from the delay. The court stressed *Pacello's* reliance on the rental income.

---

2. Estoppel

Like laches, estoppel is an equitable defense applying primarily to civil judicial and administrative enforcement actions. However, estoppel has significantly more rigorous requirements and encompasses more than enforcement agency delay. In basic terms, estoppel arises when the municipality takes action and the owner violates the regulation by relying on this action: for example, where a building permit was erroneously issued in violation of zoning regulations. Under this scenario the enforcement agency is 'estopped' from enforcing its regulations because of the prior actions.

Five basic elements are required to prove estoppel against a governmental entity—

- The municipality was aware of the true facts
- The municipality intended that its conduct be acted upon, or its conduct was such that the defendant reasonably believed that this was intended
- The defendant was unaware of the true facts
- The defendant relied on the municipality's conduct to his or her detriment
- Justice requires the application of estoppel against the municipality when weighed against the injury to the public interest

Given these stringent requirements, estoppel is an unlikely defense in code cases involving health and safety hazards.

As a general proposition, estoppel will not be applied against a governmental entity if to do so would nullify a "strong rule of policy, adopted for the benefit of the public, ..." *County of San Diego v. California Water and Electric Co.*, 30 Cal.2d 817, 829-830 (1947). Zoning ordinances are considered vital to the public interest. *Pettitt v. City of Fresno*, 34 Cal.App.3d 813, 822 (1974) (despite issuance of building permit, owner could not be allowed to violate zoning laws; thus, court did not apply estoppel). *See also La Canada Flintridge Development Corp. v. Department of Transportation*, 166 Cal.App.3d 206, 219-222 (1985) (state agency will not be estopped from imposing conditions on project where developer relied on his own misinterpretations of the law—such reliance was not reasonable).

There are volumes of court decisions discussing estoppel and vested rights. Many of these cases can be classified into one of the following four common scenarios—

a. A Valid Building Permit Is Issued, but Subsequent Changes Are Made to Zoning Ordinances. Generally, a landowner who has performed substantial work and incurred substantial expenditures in reliance on a valid building permit has acquired a vested right, and subsequent changes in zoning ordinances cannot defeat that vested right. Hence, the govern-

City of Long Beach v. Mansell, 3 Cal. 3d 462, 493 (1970) is the leading case in California on the application of estoppel to governmental entities.

Estoppel and Vested Rights

Estoppel and Vested Rights are separate legal doctrines spawned from the same notions of equity and fairness.

Estoppel and vested rights are often discussed by the courts within the same phrase. The somewhat interchangeable use of estoppel and vested rights can create confusion. Although both legal doctrines are derived from equitable concepts, estoppel and vested rights are distinct doctrines. Estoppel turns on whether it would be inequitable to allow a public agency to repudiate its prior conduct. Vested rights focuses on whether the owner has acquired a property right which cannot be abridged by the subsequent changes in government regulations.

Vested rights is generally asserted by the developer or landowner to avoid subsequent regulatory changes. And it is often affirmatively raised in litigation challenging the application of new zoning regulations before a development is built. Estoppel is often asserted where the landowner or developer detrimentally relies on an invalid permit issued in violation of other local laws. In the context of code enforcement, estoppel is generally raised as a defense after a development is built.

Estoppel and Code Enforcement

Property owners operated a bed-and-breakfast inn from their single-family home located in a rural agricultural zone. About seven months after they began operation, code enforcement inspectors issued a notice of violation for maintaining a nonpermitted use in the agricultural zone. The county eventually amended the zoning regulations to permit bed-and-breakfast inns with a special use permit. During this period county planners made various statements to the owners about whether their original use would require the special use permit. Several years later the county filed an abatement action in court to permanently enjoin the owners from maintaining the bed-and-breakfast inn without a special use permit.

On appeal, the owners asserted the defense of estoppel based on the various representations made by county staff. The court rejected this defense. The owners were aware that their business did not comply with zoning laws. The court concluded that their reliance on the statements by county staff was unreasonable. Moreover, the court concurred with the trial court's decision that adverse impacts to the community would continue if the county was estopped from enforcing the permanent injunction. "When considering the application of the doctrine with respect to zoning laws and permits, courts must balance the individual's interest against the interest of the public and community in preserving the community patterns established by zoning laws." *County of Sonoma v. Rex*, 231 Cal.App.3d 1289, 1294-1296 (1991).

ment cannot revoke the permit. *Russ Bldg. Partnership v. City and County of San Francisco*, 44 Cal. 3d 839, 845-846 (1988). This rule is based on the constitutional principle that property may not be taken without due process of law. *Urban Renewal Agency v. California Coastal Zone Conservation Com.*, 15 Cal. 3d 577, 583-584 (1975).

Last Discretionary Approval. Recent California court decisions have expanded the application of vested rights to situations where building permits are not at issue. *City of West*

Hollywood v. Beverly Tower, Inc., 52 Cal.3d 1184, 1191-1193 (1991) (local agencies cannot enforce condominium conversion regulations enacted after developer secured final subdivision map approval and permission from California Department of Real Estate).

b. The City Issues a Building Permit in Error.

Generally, the courts will not estop a city from taking an enforcement action on an invalid permit even when an owner has substantially relied on the permit, because the owner has not acquired a vested right by relying on an invalid permit. *Millbrae Assn. for Residential Survival v. City of Millbrae*, 262 Cal.App. 2d 222, 246 (1968) (where court upheld city's right to prohibit developer from continual violation despite developer's $600,000 expenditure and reliance on an invalid permit).

The court's rationale is that a building permit can confer no greater rights upon a permittee than an ordinance itself. "Estoppel may be invoked against a governmental agency only when the agency has the power to do that which it promised to do or which it led the opposing party reasonably and justifiably to believe it would do. Where, however, the procedure specified in a statute is the measure of the agency's power to act, estoppel cannot be applied to enlarge that power." *Merco Constr. Engineers, Inc. v. Los Angeles Unified Sch. Dist.*, 274 Cal.App. 2d 154, 160 (1969); *See also Magruder v. City of Redwood*, 203 Cal. 665, 674-675 (1928) (criminal enforcement action was not defeated against owner for operating commercial business in residential zone despite issuance of building permits).

"Estoppel may be invoked against a governmental agency only when the agency has the power to do that which it promised to do or which it led the opposing party reasonably and justifiably to believe it would do. Where, however, the procedure specified in a statute is the measure of the agency's power to act, estoppel cannot be applied to enlarge that power." (Merco Constr. Engineers, Inc. v. Los Angeles Unified School District)

Exceptions. For two cases where the city was estopped from revoking permits issued in error, *see Anderson v. City of La Mesa*, 118 Cal.App. 3d 657, 669 (1981) (where owner acted in good faith reliance on the city's representations, and public interest was minimal) and *Keiffer v. Spencer*, 153 Cal.App. 3d 954, 963 (1984) (where owners acted in good faith, expended large amounts of money, and relied on information and advice from the city in establishing their video arcade business).

c. City Engages in a Course of Conduct Which Creates Extensive Reliance.

A city may be estopped if it has actively encouraged a course of conduct, or has itself engaged in a course of conduct (as distinguished from a single act), inducing or encouraging reasonable reliance, particularly if the conduct causes reliance on a large group of people. *See generally, City of Imperial Beach v. Algert*, 200 Cal.App. 2d 48, 52 (city was estopped from asserting that a parcel was a public street when for the previous 12 years it made representations to the contrary); *City of Long Beach v. Mansell*, 3 Cal. 3d 462, 493 (1970) (state and city were estopped from invalidating title where thousands of homeowners had settled on land over a period of many years and where the government was aware of, but had not taken steps to resolve, the complex title problems).

Courts are hesitant to apply estoppel where public policy might be violated by setting a precedent whereby estoppel is used to circumvent well-established procedures or where the public's health or safety may be adversely affected.

d.   Other Public Policy Arguments. Courts are hesitant to apply estoppel where public policy might be violated by setting a precedent whereby estoppel is used to circumvent well-established procedures or where the public's health or safety may be adversely affected. For example, *see generally, County of San Diego v. Cal. Water, etc.*, 30 Cal. 2d 817, 829-830 (1947) (county would not be estopped where it would frustrate public policy by permitting evasion of strict statutory procedures); *Smith v. County of Santa Barbara*, 7 Cal.App. 4th 770, 775-776 (1992) (estoppel should not replace the legally established substantive and procedural requirements for obtaining permits); *Chaplis v. County of Monterey*, 97 Cal.App. 3d 249, 260 (1979) (county would not be estopped from revoking an invalid septic tank permit where the tank jeopardized public health).

D.   Statute of Limitations

Enforcement actions must be filed within the time frame established by statute. Penal Code section 802 establishes a one-year statute of limitation for the filing of misdemeanor or infraction criminal actions. Unless a specific statute sets the limitation, Code of Civil Procedure section 343, which applies to most civil causes of action alleged in a code enforcement judicial action, requires actions to be filed within three years.

Statute of limitations is a common defense which can be raised by filing a special motion to dismiss in either a criminal or civil judicial action. In the context of code enforcement cases, statute of limitations claims do not demand the dismissal of the

Zoning violations have long been recognized as continuous in nature. *City of Fontana v. Atkinson*, 212 Cal.App. 2d 499, 509 (1963). Where the crime charged is continuous in nature, if the crime is continued within the statutory period, a prosecution is not barred. *People v. Curry*, 69 Cal.App. 501, 504 (1924). Consequently, a defendant could be cited for each day a violation on his property exists during the one-year statute of limitations for misdemeanors. Many municipal code enforcement provisions include language declaring that a separate offense be charged for each day in violation.

While *Fontana* involved a civil action, it is irrelevant whether a statute of limitations is categorized under the Penal or Civil Code. Separation of statutes into codes is only for convenience. *People v. Ashley* 17 Cal.App. 3d 1122, 1126 (1971): "Statutes dealing with the same subject matter from various codes must be read together." *Beasley v. Municipal Court*, 32 Cal.App.3d 1020, 1027 (1973)).

'Maintaining'

When drafting land use regulations, it is critical to ensure that maintaining a property in violation is declared a violation of law. This is especially important given that many years may pass before the enforcement agency discovers the violation. Once the violation is discovered, the statute of limitations will start to run. (*See* discussions on pages 114-115.)

action, because most land use violations are viewed as continuous. As long as the complaint includes dates with the prescribed statutory time period, a code enforcement action is not barred by the statute of limitations.

E. Discriminatory or Selective Enforcement

When an inspector initially notifies an owner or responsible person about a violation, the issue of discriminatory enforcement is frequently raised. "How can you find a violation on my property when everyone else in my neighborhood has the same violation!" Successfully asserting discriminatory enforcement relies on constitutional guarantees prohibiting government from treating citizens differently solely on the basis of their gender, race, or some other classification the courts have deemed to be 'suspect'. To support a defense of discriminatory enforcement, an owner must prove that he or she has been deliberately and intentionally singled out because of some unjustifiable standard, such as race, religion, or the exercise of protected rights which has no rational or legitimate law enforcement interest.

F. Bankruptcy

Bankruptcy is not an absolute defense demanding the dismissal of a pending enforcement action. However, an insolvent property owner who has filed for bankruptcy presents certain investigative and procedural obstacles. Where a person or entity has filed a bankruptcy petition, the federal court has exclusive jurisdiction over all claims affecting property which is part of that estate. Moreover, in most cases the filing of a petition for involuntary or voluntary bankruptcy operates as an automatic stay to the commencement or continuation of any action, or to the enforcement of any judgment, against the debtor. 11 U.S.C section 362 (a).

This automatic stay does not apply to any action or proceeding a governmental entity has initiated or continued as part of its police or regulatory powers to enforce its law and regulations. 11 U.S.C. sections 362(b)(4) and (5). This statute appears to allow an enforcement agency to obtain an injunction requiring an owner to comply with applicable land use regulations. However, bankruptcy jurisdiction could prohibit the assessment or collection of any civil penalties.

Nonetheless, enforcement of an order to repair against an insolvent or bankrupt property owner may still prove futile. Remember, civil contempt is the process by which an agency

---

Avoiding Statute of Limitations Problems

A common practice in drafting a criminal complaint is to ensure that the dates alleged correspond with the dates of actual inspections that are within one year of the filing date of the complaint. Since they are within the one-year statute of limitations, most courts will approve those inspection dates.

Murgia v. Municipal Court, 15 Cal. 3d 286, 297 (1975) (mere laxity of enforcement or nonarbitrary selective enforcement is not a denial of equal protection). It is not a constitutional denial of equal protection (and therefore not a defense based on discriminatory or selective enforcement) that one party is prosecuted while others in violation are not. *See City of Banning v. Desert Outdoor Advertising, Inc.*, 209 Cal.App. 2d 152, 154-6 (1962). In the context of code enforcement, the claim that one owner is the subject of 'selective enforcement', because the agency did not file an enforcement action against other owners with similar code violations, is not sufficient to support this defense.

Bankruptcy's automatic stay limitations do not apply to criminal prosecution, which is excepted by U.S.C. section 362(b)(1). A bankruptcy proceeding does not shield a criminal defendant from prosecution or from the imposition of conditions as part of a criminal sentence. *Kelly v. Robinson*, 479 U.S. 36, 50 (1986) (restitution for welfare fraud not dischargeable under bankruptcy).

The elimination of nonconforming uses is one of the most fundamental problems resulting from zoning changes.

A nonconforming use is automatically exempt from the terms of a new zoning ordinance, and no application is needed for a variance or conditional use permit. *City of Los Angeles v. Gage*, 127 Cal.App. 2d 442, 453, 460 (1954) (elimination of existing uses within five years did not amount to taking of property); *Hill v. City of Manhattan Beach*, 6 Cal. 3d 279, 285-286 (1971) (land not used for building purposes would not create a nonconforming right).

enforces the terms of an injunction when the owner fails to correct violations on the property. The owner's inability, including financial inability, to carry out the requirements of the injunction or other court order is a defense to contempt proceedings. If an owner is financially unable to repair the property or otherwise comply with the injunction, the agency may be forced to obtain court orders permitting city crews or private contractors to abate the imminent health and safety hazards.

G. Nonconforming Uses and Structures

Nonconforming rights, like the equitable defenses of laches and estoppel, is probably the most common defense which can defeat an enforcement action. A nonconforming use is one that is valid when the use commences, but becomes nonconforming when subsequent regulations are enacted. The burden of the nonconforming rights defense rests entirely on the property owner and his or her ability to prove that the nonconforming use of the property continued since the change in zoning regulations. Given its direct connection to the use of the property or building, the enforcement agency should spend sufficient time at the outset of any investigation to research the use and history of a particular parcel to determine whether the issue of nonconforming rights is a viable defense.

The elimination of nonconforming uses is one of the most fundamental problems resulting from zoning changes. After all, the general purpose of zoning is eventually to end all nonconforming uses. What was once a permitted use is now no longer recognized as such in the new zoning regulations. Immediate termination of nonconforming uses can cause serious hardship and may be considered so destructive of property interests as to constitute a denial of due process. Given this background, most municipalities enact zoning regulations that impose less drastic methods to terminate nonconforming uses: (a) prohibition against rebuilding or expansion; and (b) amortization of the use within a reasonable period of time.

Establishing Nonconforming Uses in Structures. Nonconforming uses are difficult to prove where there is a lengthy passage of time between the change in the zoning regulation and the code enforcement investigation. Most nonconforming issues involve the repair of buildings. Illegal additions and conversions of garages to residential dwellings are very common in code enforcement investigations where nonconforming rights is often raised as a major issue.

Density, Illegal Dwelling Units, and Nonconforming Uses

In the mid-1980s the City of San Diego undertook a code enforcement sweep for illegal dwelling units in the Mission Beach community. Mission Beach is a moderate-income, beachfront community designed in the early 1920s and 30s. Over the years congestion has become a major problem because many owners converted garages and added dwelling units to increase their incomes from vacation rentals. The Mission Beach area has undergone nearly 10 rezonings. The most recent change established the Mission Beach Planned District with residential subareas that modified the number of permitted dwelling units.

The sweep uncovered many properties that exceeded existing density, but, given the number of zoning changes, it became critical to develop an entire zoning history for these properties. While the primary single-family dwelling might have been legal, many of the additional dwellings did not have building permits on file. However, this proved inconclusive because the city partially destroyed some of the building records prior to 1954.

The possibility existed that building permits had been issued, but no records could be found. Worksheets used by the County Assessor were more accurate as they contained notes made by the various assessors at the time of their inspections. These records often dated back to the construction of the beach bungalows in the 1920s. Other evidence used by the enforcement agency included written statements made by previous owners, photographs of garage doors, and declarations from building inspectors that attempted to date the old construction materials and techniques.

Termination of Nonconforming Uses. An enforcement agency's inquiry does not stop when the owner is able to provide sufficient facts to establish the nonconforming right to use the property according to former land use regulations. Nonconforming uses may be terminated by any of the following occurrences—

An enforcement agency's inquiry does not stop when the owner is able to provide sufficient facts to establish the nonconforming right to use the property according to former land use regulations.

Reuse of the property can be prohibited when a nonconforming use is voluntarily abandoned. *Hill v City of Manhattan Beach*, 6 Cal.3d 279, 285-286 (1971).

■ Voluntary Abandonment. If the enforcement agency can prove abandonment of the nonconforming use, the owner's claim of nonconforming rights fails. The case for abandonment, however, involves the difficult task of proving the owner or business operator's intent. Most zoning ordinances create a presumption of abandonment where the use was discontinued for a period of twelve consecutive months.

■ Expansion or Enlargement of the Use or Buildings. Where the use over the years becomes more restrictive in nature, owner may be prohibited from returning to the earlier high intensity use. Repairs and alterations may be allowed if they do not increase the size of structure or expand the use itself. Many zoning ordinances establish a limit on the repairs based on the fair market value of the building.

What Is Enlargement?

Enlargement of a nonconforming business in a residential area would detrimentally effect the neighborhood's character; a nonconforming use does not entitle owner to increase the size of permanent buildings. *Edmonds v. County of Los Angeles*, 40 Cal.2d 642, 653 (1953) (trailer court improperly expanded from 20 to 30 trailers); *contra, Ricciardi v. County of Los Angeles*, 115 Cal. App.2d 569, 576 (1953) (owner can make minor repairs to dilapidated buildings if it would not enlarge nonconforming use).

O'Mara v. Council of the City of Newark, 238 Cal.App.2d 836, 838 (1965) (measure the assessed value prior to the fire with the assessed value after the fire to determine if nonconforming zoning criteria apply).

■ Substantial Destruction. Where the building is destroyed by fire, explosion or act of God, most zoning ordinances provide for automatic loss of the nonconforming use and structure. Again some ordinances establish a limit on the destruction according to the fair market value of the building.

■ Public Nuisances. Nonconforming uses declared to be a public nuisance can be immediately abated pursuant to the municipal police powers if the enforcement agency follows procedural due process. *Department of Transportation v. Hadley Fruit Orchards, Inc.*, 59 Cal.App.3d 49, 53 (1976).

■ Amortization. Since immediate termination of certain nonconforming uses may cause financial hardship, the municipality may provide for amortization of the use after several years. The courts generally approve of this method where they find the period of amortization is reasonable given the use.

In *United Business Comm. v. City of San Diego*, 91 Cal.App.3d 156, 179-182 (1979), the court found that a seven-year amortization period for nonconforming signs was reasonable. And in another case the court ruled in favor of a billboard ordinance providing for amortization from one to four years. Here the court considered several factors: (1) the cost of the billboard; (2) its depreciated value; (3) remaining useful life; (4) remaining length of leases; and (5) harm to the public if the structure remains beyond the amortization period. *Metromedia, Inc. v. City of San Diego*, 26 Cal.3d 848, 881-884 (1981) overruled on other grounds by U.S. Supreme Court, 453 U.S. 490 (1981).

Appendix A
Forms and Documents

Appendix A
Documents

Appendix B
Code Sections

Appendix C
Flow Charts

Table of
Authorities

Glossary

Suggested
Reading

Index

Suggestion
Form

Solano Press
Books

Notes

MUNICIPAL COURT OF CALIFORNIA, COUNTY OF _____

_____ JUDICIAL DISTRICT

INSPECTION WARRANT

No. _____

The People of the State of California, to any Building Investigator of the City of _____:

Upon good cause shown to the Court:

YOU ARE HEREBY COMMANDED TO CONDUCT an inspection as authorized by section 91.0202 of the San Diego Municipal Code of the premise described as the single family wood frame structure located on San Diego assessors parcel number _____ known as 2000 Field Road, in the City of _____, County of _____, State of California. Specifically, the second story room addition located to the rear of the building, and related support work done on the ground floor.

YOU ARE AUTHORIZED to enter the premises above to inspect the interior of the structure and to take photographs of any and all of the above mentioned areas of inspection for the purpose of determining whether there are violations of Building Ordinances, including but not limited to Uniform Building Code section 301a as adopted by _____ Municipal Code section 91.0202 (building without a building permit).

This inspection shall be conducted pursuant to Code of Civil Procedure section 1822.56 in a reasonable manner for the purpose of ensuring compliance with all applicable laws. The court finds that immediate execution is reasonably necessary under circumstances shown and the requirement of twenty-four (24) hours advance notice is hereby waived for the reasons set forth in the accompanying affidavits. An inspection may be made between the hours of 8:00 a.m. and 6:00 p.m. of any day. This warrant will be effective from the date hereof for a period not to exceed fourteen (14) days.

Given under my hand this _____ day of _____, 1994.

_____
Judge of the Municipal Court
_____ Judicial District

MUNICIPAL COURT OF CALIFORNIA, COUNTY OF _____

_____ JUDICIAL DISTRICT

STATE OF CALIFORNIA   )   **AFFIDAVIT FOR INSPECTION WARRANT**

)   ss.

COUNTY OF _____   )   No._____

I, _____, who under oath, say and depose the following on this _____ day of June 1994:

That I am a Code Compliance Officer employed by the City of _____ Building Inspection Department. I have been employed by the Building Inspection Department for approximately twelve (12) years. I have obtained approximately thirty (30) college units of education in the area of building and construction. I have received ongoing in-house training in the areas of building code enforcement and investigation of building violations.

On or about November 1, 1993, the City of _____ Building Inspection Department received a complaint concerning 2000 Field Road. The complaint alleged that an addition to the rear of the residence was being constructed without a building permit. I checked the Building Inspection Department's computerized files and found no plans or permits for 2000 Field Road. I researched the County Assessor's computerized files and learned that the property is owned by _____.

On November 28, 1993, I went to 2000 Field Road. I found the only people at the residence to be day laborers installing a brick driveway. No one at the property spoke English so I left a door hanger requesting the owner call me within three (3) days.

On November 30, 1993, I received a call from the property owner. I attempted to get the owner to schedule an inspection time, however, he refused stating he was going to Los Angeles and then La Paz, Mexico for a week.

On December 14, 1993, I went to 2000 Field Road to attempt an inspection. A woman who I believe to be Mrs. _____ answered the door. I asked if I could inspect the room addition. She refused my request for the inspection stating she was just home for lunch and did not want to put the dogs up. She agreed to meet me on December 21, 1993, for an inspection at 11:30 a.m.

On or about December 21, 1993, I went to the residence for the scheduled inspection. I arrived at 11:25 a.m. and found no one home. I waited approximately forty (40) minutes and no one came to the house. I left a door hanger requesting the homeowner call me.

On or about December 27, 1993, I mailed a letter to Mr. _____ at 2000 Field Road. The letter outlined my attempts to inspect the property and informed him that I would contact the City Attorney for an inspection warrant if he did not contact me and arrange for an inspection. (See Exhibit ___.)

On or about February 13, 1994, I contacted the City Attorney Investigator for assistance with an inspection at 2000 Field Road. (See Declaration of City Attorney Investigator as Exhibit ___.) As a result of the investigator's phone call, Mr. _____ called me on February 21, 1994. He told me that he works in Los Angeles and could not meet me for an inspection. I told him that he did not have to be present for the inspection, his wife could let me into the house. He said he would check with his wife and call me back.

On or about February 26, 1994, I called the residence and received no answer. On March 4, 1994, I called the residence and left a message on the phone recorder. On April 1, 1994, I called the residence and discovered the telephone had been disconnected.

Based on my case research, I am of the opinion that an addition has been added to the rear portion of the structure at 2000 Field Road in the City of _____. This is a violation of Uniform Building Code (UBC) section 301a, which requires a building permit for such additions and UBC section 305d, which requires inspections and approvals by the building official for such additions as adopted by _____ Municipal Code section 91.0101.

It is my opinion that improper installation of electrical or mechanical devices in the addition could present a hazard to the occupants. Access to the interior of the residence located at 2000 Field Road is necessary to determine if other building code violations exist.

Given under my hand and dated this _____ day of March 1994, at _____, California.

_____

Subscribed and sworn before me
this _____ day of March 1994
at _____ AM/PM

_____
JUDGE OF THE MUNICIPAL COURT
_____ JUDICIAL DISTRICT

fcb:mar

MUNICIPAL COURT OF CALIFORNIA, COUNTY OF _____

_____ JUDICIAL DISTRICT

STATE OF CALIFORNIA	)	DECLARATION IN SUPPORT OF
	)	AFFIDAVIT FOR INSPECTION WARRANT
	) ss.	
COUNTY OF _____	)	No.

I,_____, declare under penalty of perjury that the foregoing is true and correct.

QUALIFICATIONS

I am an Investigator for the City Attorney's Office, and I am assigned to the Code Enforcement Unit. This unit is responsible for the criminal and civil enforcement of the City's land use ordinances (zoning, housing, building, fire, health, and etc.). I have been assigned to this unit since June, 1987. Previously I was employed by the County of Siskiyou, State of California for six (6) years as a resident Deputy Sheriff-Coroner. Prior to that I was employed by the City of Mt. Shasta, California for one and one-half (1 1/2) years as a police officer. I have a Bachelor of Arts Degree in Criminal Justice from California State University at Sacramento. I have accumulated over six hundred (600) hours of specialized training in criminal investigation and related law enforcement subjects. I have attended training seminars dealing with housing, zoning, fire and narcotics abatement laws.

INVESTIGATION

On or about February 13, 1994, I was contacted by _____, Code Compliance Officer for the City. She requested my assistance in getting an inspection warrant for 2000 Field Road in the City of _____. I was given a copy of a letter written to the property owner dated December 27, 1993, that outlined her attempts to inspect.

On or about February 19, 1994, I telephoned the property owner. He agreed to call the Code Compliance Officer to schedule an inspection. On February 25, 1994, I received a call from the Code Compliance Officer who told me that the owner had called and would arrange an inspection.

On or about March 26, 1994, I learned that the owner had not scheduled an appointment. I called him at home and attempted to get a date and a time for an inspection. He refused to set a time and indicated he would call us later. On April 2, 1994, the owner had not scheduled an appointment so I attempted to call him at home. I learned that the telephone had been disconnected.

On April 24, 1994, I went to 2000 Field Road to talk to him. I was met at the front door by two males in their early twenties. They told me that they were staying at the house. I asked if _____ was home and one of the males replied, "yes." I identified myself and asked if I could speak to him. One of the males went upstairs to get Mr. _____. He returned a short time later and told me he was not home. I left my business card and asked them to have Mr. _____ call me. To this date I have not heard from him.

Given under my hand and dated this _____ day of March 1994, at _____, California.

_____

THE CITY ATTORNEY
CITY OF SAN DIEGO

SUSAN M. HEATH
SENIOR CHIEF DEPUTY CITY ATTORNEY

DAVID C. JAMES
ASSISTANT CHIEF DEPUTY CITY ATTORNEY

John W. Witt
CITY ATTORNEY

CRIMINAL DIVISION
1200 THIRD AVENUE, SUITE 700
SAN DIEGO, CALIFORNIA 92101-4106
TELEPHONE (619) 533-5500
FAX (619) 533-5505

N O T I C E

An interior and exterior inspection of _____ (address) will be conducted by the City of San Diego (Dept.) Department on (date & time).

This inspection will be done pursuant to an Inspection Warrant issued by the San Diego Municipal Court. A copy of the warrant will be delivered at the time of service.

It is a misdemeanor to willfully refuse to permit an inspection authorized by warrant. CCP §1822.56

This Notice serves as the required 24-hour notice of intent to execute the above-mentioned warrant. CCP §1822.56

_____
Dennis J. Smith
Senior Criminal Investigator

[mgr] form
2301

CENTER FOR MUNICIPAL DISPUTE RESOLUTION

1200 Third Avenue • Suite 500 • San Diego, CA 92101 • 619/533-5625

On February 2, 1994, John Smith, owner of property at 222 Every Way, met with Sam Saw, from Building Inspection and Susan Quinn, Mediator, to discuss the issue of building violations on the property. As a result of this compliance mediation the following good-faith agreement has been reached:

1. John agrees to attend Homeowner's Night at 1222 1st Avenue, 3rd Floor, which is held on Thursdays from 5-8 PM. The number to call for an appointment is 236-6270. He will go no later than March 19, 1994.

2. Sam agrees to call John at 555-1212 no later than March 4, 1994 with costs and lists of contacts for "Plan Runners" to assist in taking John's plans through the process.

4. Sam will inform the Building Inspection Department that John will obtain proper permits for the construction of his back deck by April 1, 1994. Final inspection of the deck will be completed by August 31, 1994.

5. John understands that if the property is not in compliance by August 31, 1994, the Building Inspection Department will make certain that the County Recorder records on the deed that the property may not be sold until the permit is obtained and inspection is complete.

_____
John Smith, Property Owner

_____
Sam Saw
Building Inspection

_____
Susan Quinn, Mediator

February 2, 1994
_____
Date

TRAIN\AGRMNT.SPL

OFFICE OF CITY ATTORNEY
CRIMINAL DIVISION
CODE ENFORCEMENT UNIT
1200 THIRD AVENUE, SUITE 700
SAN DIEGO, CALIFORNIA 92101-4106

NOTICE TO DEFENDANT
_____ _____

A COMPLAINT HAS BEEN FILED AGAINST YOU CHARGING A VIOLATION OF

_____

_____

VIOLATION DATE(S)_____

YOU ARE HEREBY NOTIFIED TO APPEAR IN THE MISDEMEANOR ARRAIGNMENT DEPARTMENT OF THE MUNICIPAL COURT, ROOM 1008,

220 WEST BROADWAY, SAN DIEGO, ON_____AT _____AS A

DEFENDANT IN SAID ACTION PROSECUTED BY THE PEOPLE OF THE STATE OF CALIFORNIA.

_____   **APPEARANCE IS MANDATORY**
_____   Failure to appear as above notified may result in a
_____   WARRANT OF ARREST being issued against you.
_____

CA-2003 (REV. 9-93)

MUNICIPAL COURT OF CALIFORNIA, COUNTY OF SAN DIEGO

SAN DIEGO JUDICIAL DISTRICT
CODE ENFORCEMENT

THE PEOPLE OF THE STATE OF   )   No.

CALIFORNIA,   )

)

Plaintiff,   )

)   **AMENDED**

v.   )   **CRIMINAL COMPLAINT**

_____,   )

)

Defendants   )

_____   )

)

       The undersigned, certifying upon information and belief, complains

COUNT ONE:

       That on or about November 3, 1992, at _____, in the City of San Diego, County of San Diego, State of California, defendant committed a misdemeanor by maintaining a structural addition, <u>to wit</u>: construction of a second story addition to the original dwelling unit which lacks a permit, in violation of section 301(a) of the Uniform Building Code as adopted by San Diego Municipal Code section 91.0101, in violation of San Diego Municipal Code section 91.0205.

COUNT TWO:

       That on or about November 3, 1992, at _____, in the City of San Diego, County of San Diego, State of California, defendant committed a misdemeanor by maintaining a structural addition, <u>to wit</u>: construction of an additional room on the east side of the dwelling unit which lacks a permit, in violation of section 301(a) of the Uniform Building Code as adopted by San Diego Municipal Code section 91.0101, in violation of San Diego Municipal Code section 91.0205.

COUNT THREE:

       That on or about November 3, 1992, at _____, in the City of San Diego, County of San Diego, State of California, defendant committed a misdemeanor by maintaining a structural addition, <u>to wit</u>: construction of an additional bathroom to the west side area of the dwelling unit which lacks a permit, in violation of section 301(a) of the Uniform Building Code as adopted by San Diego Municipal Code section 91.0101, in violation of San Diego Municipal Code section 91.0205.

COUNT FOUR:

       That on or about November 3, 1992, at _____, in the City of San Diego, County of San Diego, State of California, defendant committed a misdemeanor by maintaining a structural addition, <u>to</u>

COUNT ELEVEN:

That on or about February 10, 1993, at _____, in the City of San Diego, County of San Diego, State of California, defendant committed a misdemeanor by maintaining a structural addition, <u>to wit</u>: construction of an additional room on the east side of the dwelling unit which lacks a permit, in violation of section 301(a) of the Uniform Building Code as adopted by San Diego Municipal Code section 91.0101, in violation of San Diego Municipal Code section 91.0205.

COUNT TWELVE:

That on or about February 10, 1993, at _____, in the City of San Diego, County of San Diego, State of California, defendant committed a misdemeanor by maintaining a structural addition, <u>to wit</u>: construction of an additional bathroom to the west side area of the dwelling unit which lacks a permit, in violation of section 301(a) of the Uniform Building Code as adopted by San Diego Municipal Code section 91.0101, in violation of San Diego Municipal Code section 91.0205.

COUNT THIRTEEN:

That on or about February 10, 1993, at _____, in the City of San Diego, County of San Diego, State of California, defendant committed a misdemeanor by maintaining a structural addition, <u>to wit</u>: installation of new stucco on the dwelling unit which lacks a permit, in violation of section 301(a) of the Uniform Building Code as adopted by San Diego Municipal Code section 91.0101, in violation of San Diego Municipal Code section 91.0205.

COUNT FOURTEEN:

That on or about February 10, 1993, at _____, in the City of San Diego, County of San Diego, State of California, defendant committed a misdemeanor by maintaining a structural addition, <u>to wit</u>: installation of new plywood siding to the detached garage which lacks a permit, in violation of section 301(a) of the Uniform Building Code as adopted by San Diego Municipal Code section 91.0101, in violation of San Diego Municipal Code section 91.0205.

COUNT FIFTEEN:

That on or about February 10, 1993, at _____, in the City of San Diego, County of San Diego, State of California, defendant committed a misdemeanor by maintaining electrical wiring, device, appliance or equipment on any building, structure, or premises, <u>to wit</u>: installed new electrical wiring and outlets in second story addition, which lacks a permit required by San Diego Municipal Code section 92.0201A, in violation of San Diego Municipal Code section 92.0108B.

COUNT SIXTEEN:

That on or about February 10, 1993, at _____, in the City of San Diego, County of San Diego, State of California, defendant committed a misdemeanor by maintaining electrical wiring, device, appliance or equipment on any building, structure, or premises, <u>to wit</u>: installed new or altered existing electrical wiring in the original dwelling unit, which lacks a permit required by San Diego Municipal Code section 92.0201A, in violation of San Diego Municipal Code section 92.0108B.

COUNT SEVENTEEN:

That on or about February 10, 1993, at _____, in the City of San Diego, County of San Diego, State of California, defendant committed a misdemeanor by maintaining a plumbing system or part thereof within or on any building, structure, or premises, <u>to wit</u>: plumbing lines in the 3/4 bathroom, which lacks a permit issued by the Department of Building Inspection as required by San Diego Municipal Code section 93.0301(a), in violation of San Diego Municipal Code section 93.0109.

COUNT EIGHTEEN:

That on or about February 10, 1993, at _____, in the City of San Diego, County of San Diego, State of California, defendant committed a misdemeanor by maintaining a forced air furnace which lacks a heating or ventilation permit required by San Diego Municipal Code section 93.0302(a), in violation of San Diego Municipal Code section 93.0109.

I certify under penalty of perjury that the foregoing is true and correct.

Dated _____, at San Diego, California.

_____
(COMPLAINANT)

Pursuant to Penal Code section 1054.5(b), the People are hereby informally requesting that defendant's counsel provide discovery to the People as required by Penal Code section 1054.3.

CRIMINAL COMPLAINT FILED: _____

CODE ENFORCEMENT

PROPOSED OFFER AND ISSUING SHEET

_____
Defendant/#

CHARGES ISSUED:

SDMC § 91.0205 x 10
SDMC § 92.0108B x 4
SDMC § 93.0109 x 4

_____
Co-Defendant/#

MJL / 04-07-93
Issued By/Date

_____18_____
Total Counts

CE CASE#_____

1. Plead guilty or no contest to Counts Ten through Eighteen, dismiss Counts One through Nine.
2. Harvey waiver
3. ISS 3 years on the following terms and conditions:
    a. Fine/Custody: $2,000
    b. Under the direction of the Neighborhood Code Compliance Department regarding property located at_____:
        (1) Obtain necessary building, electrical, plumbing or mechanical permits for all work done without proper permits including the second story addition; the electrical wiring within both the original structure and addition; the 3/4 bath located at west side of the original structure; the forced air furnace installed in the second story addition; the room addition on east side of the original structure; the stucco on the dwelling unit; the plywood siding to the garage; and
            • Obtain necessary inspections and approvals for all work done under the permits required in item 3.b.1); or
        (2) Remove/demolish all unpermitted work including the second story addition; the electrical wiring within both the original structure and addition.
    c. Pay to the City of San Diego $850 for administrative citations, numbers 00694, 00779 and 00782 issued on April 6, 1992, May 11, 1992 and June 15, 1992, respectively.
    d. Violate no same or similar building laws and regulations as to any property owned, leased or maintained within the City of San Diego.
    e. Return to court within approximately 45 days with proof of all required permits.
    f. Return to court within approximately 45 days with proof of final approvals or removal/demolition of all unpermitted work.
    g. Inspections: Allow Neighborhood Code Compliance inspectors from the City of San Diego access to the property and premises to inspect and take pictures to monitor compliance with terms of probation.
        (1) Time: Between 8AM-6PM.
        (2) 24 hour notice required.

(3) Pursuant to San Diego Municipal Code sections 13.0401-0409 defendant shall pay the reinspection fee for each inspection made by City inspectors to determine compliance with the terms of probation. Payment shall be made as directed in the Notification of Reinspection Fee.

RH Hearing Date:_____   Plead:_____

Continuance Date:_____   TSD:_____

I HAVE READ AND UNDERSTAND AND ACCEPT THE ABOVE
TERMS AND CONDITIONS OF PROBATION.

_____   _____
Defendant   Date

_____   _____
Defendant   Date

JOHN W. WITT, City Attorney
SUSAN HEATH, Senior Chief Deputy
MARY JO LANZAFAME, Deputy City Attorney

    Code Enforcement Unit
    City Attorney's Office
    1200 Third Avenue, Suite 700
    San Diego, California 92101
    Telephone: 533-5500

Attorneys for Plaintiff

MUNICIPAL COURT OF CALIFORNIA, COUNTY OF SAN DIEGO

SAN DIEGO JUDICIAL DISTRICT

THE PEOPLE OF THE STATE OF CALIFORNIA,)) Plaintiff,)) v.)) _____,)) Defendant.) _____)	No. _____ **NOTICE OF LIS PENDENS** (GOVERNMENT CODE § 65908)

    NOTICE IS HEREBY GIVEN that in the above-entitled action, now pending in the above-entitled Court, Plaintiff has instituted a judicial action to enforce the City of San Diego's zoning regulations. This action concerns the real property known and described as:

Dated: _____   JOHN W. WITT, City Attorney

                                          By _____
                                            Mary Jo Lanzafame
                                            Deputy City Attorney

JOHN W. WITT, City Attorney
SUSAN M. HEATH, Senior Chief Deputy
MARY JO LANZAFAME, Deputy City Attorney

     Code Enforcement Unit
     City Attorney's Office
     1200 Third Avenue, Suite 700
     San Diego, CA 92101
     Telephone: 533-5500

Attorneys for Plaintiffs and
Real Party In Interest

SUPERIOR COURT OF THE STATE OF CALIFORNIA

THE COUNTY OF SAN DIEGO

THE PEOPLE OF THE STATE OF CALIFORNIA,)
 	
    Plaintiff,)
 	
THE CITY OF SAN DIEGO,)
a municipal corporation,)
 	
    Plaintiff and)
    Real Party In Interest,)
 	
    v.)
 	
_____; and)
DOES I THROUGH XX, inclusive,)
 	
    Defendants.)
_____)
	No.
	
	COMPLAINT FOR INJUNCTION
	AND OTHER EQUITABLE RELIEF

    THE PEOPLE OF THE STATE OF CALIFORNIA as plaintiff, and THE CITY OF SAN DIEGO, a municipal corporation and a chartered city, as plaintiff and Real Party In Interest each allege:

    1. At all times mentioned in the pleadings, real party in interest, THE CITY OF SAN DIEGO was and now is a municipal corporation and a chartered city organized and existing under the laws of California.

    2. Defendants DOES I through XX are sued as fictitious names, their names and capacities being unknown to plaintiffs. When the true names and capacities are ascertained, plaintiffs will amend this Complaint by inserting their true names and capacities.

    3. The owner of record of the real property at _____, San Diego, California is listed on the County Assessor's Records as _____. The legal description of the property according to the Quitclaim Deed is:

    4. Plaintiffs are informed and believe that _____ and all other defendants are legally responsible for the maintenance and repair of the property located at _____, San Diego, California.

    5. Wherever in this Complaint reference is made to any act of defendant, such allegation shall be deemed to mean defendant or his officers, agents, managers, representatives, employees or DOES I through XX, did or

authorized such acts while actively engaged in the operation, management, direction or control of the affairs of defendant while acting within the course and scope of their duties.

FIRST CAUSE OF ACTION
VIOLATIONS OF THE SAN DIEGO MUNICIPAL CODE

6. Plaintiff CITY OF SAN DIEGO brings this action pursuant to section 12.0202 and 101.0212E of the San Diego Municipal Code which authorizes the City to enforce any violation of its Municipal Code by seeking an injunction in the Superior Court.

7. On June 28, 1993, San Diego County Department of Health Services Vector Control Technicians inspected the property located at _____, San Diego, California. At that time, the inspector determined that there was an infestation of rats at _____ as evidenced by copious amounts of rat feces observed from the curb to the front door. The inspector further observed an abundance of trash and debris in both the front and back yards that could provide harborage for rats. Access to the interior of _____ was denied but the inspector's observation through the window led him to the conclusion that similar accumulations of trash and debris inside provide additional harborage for rats. An inspection of both addresses revealed evidence of rat feces on both properties but neither property had harborage for rats.

8. Defendant has caused, permitted and allowed the following violations to remain on the property:

a. San Diego Municipal Code section 54.0210—failing to maintain the premises free from waste material.

b. San Diego Municipal Code section 44.0341—failing to maintain the premises free of rats.

c. San Diego Municipal Code section 44.0349(c)—placing, leaving, dumping or permitting to accumulate or remain in any building or premises garbage, rubbish, trash or manure,
so that the same shall or may afford food, harborage, shelter or breeding place for rats.

d. San Diego Municipal Code section 44.0350—failure to pile junk and debris in an even and orderly manner upon racks elevated not less than eighteen inches above the ground and away from walls of buildings so that those materials will not afford a shelter or harborage for rats.

e. San Diego Municipal Code section 101.0707F—failing to maintain the proper storage of items not incidental to the residential use of the property, such as junk and miscellaneous debris.

f. California Health and Safety Code section 17920.3(a)(12)—maintaining a dwelling unit which is infested with insect, vermin or rodents as determined by a health officer.

g. California Health and Safety Code section 17920.3(j)—maintaining premises on which an accumulation of junk, dead organic matter, debris, garbage, rodent harborages, combustible materials or similar materials or conditions constitutes a fire, health or safety hazard.

SECOND CAUSE OF ACTION
MAINTENANCE OF A PUBLIC NUISANCE

9. Plaintiffs incorporate by reference allegations ONE through FOUR, SIX and SEVEN, in this second cause of action.

10. Plaintiffs bring this action pursuant to section 731 of the California Code of Civil Procedure in the name of THE PEOPLE OF THE STATE OF CALIFORNIA, to abate a public nuisance.

11. Defendant has caused and maintained a continuing public nuisance on the property since at least June 28, 1993. This condition renders the property a public nuisance because of the extreme accumulation of junk, trash and debris piled. . . . .next to the building and in the front and back yards, providing a harborage for rats.

12. Defendant's maintenance of the property in the condition described above is a continuing public nuisance as defined in California Civil Code sections 3479 and 3480. Defendant's property affects the entire community and neighborhood. Its current condition is injurious to health, offensive to the senses, and obstructs the

free use of the property and neighboring properties by interfering with the comfortable enjoyment of life or property. Such a condition is objectional to the neighborhood and community in whole.

13. Defendant was notified of the violation of the San Diego Municipal Code and State of California Health and Safety Code by a written notice on September 16, 1993. Defendant has not corrected the violations nor have they indicated to plaintiff any intention to permanently correct these violations. Therefore, plaintiffs are informed and believe that defendant will continue to maintain the property in the above-described condition, thereby causing irreparable injury and harm to the public's health, safety and welfare.

14. Plaintiffs have no adequate remedy at law.

15. Plaintiffs are informed and believe that the defendant will not correct these violations or abate the nuisance within a reasonable time. If it becomes necessary for plaintiffs to correct the violations or abate the nuisance, the City will incur substantial costs. As part of its prayer, plaintiffs request recovery of its costs to correct these _____ violations or abate the nuisance and establish a prior lien on the property for such costs.

WHEREFORE, PLAINTIFFS PRAY FOR JUDGMENT AS FOLLOWS:

1. That the property subject to this Complaint located at _____, San Diego, California and the existing conditions thereon be declared in violation of:

San Diego Municipal Code sections:

44.0119(a)	44.0350
44.0341	101.0407F
44.0349(c)	

and,

California Health & Safety Code section:

17920.3a12(2)

2. That defendant, his successors and assigns, be permanently enjoined from maintaining these San Diego Municipal Code and California Health and Safety Code violations;

3. That defendant's property be declared a continuing public nuisance;

4. That defendant be permanently enjoined from maintaining a public nuisance at their property;

5. That defendant be ordered to abate all conditions which cause the nuisance, or alternatively, that plaintiff CITY OF SAN DIEGO or its contractors be authorized to accomplish the work and recover the costs from defendant, his successors and assigns;

6. That recordation of an abstract of the judgment in this case constitutes a prior lien over any lien that may be held on the property by any defendant to this action; . . . .

7. That plaintiff CITY recovers costs of this suit from defendant, his successors and assigns; and

8. That plaintiffs are entitled to such other relief as the Court deems proper.

Dated: _____, 1993

JOHN W. WITT, City Attorney

By _____
    Mary Jo Lanzafame
    Deputy City Attorney

Attorneys for Plaintiffs
and Real Party In Interest

SUPERIOR COURT OF CALIFORNIA, COUNTY OF SAN DIEGO

STATE OF CALIFORNIA

THE PEOPLE OF THE STATE OF CALIFORNIA,	)))	No. _____
	)	I/C JUDGE WAYNE L. PETERSON
Plaintiff,	))	
THE CITY OF SAN DIEGO,	)	ORDER GRANTING
a municipal corporation,	)	PRELIMINARY
	)	INJUNCTION
Plaintiff and	)	
Real Party In Interest,	))	
v.	))	
_____; and	)	
DOES I through XX, inclusive,	))	
Defendants.	)	
_____	)	

INTRODUCTION

The motion of plaintiffs for an order granting preliminary injunction having come regularly for hearing before the Honorable Wayne L. Peterson on December 28, 1993 at 9:30 a.m. in Department 16 of the San Diego Superior Court, notice duly and regularly given, Mary Jo Lanzafame appearing as attorney for the plaintiffs, defendant appearing in propria persona and upon reading the complaint on file in this action, the supporting declarations, points and authorities, it appears to the satisfaction of the court that this is a proper case for granting a preliminary injunction.

IT IS HEREBY ORDERED that during the pendency of this action or until further order of the Court, defendant _____, his agents, servants, employees, representatives and all persons acting in concert or participating with or for him with actual or constructive notice of this injunction, are hereby enjoined from engaging in or performing, directly, or indirectly, the following:

   1. violating any and all applicable health ordinances, regulations and laws of the City of San Diego and State of California at _____, San Diego, California;

   2. violating state housing laws at _____ by maintaining the residential dwelling in a substandard condition to the extent that it endangers life, limb, health, property, safety or welfare of the public or the occupant;

   3. accumulating trash, debris and garbage inside and outside of the dwelling;

   4. accumulating combustible materials inside the dwelling;

   5. maintaining refuse outside of refuse containers;

6. failing to maintain the interior and exterior of the premises free of rats; and

7. storing items or material in the front, rear or side yards which are not legally stored nor incidental to residential use.

IT IS FURTHER ORDERED that, under the direction of the Neighborhood Code Compliance and Health Departments, defendant, his agents, employees, and representatives, and all persons acting in concert or participating with him, are hereby restrained and enjoined from engaging in or performing any and all of the following:

8. Accumulating and storing materials on the property to the extent that it provides a shelter or harborage for rats.

IT IS FURTHER ORDERED that defendant <u>immediately</u> perform the following acts:

9. Remove all trash, rubbish, junk and debris from the yard areas so that only dirt, grass, plants, natural vegetation and any previously existing pavement remain in the yard areas.

10. Eliminate the infestation of rats.

11. Remove all material inside the dwelling and garage which the County Health Official determines will provide a harborage for rats.

12. If the defendant fails to perform the above acts, items NINE through ELEVEN, within fifteen days from the date this order is personally served, then City crews are authorized to abate the following imminent health hazards:

a. Remove all waste, accumulated material and miscellaneous debris from the exterior premises that is not legally stored nor incidental to residential use.

b. Remove all accumulated material, including lumber, boxes, barrels, bricks, stones, junk, debris or similar items, from the dwelling, garage and exterior of the premises, which afford a shelter or harborage for rats.

13. Any remaining items or material, with the exception of inoperable vehicles, removed from the subject property by City crews shall be deemed valueless and may be disposed of at a proper refuse site.

14. Defendant _____ shall do nothing that will prevent, impair, frustrate, obstruct or delay the efforts of City crews from performing the above acts, items 12 a and b.

15. In the event the defendant interferes or otherwise hinders the City's actions authorized by this order, the San Diego Police Department or San Diego County Sheriff are authorized to remove the defendant from the property while such action is ongoing.

16. Allow City personnel to inspect the property, with a written twenty-four hour notice, between 8:00 a.m. and 6:00 p.m., so that any imminent health hazards can be monitored.

17. All costs incurred by the City of San Diego in abating the nuisance at the defendant's property will be assessed as a special assessment against the property pursuant to Government Code section 38773.5.

Dated_____

_____
JUDGE OF THE SUPERIOR COURT

Appendix B
Local Code Sections

Appendix A
Documents

Appendix B
Code Sections

Appendix C
Flow Charts

Table of
Authorities

Glossary

Suggested
Reading

Index

Suggestion
Form

Solano Press
Books

Notes

Source: City of San Diego

CHAPTER ONE
ARTICLE TWO
Code Enforcement
Judicial and Administrative Remedies

("General Procedures" added 1–8–90 by O–17408 N.S.)
(Retitled 8–10–93 by O–17956 N.S.)

DIVISION TWO
Enforcement Authority and Powers

("Notice" added 1–8–90 by O–17408 N.S.)
(Retitled 8–10–93 by O–17956 N.S.)

§ 12.0101 Declaration of Purpose

The Council finds that the enforcement of the Municipal Code and applicable state codes throughout the City is an important public service. Code Enforcement is vital to protection of the public's health, safety and quality of life. The Council recognizes that enforcement starts with the drafting of precise regulations that can be effectively applied in administrative enforcement hearings and judicial proceedings. The Council further finds that a comprehensive code enforcement system that uses a combination of judicial and administrative remedies is critical to gain compliance with code regulations. Failure to comply with an administrative code enforcement action may require the City Attorney to file a judicial action to gain compliance.

("Declaration of Purpose" added 8–10–93 by O–17956 N.S.)

§ 12.0102 General Enforcement Authority

The City Manager, the City Clerk or any of their designated Enforcement Officials have the authority and powers necessary to gain compliance with the provisions of the Municipal Code and applicable state codes. These powers include the power to issue Notices of Violation and field citations, inspect public and private property and use whatever judicial and administrative remedies are available under the Municipal Code or applicable state codes.

("General Enforcement Authority" added by O–17956 N.S.)

§ 12.0103 Notice of Violation

Whenever a Director determines that a violation of the Municipal Code or applicable state codes exists, the Director or Enforcement Official may issue a Notice of Violation to a Responsible Person. The Notice of Violation shall include the following information:

1. The name of the property's record owner;

2. Street address;

3. The code sections in violation;

4. A description of the property's condition which violates the applicable codes;

5. A list of necessary corrections to bring the property into compliance;

6. A deadline or specific date to correct the violations listed in the Notice of Violation;

7. Reference to the potential consequences should the property remain in violation after the expiration of the compliance deadline including, but not limited to: criminal prosecution, civil injunction, administrative abatement, civil penalties, revocation of permits, recordation of the Notice of Violation and withholding of future municipal permits.

("Notice of Violation" added (portions previously contained in former Sec. 44.0122) 8–10–93 by O–17956 N.S.)

§ 12.0104 Authority to Inspect

A Director and any designated Enforcement Official are authorized to enter upon any property or premises to ascertain whether the provisions of the Municipal Code or applicable state codes are being obeyed, and to make any examinations and surveys as may be necessary in the performance of their enforcement duties. These may include the taking of photographs, samples or other physical evidence. All inspections, entries, examinations and surveys shall be done in a reasonable manner. If an owner, occupant or agent refuses permission to enter or inspect, the Enforcement Official may seek an administrative inspection warrant pursuant to the procedures provided for in California Code of Civil Procedure Section 1822.50 through 1822.59.

(Added 8–10–93 by O–17956 N.S.)

§ 12.0105 Power to Arrest

A Director or any designated Enforcement Official is authorized to arrest without a warrant any person whenever the Enforcement Official has reasonable cause to believe that the person has committed a violation of the Municipal Code or applicable state codes in his or her presence. Pursuant to Penal Code Section 836.5 the Enforcement Official can only arrest a person by issuing a misdemeanor field citation.

(Added 8–10–93 by O–17956 N.S.)

DIVISION TWO
Judicial Remedies
(Added 8–10–93 by O–17956 N.S.)

§ 12.0201 Criminal Violations— Misdemeanors and Infractions

It shall be unlawful for any person to violate any provision or to fail to comply with any of the requirements of this Code. A violation of any of the provisions or failing to comply with any of the mandatory requirements of this Code shall constitute a misdemeanor; except that notwithstanding any other provision of this Code, any such violation constituting a misdemeanor under this Code may, in the discretion of the City Attorney, be charged and prosecuted as an infraction; and, with the further exception that any violation of the provisions relating to parking, operation of bicycles, operation of motor vehicles, and use of freeways, highways and streets by animals, bicycles, motor vehicles or pedestrians shall constitute an infraction. Any person convicted of a misdemeanor under the provisions of this Code, unless provision is otherwise herein made, shall be punishable by a fine of not more than one thousand dollars ($1000) or by imprisonment in the County Jail for a period of not more than six months or by both fine and imprisonment. Any person convicted of an infraction under the provisions of this Code, unless provision is otherwise herein made, shall be punishable by fine only as follows: Upon a first conviction, by a fine of not exceeding two hundred fifty dollars ($250) and for a second conviction or any subsequent conviction within a period of one year, by a fine of not exceeding five hundred dollars ($500).

Each such person shall be charged with a separate offense for each and every day during any portion of which any violation of any provision of this Code is committed, continued or permitted by such person and shall, upon conviction, be punished accordingly.

(Renumbered from Sec. 13.0201 and retitled 8–10–93 by O–17956 N.S.)

§ 12.0202 Civil Violations— Injunctions and Civil Penalties

(a) In addition to any other remedy provided by this Code, any provision of this Code may be enforced by injunction issued by the Superior Court upon a suit brought by The City of San Diego.

(b) As part of a civil action filed to enforce provisions of this Code, a court may assess a maximum civil penalty of two thousand five hundred dollars ($2,500) per violation of the Municipal Code for each day during which any person commits, continues, allows or maintains a violation of any provision of this Code.

(Renumbered from Sec. 13.0202 and retitled 8–10–93 by O–17956 N.S.)

§ 12.0203 Code Enforcement Performance Bond

As part of any court action, the City has the authority to require a Responsible Person to post a performance bond to ensure compliance with the Municipal Code, applicable state codes or any judicial action.

(Added 8–10–93 by O–17956 N.S.)

§ 12.0204 Judicial Abatement

Pursuant to California Government Code Section 38773, the City has the authority to judicially abate public nuisances by filing criminal or civil actions. The City also has the authority to make the expense of abatement of the nuisance a special assessment, or a lien against the property on which it is maintained and a personal obligation against the property owner, in accordance with California Government Code Section 38773.1 or 38773.5.

(Added 8–10–93 by O–17956 N.S.)

§ 12.0205 Treble Damages for Subsequent Abatement Judgments

Pursuant to California Government Code Section 38773.7, upon the entry of a second or subsequent civil or criminal judgment within a two–year period that finds an owner of property responsible for a condition that may be abated in accordance with California Government Code Section 38773.5, a court may order the owner to pay treble the costs of the abatement. These costs shall not include conditions abated pursuant to Section 17980 of the California Health and Safety Code.

(Added 8–10–93 by O–17956 N.S.)

CHAPTER NINE
ARTICLE ONE

DIVISION ONE
Title, Scope and Adoption
(Added 11–20–89 by O–17390 N.S.)

§ 91.0101 Title and Adoption

(a) Title and Adoption. Subject to the exceptions listed in Section 91.0101 (b) through (e), the "Uniform Building Code, 1991 Edition", and the Uniform Building Code Standards, 1991 Edition, insofar as applicable to the Uniform Building Code, 1991 Edition, both published by the International Conference of Building Officials, are hereby adopted and, taken together with the provisions of Chapter IX, Article 1 of the San Diego Municipal Code, shall be known as the Building Code of The City of San Diego, California (hereinafter "This Code"). This Code shall: regulate the erection, construction, enlargement, alteration, repair, moving, removal, demolition, conversion, occupancy, equipment, use, height, area and maintenance of all privately owned buildings or structures in the City of San Diego, California; provide for the issuance of permits and collection of fees therefor; and provide penalties for violations of This Code. Each of the regulations, provisions, penalties, conditions and terms of the "Uniform Building Code, 1991 Edition, and the Uniform Building Code Standards, 1991 Edition insofar as applicable to the Uniform Building Code, 1991 Edition, published by the International Conference of Building Officials," are on file in the office of the City Clerk, as Documents No. OO–17773–1 and OO–17773–2 respectively, and are referred to, adopted and made a part of this Article as if fully set forth in this Article.

The adoption of the Uniform Building Code, 1991 Edition, shall in no way limit, prohibit, impede or prevent the City Council from adopting ordinances limiting or preventing the issuance of any type, number, or geographical distribution of permits for construction or demolition of any facility for which a permit is required.

(b) Chapters not Adopted. Chapter 31, entitled "Accessibility", of the Uniform Building Code, 1991 Edition, is not adopted by The City of San Diego.

(c) Sections not Adopted. The following Sections or Subsections of the Uniform Building Code, 1991 Edition, are not adopted by the City of San Diego:

SECTION 101	TITLE
SECTION 103	SCOPE
SECTION 104	APPLICATION TO EXISTING BUILDINGS AND STRUCTURES
	(b) Additions, Alterations or Repairs
	(c) Existing Installations
	(e) Moved Buildings and Temporary Buildings
	(f) Historic Buildings
SECTION 106	MODIFICATIONS
SECTION 201	CREATION OF ENFORCEMENT AGENCY
SECTION 202	POWERS AND DUTIES OF BUILDING OFFICIAL
SECTION 203	UNSAFE BUILDINGS OR STRUCTURES
SECTION 204	BOARD OF APPEALS
SECTION 205	VIOLATIONS
SECTION 301	PERMITS
	(b) Exempted Work
SECTION 302	APPLICATION FOR PERMIT
	(b) Plans and Specifications
SECTION 303	PERMITS ISSUANCE
SECTION 304	FEES
SECTION 305	INSPECTIONS
	(d) Approval Required

TABLE 3–A	BUILDING PERMIT FEES
SECTION 2903	EXCAVATION AND FILLS
	(a) General
SECTION 3203	ROOF COVERING REQUIREMENTS
SECTION 3803	SPRINKLER SYSTEM SUPERVISION ALARMS
SECTION 3805	STANDPIPES
	(b) Where Required
TABLE 38–A	STANDPIPE REQUIREMENTS

(d) Appendix Chapters Adopted. The following Appendix Chapters of the Uniform Building Code, 1991 Edition, are adopted by The City of San Diego. The remaining Appendix Chapters have not been adopted.

CHAPTER 11	AGRICULTURAL BUILDINGS
CHAPTER 29	WATERPROOFING AND DAMPPROOFING FOUNDATIONS
CHAPTER 38	BASEMENT PIPE INLETS
CHAPTER 49	PATIO COVERS
CHAPTER 55	MEMBRANE STRUCTURES

(e) Appendix Sections not Adopted. The following Sections of the Uniform Building Code Appendix, 1991 Edition, are not adopted by The City of San Diego:

SECTION 2918	FLOOR WATERPROOFING
	(b) Waterproofing Materials

(f) the last four digits of the section numbers adopted in This Code correspond to the Uniform Building Code, 1991 Edition, sections they replace.

(Amended 8–10–93 by O–17959 N.S.)

DIVISION TWO
Organization and Enforcement
(Added 11–20–89 by O–17390 N.S.)

§ 91.0201 Creation of Enforcement Agency

The Neighborhood Code Compliance Department as established in Municipal Code Section 22.1801 shall have the primary responsibility for the enforcement of the Building, Electrical, Plumbing and Mechanical Codes as they apply to existing structures within the City of San Diego. The Director of the Neighborhood Code Compliance Department together with the Building Official shall coordinate and develop programs and policies for the consistent and uniform enforcement of these codes.

(Added 8–10–93 by O–17959 N.S.)

§ 91.0202 Enforcement Powers and Duties of Building Official and Neighborhood Code Compliance Director

(a) General. The Building Official and Director of the Neighborhood Code Compliance Department are authorized to enforce all provisions of the Building, Electrical, Plumbing and Mechanical Codes and appoint inspectors, technical experts, Enforcement Officials and other employees as may be necessary to carry out enforcement functions.

(b) Interpretation and Administrative Rules. Only the Building Official shall have the power to render interpretations of the Building, Electrical, Plumbing and Mechanical Codes. The Director of Neighborhood Code Compliance Department and Building Official have the power to adopt policies and regulations reasonably necessary to clarify the application of these codes. The interpretations, rules and regulations shall be in conformity with the intent and purposes of the Building, Electrical, Plumbing and Mechanical Codes.

(c) Enforcement Authority.

(1) Whenever the Director of the Neighborhood Code Compliance Department or Building Official determine that a building or structure violates any of the provisions of Articles 1, 2 or 3 of this Chapter, the Director or Building Official and their designated Enforcement Officials may exercise any of the enforcement powers as set forth in Division 1, Article 2 of Chapter I of this Code.

(2) In addition to the general authority to inspect private property provided in Section 12.0103 of this Code, the Director or Building Official has the authority to enter a building, structure or premises to determine:

(A) whether a building is unsafe, substandard, dangerous as defined in this Division; and

(B) whether a building is of unreinforced masonry bearing wall construction.

(3) The Building Official or Director of the Neighborhood Code Compliance Department may report relevant violations of Articles 1, 2 or 3 of this Chapter to the State Contractors License Board or other appropriate licensing or regulatory agency.

(4) The Building Official or Director of the Neighborhood Code Compliance Department may issue a stop work notice pursuant to Section 91.0202(d) where appropriate.

(d) Sections 202(d), (e), (f) and (g) of the 1991 Uniform Building Code has been adopted without change pursuant to Section 91.0101(a).

(e) Restoration and Mitigation. In addition to the remedies provided in Chapter I of this Code the Building Official or Director of the Neighborhood Code Compliance Department may order the reasonable restoration of a building, premises and any adjacent and affected site to its lawful condition or require reasonable mitigation. These requirements can be attached as conditions to applicable permits or enforcement actions and orders as appropriate.

(1) Any restoration or mitigation imposed by the Building Official or Director shall be at the sole cost of the Responsible Person.

(2) Mitigation may be appropriate where the Building Official or Director determines that restoration of the building, premises or adjacent site to its lawful condition is not feasible or that irreparable damage has been done to a structure, environmentally sensitive area or habitat or historical structure.

(3) Mitigation may include the purchase or exchange of like-kind real property and structures of a similar or greater quality and value.

(4) The Building Official or Director may require a combination of restoration and mitigation of the building, premises or site depending upon the circumstances.

(5) The Building Official or Director may promulgate additional administrative guidelines and regulations to implement and clarify the authority to require restoration and mitigation.

(Retitled to "Enforcement Powers and Duties of Building Official and Neighborhood Code Compliance Director" and amended 8–10–93 by O–17959 N.S.)

§ 91.0205 Violations and Enforcement Remedies

(a) It is unlawful for any person, firm or corporation to erect, construct, enlarge, alter, repair, move, improve, remove, convert or demolish, equip, use, occupy or maintain any building or structure, or cause the same to be done, in violation of any provision of this Article or contrary to any order or permit issued by the Director of the Neighborhood Code Compliance Department or Building Official.

(b) Violations of this Article may be prosecuted as misdemeanors subject to the penalties provided in Municipal Code Section 12.0201. The Director of Neighborhood Code Compliance or Building Official may also seek injunctive relief and civil penalties in the Superior Court pursuant to Municipal Code Section 12.0202 or pursue any administrative remedy provided in Chapter I of this Code.

(c) Violations of this Article shall be treated as strict liability offenses regardless of intent.

(Retitled to "Violations and Enforcement Remedies" and amended 8–10–93 by O–17959 N.S.)

CHAPTER TEN
ARTICLE ONE

DIVISION TWO

§ 101.0201 Zone Map Required

It shall be the duty of the Planning Department of The City of San Diego to prepare a zone map of said City specifically outlining thereon the various districts brought within the zones herein outlined. Each zone shall be shaded in a different color, and shall clearly show the boundaries of each zone. The map shall also contain a legend specifically describing the restrictions and limitations of each zone, in so far as they determine the location and locations of commerce, trades and enterprises, and the location of all buildings arranged or intended for special uses in The City of San Diego.

(Incorp. 1–22–52 by O–5046 N.S.)

§ 101.0203 Zoning Authorization

Whenever the public necessity, convenience or general welfare, or good zoning practice justifies such action, and after due consideration and report on the same by the Planning Commission, the City Council may, by ordinance, in accordance with Section 111.0805, include or place any property within The City of San Diego into any zone as established, created and defined in Chapter X, Article 1 of the San Diego Municipal Code.

(Retitled to "Zoning Authorization" and amended 11–23–92 by O–17868 N.S.)

§ 101.0212 Enforcement Authority and Remedies

(a) Enforcement Authority. The Directors of the Planning Department and the Neighborhood Code Compliance Department are authorized to administer and enforce the provisions of this Chapter. The Directors shall coordinate and develop programs and policies for the consistent and uniform enforcement of this Chapter. The Directors and their designated Enforcement Officials may exercise any enforcement powers as set forth in Division 1, Article 2 of Chapter I of this Code. The Directors may also promulgate policies and regulations reasonably necessary to implement the intent and provisions of this Chapter.

(b) General Prohibitions and Enforcement Remedies. It is unlawful for any person to violate the provisions of this Chapter in the following manner:

(1) to erect, place, construct, reconstruct, convert, establish, alter, maintain, use, or enlarge any building, structure, improvement, lot, or premises in any manner contrary to any provision contained in this Chapter; or

(2) to do any act without any required permit, or contrary to the permit conditions which have been issued pursuant to this Code; or

(3) to do any act or maintain any structure or improvement without a variance or special permission as required by this Code, or contrary to any condition imposed by a variance or special permission (or amendment) properly issued according to the provisions of this Code.

Violations of this Chapter may be prosecuted as misdemeanors subject to the fines and custody provided in Municipal Code Section 12.0201. A Director may also seek injunctive relief and civil penalties in the Superior Court pursuant to Municipal Code Section 12.0202 or pursue any administrative remedy provided in Chapter I of this Code.

(c) Property Owner's Responsibility and Strict Liability Violations. It is unlawful for property owners to maintain or use, or allow to be maintained or used, their real property and appurtenances in violation of any provision of this Chapter. Violations of this Chapter shall be treated as strict liability offenses regardless of intent.

(d) Restoration and Mitigation. The Directors of the Planning and Neighborhood Code Compliance Department, in addition to other remedies provided in Chapter I of this Code, may order the reasonable restoration of a building, premises and any adjacent and affected site to its lawful condition or require reasonable mitigation. These requirements can be attached as conditions to applicable permits or enforcement actions and orders as appropriate.

(1) Any restoration or mitigation imposed by a Director shall be at the sole cost of the Responsible Person.

(2) Mitigation may be appropriate where a Director determines that restoration of the building, premises or adjacent site to its lawful condition is not feasible or that irreparable damage has been done to a structure, environmentally sensitive area or habitat or historic structure.

(3) Mitigation may include the purchase or exchange of like-kind real property and structures of a similar or greater quality and value.

(4) A Director may require a combination of restoration and mitigation of the building or premises depending upon the circumstances.

(5) A Director may promulgate additional administrative guidelines and regulations to implement and clarify the authority to require restoration and mitigation.

(e) Invalid Permits. Whenever the Director of the Planning Department or Neighborhood Code Compliance Department determines that a previously issued permit or license violates this Chapter or any other provision of the Municipal Code or applicable state codes, the Director shall invalidate the previously issued permit or license.

(Retitled to "Enforcement Authority and Remedies" and amended 8–10–93 by O–17960 N.S.)

Appendix C
Flow Charts

Appendix A
Documents

Appendix B
Code Sections

Appendix C
Flow Charts

Table of
Authorities

Glossary

Suggested
Reading

Index

Suggestion
Form

Solano Press
Books

Notes

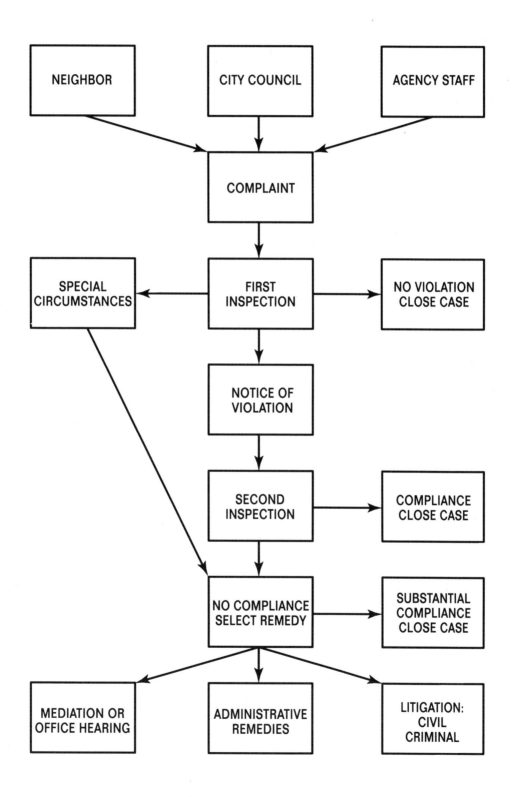

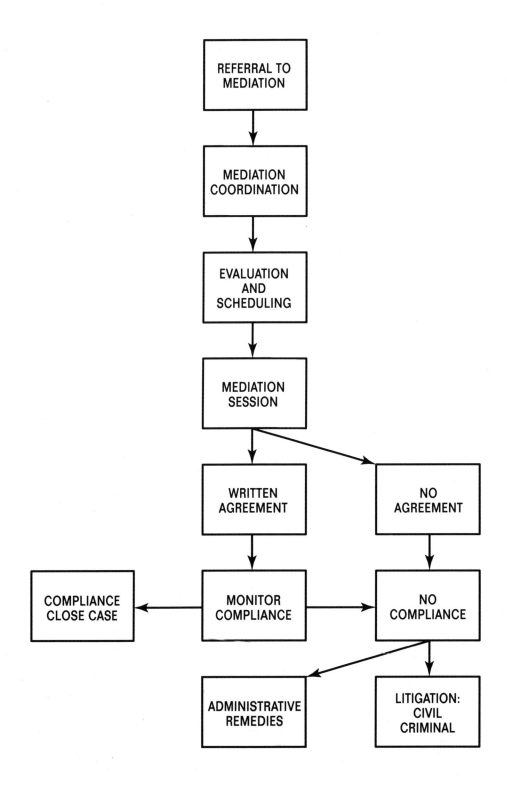

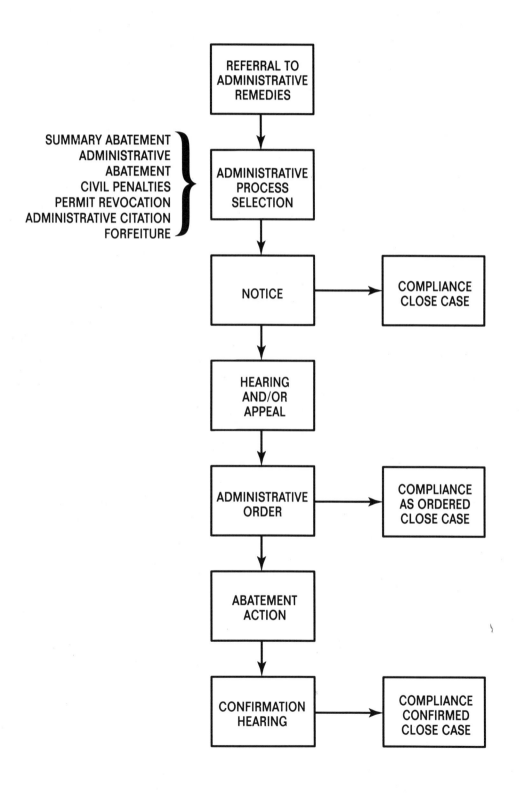

SUMMARY ABATEMENT
ADMINISTRATIVE
ABATEMENT
CIVIL PENALTIES
PERMIT REVOCATION
ADMINISTRATIVE CITATION
FORFEITURE

REFERRAL TO
ADMINISTRATIVE
REMEDIES

ADMINISTRATIVE
PROCESS
SELECTION

NOTICE

COMPLIANCE
CLOSE CASE

HEARING
AND/OR
APPEAL

ADMINISTRATIVE
ORDER

COMPLIANCE
AS ORDERED
CLOSE CASE

ABATEMENT
ACTION

CONFIRMATION
HEARING

COMPLIANCE
CONFIRMED
CLOSE CASE

Litigation

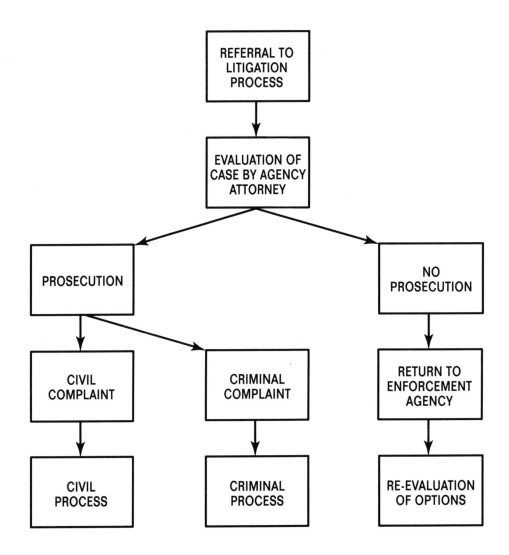

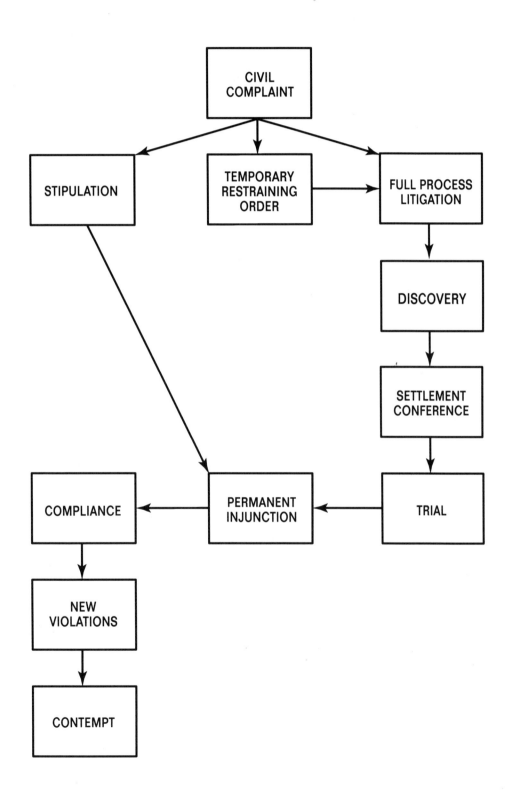

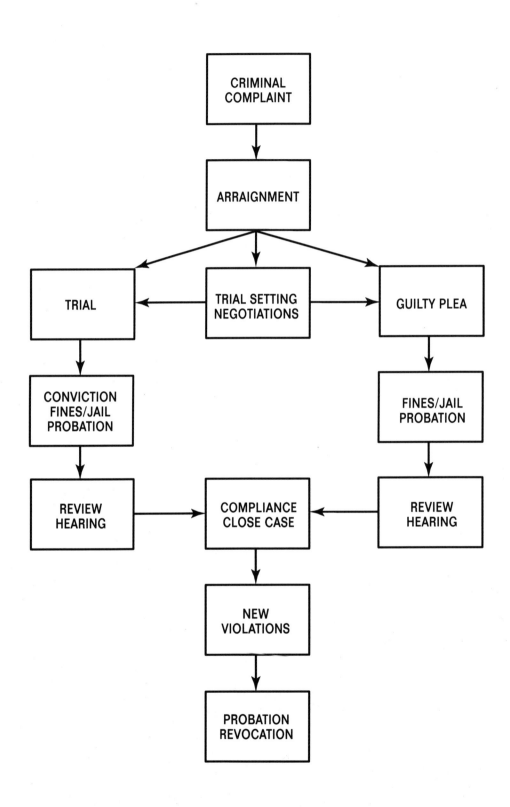

Table of Authorities

Appendix A

Appendix B

Appendix C

Table of
Authorities

Glossary

Suggested
Reading

Index

Suggestion
Form

Solano Press
Books

Notes

Abatement
Removal or elimination of a noncomplying use or structure. Abatement can be undertaken on private property after an enforcement agency obtains permission through a court proceeding or administrative hearing. Abatement generally refers to removal of the condition which causes a public nuisance. Removal is usually carried out by the enforcement agency or by the agency's contractor.

Admissions
Statements made by the defendant in a court proceeding which can be used as evidence against the defendant.

Amortization
Return of value over time for investing in an improvement on property. In zoning regulations, an amortization period establishes a specific deadline for a particular use or structure to be removed. This period provides the property owner with a reasonable return on investment prior to the abatement of a structure.

Building Permit
Document granted by a ministerial process which allows the construction or modification of a building or structure; building permits are one of the means used by enforcement agencies to control compliance with building and zoning codes.

California Building Standards Code
Statewide building standards administered by the California Building Standards Commission.

Cause of Action
Legal basis for filing a civil lawsuit, public nuisance, State Housing Law, etc. Civil complaints generally include several causes of action against the property owner in code compliance cases.

Certificate of Occupancy
Building certification required by the Uniform Building Code and administered by the Building Official indicating that work has been completed in compliance with building and zoning codes.

Certified Grant Deed
Document, certified by the County Recorder as a valid public record, establishing property ownership.

Charter City
City organized under a charter adopted by a majority vote according to provisions of state law. The charter operates as the city's constitution. A city without a charter must follow the general laws of the state in all situations.

Code
Laws organized in a systematic fashion for easy reference. Code is often synonymous with ordinances and regulations.

Community–Oriented Policing
Law enforcement strategy which stresses community involvement to resolve neighborhood crime issues. Officers work closely with the community to identify problems and use all available resources, including code enforcement, to address the root causes of the crime-related problem. Also known as Problem-Oriented Policing.

Conditional Use Permit
Discretionary permission issued by a local land use authority wherein a specific use is approved as long as equally specific conditions of establishment and operation are met. Also called a Special Use Permit.

Contempt
Defiance of a court order, generally resulting in a judge imposing additional fines and/or time in jail.

Continuous Violation
Violation of a law or regulation which exists over a period of time, such as the ongoing nature of building and zoning code violations. Distinct from other violations of law which occur as instantaneous events, such as most traffic violations.

Criminal Offense

Violations of law (state statutes or municipal ordinances) which can be enforced by filing a criminal complaint where the penalty could include fine and/or imprisonment.

Declaration

Formal document written by the enforcement agent under penalty of perjury describing the agent's observations and investigation.

Discovery

Legal procedures which govern the exchange of information between the parties in any judicial or administrative proceeding. In the code enforcement context, the property owner's attorney would likely request copies of all public documents (notices of violation, letters, memoranda, etc.) which are relevant to the enforcement action. Due process demands that most of this information be shared.

Discretionary

Administrative procedure where the decision maker (for example, a Planning Commission) may approve, approve with condition, or deny a permission (i.e., conditional use permit). A conditional use permit is an example of the exercise of discretionary authority by a local land use authority.

Discriminatory Enforcement

Defense to an enforcement action based on discriminatory reasons (for example, race, religion, etc.). If the owner can satisfy the elements for this legal defense, a judge could dismiss the action.

Drug Abatement

Specialized public nuisance statute where municipal attorneys can file a civil complaint in Superior Court against property owners for allowing continuous drug activities to occur on their properties.

Due Process

Constitutional principle which requires that all government procedures be fair. For example, all administrative hearing procedures must provide the appropriate people with adequate notice and an opportunity for a fair hearing.

Estoppel

Legal defense, commonly associated with civil enforcement actions, where the property owner reasonably relied upon the municipality's actions. A common estoppel scenario is where a city issues a building permit in error. Before a judge or administrative hearing officer can dismiss the enforcement, the property owner must satisfy all of the legal elements of estoppel.

Evidentiary Hearing

Court proceedings where evidence is presented about whether a property violates applicable land use regulations. In the context of criminal prosecution, an evidentiary hearing can be held to determine whether a defendant has violated terms of probation imposed for previous code violations.

Ex parte

Court proceedings where the prosecutor or municipal attorney can attend without the defendant being present only if the defendant is given adequate notice.

Failure to Appear

Defendant in a criminal case fails to attend the first proceeding in arraignment court after signing a field citation or receiving a notify warrant. Failure to appear could result in additional criminal charges.

Field Citation

Criminal citation for code violations, either infractions or misdemeanors, given by enforcement agents to the property owner or other responsible person. Field citations are issued in a fashion similar to traffic tickets, except that the penalties could be more severe if the violations charged are misdemeanors.

General Law City

Cities organized and incorporated under the general laws of the state. Distinguished from 'Charter Cities' or 'Home Rule Cities', which modify the effect of certain state laws through the adoption of charters.

Highly–Regulated Businesses

Classification of businesses created by the courts where inspections and searches can generally occur in most situations without the need for inspection warrants.

Home Rule City

Synonymous with 'Charter City'.

Implementation

Activities generally conducted by the staff of a public agency to carry out a land use regulation. These may include issuing permits, reviewing development plans, and monitoring permit conditions.

Infraction
Criminal offense where the penalties under state law are relatively minor (a maximum fine of $250 for the first infraction with no possibility of jail time). For example, most traffic violations are infractions.

Injunction
Civil order where the judge compels a party to correct outstanding code violations. Injunctions vary according to the seriousness of the hazard and the time permitted to correct the violations. Temporary Restraining Orders, Preliminary Injunctions, and Permanent Injunctions are different types of injunctions.

Judicial Notice
Doctrine under the Rules of Evidence which requires a judge to take 'Judicial Notice' of certain indisputable documents or facts as outlined in the Evidence Code. Attorneys use judicial notice as an evidentiary strategy to prove the existence of a document without having to bring a copy to the court hearing.

Laches
Defense to an enforcement action based on the enforcement agency's unnecessary delay in filing the action. Laches is a defense more common to civil enforcement actions than to criminal or administrative actions.

Lien
Legal document generally recorded against real property to secure the payment of a debt. Some state laws and local ordinances authorize the assessment of liens to enable the enforcement agency to recover abatement costs or civil penalties.

Lis Pendens
Legal document which informs any prospective purchasers that this property is the subject of an enforcement action. A *Lis Pendens* is simultaneously recorded when the enforcement agency commences the criminal, civil, or administrative enforcement action. Synonymous with 'Notice of Pending Action'.

Mediation
Administrative remedy where the enforcement agency uses the help of a neutral third party to obtain a written compliance agreement. In contrast to Arbitration, the mediator does not make a decision, but facilitates the communication and negotiations between the enforcement agency and the violator.

Ministerial Process
Administrative procedures, usually where a public agency has no discretion when issuing a permit and no ability to impose conditions. Issuance of a building permit is commonly done through a ministerial process.

Miranda
Legal limitation in subsequent criminal proceedings on the use of statements made by a defendant during informal questioning by police unless the officer gives a specific statement of rights and warnings. *Miranda* refers to the U.S. Supreme Court case which established this rule of law.

Misdemeanor
Criminal offense where the judge is authorized to send violators to jail and to impose fines of up to $1,000 per day for each code violation.

Mitigation Monitoring
Mandate imposed on municipalities by the Public Resources Code which requires a municipality to monitor a developer's compliance with mitigation measures imposed as part of an Environmental Impact Report adopted through CEQA review.

Nonconforming
Use or structure which does not comply or conform to current zoning regulations, where the nonconformity did not result from the landowner's actions but from a change in the regulations themselves.

Notice of Violation
Notice or warning informing an owner or user of a property about the existence of code violations.

Permit
Document issued by an agency which allows a use, event, or structure. Permission and permit are used interchangeably throughout this text. A Conditional Use Permit and a Building Permit are types of land use–related permits.

Plain View
Legal doctrine associated with inspection or search of private property which permits an enforcement

agent to observe violations open to public view—for example, an abandoned vehicle parked in a driveway visible from the sidewalk.

Police Power
Constitutional authority given to municipalities to adopt, implement, and enforce laws and ordinances designed to protect the public's health, safety, and welfare. The adoption of building and zoning ordinances are commonly considered by the courts as a reasonable exercise of the police power.

Policy
Statement of goals or objectives by a public agency or its legislative body which acts as a guideline for the implementation and enforcement of ordinances and regulations. Unlike regulations, laws, or permits, policies are nonbinding.

Preemption
Legal principle which declares that a state law is superior to a local ordinance. The effect of preemption is to invalidate the local law.

Privacy [Reasonable Expectation of]
Legal principle associated with the inspection or search of private property that determines whether or not a valid search has occurred according to the Fourth Amendment to the U.S. and California Constitutions. For example, if government agents inspect a place where a reasonable person would have an objective expectation of some degree of privacy (for example, the interior of one's home), this principle holds that a search has happened within the context of the Fourth Amendment and that a warrant should be obtained before conducting such a search.

Probable Cause
Legal principle associated with the search of private property to collect evidence for criminal prosecution. Under the Fourth Amendment to the U.S. and California Constitutions, search warrants can be issued if a neutral judge determines that sufficient facts exist to establish 'probable cause' that evidence of a crime can be found.

Probation
Terms of a criminal conviction which often require a defendant to correct outstanding code violations,

pay a fine, and avoid activities or conduct which might create code violations in the future.

Procedure
Method or manner to carry out some type of action. Procedure and process are synonymous. In the land use context, procedures are the rules which tell property owners or developers how to obtain a permit or develop their land. In a judicial context, procedure is how a case proceeds through the judicial system.

Prosecution
Act of commencing and pursuing a criminal action against a person or corporation for violations of law.

Prosecutorial Discretion
Legal principle or ethical standard applied by prosecutors when deciding whether or not to file a criminal complaint.

Prospective Regulations
Regulations which act on only those events which take place after their adoption. Prospective regulations do not operate retroactively nor do they apply to nonconforming properties.

Public Nuisance
Legal principle which prohibits unreasonable, noxious, or disturbing activities that affect a community or neighborhood.

Rebuttable Presumption
Legal principle which affects the burden of proving a case in an administrative or judicial hearing. Where the law establishes a rebuttable presumption, the enforcement agency's case is complete merely by satisfying the terms of the presumption; however, the defendant has the opportunity to produce contrary evidence to rebut the agency's case.

Receivership
Judicial remedy available in civil enforcement actions where the judge appoints a receiver to manage the property while the court action is pending. Receivership is an extraordinary remedy used by the courts on rare occasions to rehabilitate significantly substandard residential properties.

Redevelopment
Body of law designed to eliminate urban blight within designated target areas of a city according to spec-

ified provisions of the Community Redevelopment Act. Redevelopment agencies created by this process can then use extraordinary financial powers and eminent domain.

Red Light Abatement
Specialized public nuisance statute which prohibits the continuous and repeated use of real property for illegal acts of gambling and/or prostitution.

Regulations
Laws set forth and adopted by a legislative body according to specified legal procedures. State statutes and local ordinances can be two different levels of regulations.

Remedial Regulations
Laws which act retroactively or require remedial actions on the part of the owners of nonconforming properties.

Remedies
Enforcement options available to a public agency to gain compliance with a law or regulation.

Revocation, Permit
Administrative procedure used by an enforcement agency to rescind a permit due to violations of the permit or any other applicable regulation by the permittee.

Revocation, Probation
Criminal procedure used by judges to revoke probation imposed for a previous conviction based on new violations of the law.

Selective Enforcement
Defense to code enforcement action where the violator claims that the enforcement agency's action is based on arbitrary reasons. Synonymous with 'Discriminatory Enforcement'.

State Housing Law
Statewide standards for the construction and maintenance of habitable dwellings (homes, apartment buildings, hotels and motels, etc.) established in the California Health and Safety Code section 17910 *et seq*.

Statute
Law or regulation enacted by the state legislature.

Statute of Limitations
Defense to a civil or criminal court action where the complaint was filed after the time limit established in the applicable state statute.

Stop Work Order
Order issued by a Building Official as authorized by the Uniform Building Code requiring that construction be ceased due to apparent code violations.

Subdivision Map Act
Procedures and requirements established in state law for dividing land for the purposes of sale, lease, or financing (Government Code section 66410 *et seq.*).

Summons
Legal document notifying the defendant that a civil complaint has been filed against that person. The summons must be delivered to the defendant by one of the methods specified in state law. The summons is generally served simultaneously with a copy of the complaint.

Temporary Restraining Order
Court order in the early stages of a civil enforcement action requiring the defendant to abate imminent health and safety hazards on his or her property while the litigation continues. A TRO is a type of injunction.

Unfair Business Practice
Statute making it unlawful for anyone to engage in a business practice which violates state or local laws and which imposes significant civil penalties for such violations. For example, the courts—having found that a developer who violated the Subdivision Map Act when subdividing land engaged in an unfair business practice—have imposed significant penalties.

Vested Right
Legal doctrine which allows a developer to continue a project according to the zoning and building laws at the time work on the project commenced. The developer does not have to follow new laws if substantial work has been performed and substantial liability has been incurred in good faith reliance on a permit issued by an agency. The developer essentially obtains a right to proceed based on the 'vesting' date of the project.

Warrant, Arrest

Criminal order issued by a judge according to the requirements of state law directing the police or marshall to physically arrest a person for violations of law. Arrest warrants, sometimes referred to as 'bench warrants', are common where the defendant fails to make a scheduled court appearance date.

Warrant, Inspection

Administrative procedure, established in state law and based on the Fourth Amendment to the U.S. Constitution, which allows enforcement agents to inspect private property according to the terms and limitations outlined in the warrant. Judges must review affidavits and declarations from the enforcement agents to determine whether sufficient 'reasonable cause' exists to issue the inspection warrant. Although similar to the constitutional basis for a criminal search-and-seizure warrant, the inspection warrant only permits inspections and not the seizure of evidence.

Warrant, Notify

Criminal notice issued by the prosecutor informing the defendant that a criminal complaint has been filed and establishing the first appearance date in arraignment court.

ACRONYMS

AACE
American Association of Code Enforcement

ADA
Americans with Disabilities Act

BOCA
Building Officials and Code Administrators, International

CALJIC
California Jury Instructions—Criminal

CAL–OSHA
California Occupation Safety & Health Administration

CCED
California Code Enforcement Council

CEQA
California Environmental Quality Act

CMDR
Center for Municipal Dispute Resolution, San Diego

FTB
California Franchise Tax Board

HCD
California Department of Housing and Community Development

ICBO
International Conference of Building Officials

OSHA
Federal Occupational Safety & Health Administration

TRO
Temporary Restraining Order

UBC
Uniform Building Code

As a practical guide, this book does not pretend to provide a complete background in all of the areas of planning and law that code enforcement touches upon. Listed below are books and articles which are referenced within the preceding text or which can be consulted as source of additional information.

BOOKS

California Civil Procedure before Trial
Third Edition, 1993
Eric G. Wallis and Donald R. Briggs (CEB Editor)

Two-volume practice guide, with regular supplements and updates, focusing on legal issues during the early stages of civil litigation—filing the civil complaint, serving the summons, discovery, etc. A good desk reference.

Published by California Continuing Education of the Bar, 2300 Shattuck Avenue, Berkeley, California 94704.

California Criminal Law—Procedures and Practice
1986 (1992 Update)
Anne Harris (CEB Editor for 1986) & Garrick Byers (CEB Editor for 1992 Update)

One-volume practice guide, with regular supplements and updates, focusing on criminal procedural issues—arraignment, motions, discovery, etc.

Published by California Continuing Education of the Bar, 2300 Shattuck Avenue, Berkeley, California 94704.

California Criminal Law
Second Edition, 1988
B.E. Witkin and Norman Epstein

Comprehensive, six-volume treatise, with annual supplements, by Bernie Witkin of San Francisco. A good starting point for researching any criminal law issue.

Published by Bancroft-Whitney Company, 3250 Van Ness Avenue, P.O. Box 7005, San Francisco, California 94120-7005.

California Land Use & Planning Law
1994 (Fourteenth) Edition (now includes Curtin's *Subdivision Map Act* manual)
by Daniel J. Curtin, Jr.

A summary and discussion of the substantive and procedural features of California's land use and planning law. Includes analysis of the latest statutes and most recent case law, as well as an expanded chapter on the Subdivision Map Act.

Available from Solano Press Books, P.O. Box 773, Point Arena, CA 95468. A catalog and ordering information are provided at the end of this book.

California Land Use Procedure
September 1991
by J.R. Ramos

A comprehensive guide for both staff and applicant to the steps of processing land use applications. Includes sample checklists and hypothetical findings used to defend a decision.

Published by Shepard's McGraw-Hill, Inc., Colorado Springs, Colorado.

The California Municipal Law Handbook
1994, Second Edition
League of California Cities—City Attorney Division, Jo Anne Speers, General Counsel for the League

An excellent book offering municipal law practitioners a "source of first resort" when researching a given area of California municipal law including land use.

Published by League of California Cities, 1400 K Street, Sacramento, California 95814.

Guide to California Planning
1991 Edition
by William Fulton

An extensive account of what land use planning is supposed to be and what it is in California, including the processes and laws that must be observed, and how these processes and laws are used for bet-

Suggested Reading

ter of for worse. Prepared for those members of the general public and for students who wish to understand the fundamentals of the current practice of land us planning in California.

Available from Solano Press Books, P.O. Box 773, Point Arena, California 95468. A catalog and ordering information are provided at the end of this book.

Longtin's California Land Use
Second Edition, 1987
(two volumes with annual supplement)
by James Longtin

This publication should be consulted by those interested in a detailed legal analysis of the California land use law.

Available From Local Government Publications, P.O. Box 306, Malibu, California (800 345-0899).

Redevelopment in California
1994 Edition
by David F. Beatty, Joseph E. Coomes, Jr., et al.

A guide to detailed provisions of the Community Redevelopment Law and to the authority given cities and counties to establish and manage redevelopment agencies and to prepare, adopt, implement and finance redevelopment projects. Includes a full analysis of the Community Redevelopment Law Reform Act of 1993 and a new section on the economics of redevelopment.

Available from Solano Press Books, P.O. Box 773, Point Arena, California 95468. A catalog and ordering information are provided at the end of this book.

California Practice Guide: Enforcing Judgments and Debts (The Rutter Group 1988)
Rick Schwartz and Judge Alan M. Ahart

Two-volume practice guide, with annual supplements, in a user-friendly outline format. Includes many practice tips as well as case citations. Generally part of The Rutter Group's annual training seminars given throughout the state.

Published by The Rutter Group, Ltd. (TRG), 15760 Ventura Boulevard, Suite 630, Encino, California 91436.

California Practice Guide: Civil Procedure Before Trial (The Rutter Group 1993)
Judge Robert Weil (Ret.) and Judge Ira Brown (Ret.)

Multi-volume practice guide, with annual supplements in The Rutter Group outline format. The definitive practice guide written by former law and motion department judges for San Francisco (Brown) and Los Angeles (Weil).

Published by The Rutter Group, Ltd. (TRG), 15760 Ventura Boulevard, Suite 630, Encino, California 91436.

ARTICLES

"Broken Windows," by James Q. Wilson and George L. Kelling, *Atlantic Monthly*, March 1982.

"Charter Cities in California—A growing 'Statewide Concern'?", Richard Hiscocks and Marie Backes, *University of San Francisco Law Review*, Vol. 16 (Summer 1982).

"Making Neighborhoods Safe," by Professor James Q. Wilson and Kennedy School of Government Fellow George L. Kelling, *Atlantic Monthly*, February 1989.

"Code Enforcement: Curbing the Deterioration of Our Urban Environment," Joseph M. Schilling, *CEB Land Use Forum*, Fall, 1992.

"Oakland's Solution to Drug Nuisance Buildings," Jayne Williams, Joyce Hicks, and Charles Vose, *CEB Land Use Forum*, Fall, 1992

"Strategies for Implementing and Enforcing Conditional Use Permits," by Joseph M. Schilling, *CEB land Use Forum*, Fall, 1992.

GOVERNMENT AND ASSOCIATION PUBLICATIONS, STUDIES, AND POSITION PAPERS

Ahlbrandt, Professor Roger S., "Flexible Code Enforcement: A Key Ingredient in Neighborhood Preservation Programming," Washington, D.C., National Association of Housing and Redevelopment Officials (1976).

Schilling, Joseph M., "Criminal Enforcement of Municipal Land-Use Ordinances," Sacramento, League of California Cities Annual Conference (1986).

_____, "Drug Abatement—Civilizing Drug Dealers," Washington, D.C., National Institute of Municipal Law Officers Mid-Year Conference (1988).

Shames, Michael, "Municipal Code Enforcement in San Diego—A New Prescription to Protect the Neighborhood Environment" (Report to the City Council of San Diego, April 17, 1990, City Clerk Document No. RR-275508).

Silva-Martinez, Diane, "Administrative Remedies—The San Diego Experience," National Institute of Municipal Law Officers Annual Conference (1991).

A

AACE. *See* American Association of Code Enforcement

abandonment
    establishing for nonconforming use, 170
    See also nonconforming uses; public nuisance

abatement
    administrative abatement, 93, 97-99
    completion of satisfying compliance, 4, 6
    costs assessment for, 99, 100-101
    costs recovery for, 149, 150
    drug abatement, 140-141
    enforcement agency authority for, 19, 23
    forcible entry provisions for, 100
    inventory and security procedures for, 100
    judicial, 146
    red light abatement, 140
    remedial regulations for, 35
    scope and practices for, 100
    summary abatement, 97-98
    summary, compared to administrative, 97
    See also compliance; public nuisance; repairs

access, consideration of for permit issuance, 43-44

administrative enforcement hearings
    as administrative remedy, 93
    defiance of, 102
    validity of land use regulation during, 158
    use and provisions of, 102-105
    See also enforcement; hearings

administrative enforcement order, compared to court order, 103

administrative inspections
    field inspections without warrant, 70-74
    Fourth Amendment applicability to, 68-69
    of highly-regulated businesses, 73-74
    See also field inspection

administrative inspection warrant
    for entering private property, 67
    inspector's declaration required for, 77
    practice and procedures for, 74, 75, 77-79
    reasonable cause required for issuing, 76
    scope of, 78-79
    use of for gaining compliance, 75-78

administrative remedies
    formal compared to informal, 93
    overview of, 93
    use of in enforcement process, 83-84
    See also remedies

administrators
    relationship of to code enforcement, 5
    See also enforcement agencies; management

adoption process, knowledge of required for code enforcement, 3

adult businesses
    municipal authority for regulating, 16, 159, 160
    object-based enforcement for, 52
    See also businesses; red light abatement

aesthetics, municipal authority for regulating, 16, 31

agencies. *See* enforcement agencies

air quality regulations, responsibility to enforce, 3

American Association of Code Enforcement (AACE), 10

Americans with Disabilities Act, effect of on local codes, 3

amortization
    for nonconforming use, 170-171
    See also nonconforming uses

apartment buildings
    HCD standards authority for, 20
    inspection procedures for, 70, 71
    See also housing

appeals
    allowed for administrative decisions, 104

appeals *(continued)*
    See also defense; due process

application, provisions for in regulatory process, 32

arbitration
    compared to mediation, 95
    See also mediation; remedies

arrest warrant
    for initiating criminal action, 118-120
    notify warrant alternative for, 120
    See also criminal prosecution; notify warrant

Attorney General, authority of for enforcing Coastal Act, 25

authorities of regulation, for local zoning code, 19

B

bankruptcy
    as defense to enforcement, 167-168
    effect of on civil penalties, 158
    See also civil injunctions

bathhouses, 23, 140
    See also abatement

Beaver Cleaver Trap, 37

bed-and-breakfast inns, 164

best evidence rule
    consideration of in criminal prosecution and civil actions, 124
    See also criminal prosecution; evidence

binoculars
    legality of for inspections, 71-72
    See also field inspection

blight
    municipal authority for regulating, 16, 31
    redevelopment law authority over, 24
    strategic enforcement procedures for, 52
    volunteer efforts for reducing, 56
    See also neighborhood deterioration

BOCA (Building Official and Code Administrator Int'l) codes, 22
Broken Window Theory, 8, 112
budgeting
consideration of in regulatory cycle, 6
consideration of in regulatory response, 39-41, 49
procedures for establishing, 53-56
regulatory needs assessment and, 29-30
See also costs
building code
annual inspections for enforcing, 76
health and safety concerns for, 5
local flexibility limitations for, 22
municipal authority for regulating, 17, 20
upholding with remedial regulations, 35
See also Uniform Building Code
building inspection department, for processing citizen complaints, 4
building inspectors
code enforcement responsibilities of, 9, 10
See also enforcement officials; field inspection
building permits
issuance of as ministerial action, 37
municipal authority for issuing, 16, 17
process and requirements for, 20
See also permits
building regulations
local flexibility for, 21-22
municipal authority for enacting, 16
See also regulations
building violations
agency response to, 49, 50
See also violations
businesses
aerial surveillance of, 72
highly-regulated, annual inspections for, 76
highly-regulated, inspections for, 73-74
inspection procedures for, 71
ordinance challenges by, 160-161
unfair business practices penalties for, 138-140
See also unfair business practices; specific businesses
business license
enforcement for, 115

business license *(continued)*
issuance of as self-enforcing condition, 42
See also licenses; permits

C

CAI. *See* Community Associations Institute
California, land use regulatory scheme in, 16-25
California Building Standards Code
allowance for changes to, 21
See also Uniform Building Code
California Coastal Act
authority and objectives of, 24-25
civil enforcement actions under, 141
evaluation of in enforcement process, 7, 13
regulation and enforcement under, 17
California Code Enforcement Council (CCEC), 10
California Environmental Quality Act (CEQA)
applicability of to land use regulation, 17, 18
evaluation of in enforcement process, 7, 13
mitigation monitoring under, 23-24, 53
California Government Code.
See Government Code
California Jury Instruction— Criminal (CALJIC), 123
California Rules of Court, section 379, 143
California Subdivision Map Act.
See Subdivision Map Act
CALJIC. *See* California Jury Instruction—Criminal
catalog of zones
establishment of in zoning code, 18-19
See also zones; zoning code
cause of action
determining for civil injunction, 136-141
See also civil injunctions
CCEC. *See* California Code Enforcement Council
cease-and-desist order
as administrative remedy, 103
See also administrative remedies; stop work order

CEB. *See* Continuing Education of the Bar, California
CEQA. *See* California Environmental Quality Act
certificate of occupancy.
See occupancy certification
certification
for inspectors, 50, 57
with rotational training, 57
See also field inspection; investigation
certified grant deed
use of for proving property ownership, 126-127
See also criminal prosecution
CEU. *See* Code Enforcement Unit
Charter cities, 14
constitutional regulatory authority of, 14-16
See also cities
checklist
for preliminary investigation, 64
See also investigation
cities
Charter cities, 14-16
General Law, compared to Charter, 14
judicial abatement by, 146
requirements of under CEQA, 23-24
See also municipalities
citizen. *See* public
city attorney. *See* municipal attorney
civil action
to abate public nuisance, 23
as enforcement remedy, 17, 83, 103
lis pendens filing in, 141-142
See also penalties; remedies
civil complaints
lis pendens recorded with filing of, 142
See also complaints; criminal complaints
civil injunctions
additional remedies for use with, 148-153
advantages of using, 126
for gaining compliance, 6, 7, 135-153
prohibitory vs. mandatory, 143
temporary restraining order, 110-111, 135-136, 142, 143-144
vs. criminal prosecution, 110-110
See also criminal prosecution; injunctive relief
civil procedures, 141-148
overview of, 141-143

Drug Abatement Act, 23
drug use, neighborhood deterioration and, 8
'Duck Test', 19
due process
    for administrative action, 96, 98
    analysis of for criminal complaints, 121-122
    as basis for enforcement challenges, 160, 161
    consideration of in code enforcement, 9
    consideration of in processing complaints, 116
    for permit recision, 38
    required for administrative hearings, 103
    requirements of for administrative abatement, 99
    for zoning prosecutions, 122
    See also Fourth Amendment; privacy rights
dwellings. *See* housing

E

earthquake. *See* seismic safety
economics, relationship of to code enforcement, 5, 9
efficiency
    increasing with strategic planning, 51-53
    in proactive enforcement program, 54
    See also costs
emergency circumstances
    following natural disaster, 10
    inspection procedures for, 70
    summary abatement allowed for, 97-98
    warrantless inspection allowed for, 74
    See also abatement
enabling legislation.
    See legislative process; police power
enforcement
    authority for, 16, 17
    budgeting concerns for, 53-55
    by redevelopment agencies, 24
    with civil injunctions, 135-153
    community deterioration and, 8
    complexities of, 7-9
    comprehensive, defined, 4-7
    contemporary procedures for, 3-4, 10, 19
    coordination of, 7, 50-51

enforcement *(continued)*
    costs recovery for, 148, 149, 150, 152
    criminal prosecution for, 109-132
    defenses to, 157-171
    discretionary considerations, 57-58
    discriminatory/selective, 167
    enforceability vs. defensibility of, 39
    evaluation policy/procedures, 5, 84
    as form of law enforcement, 7-9, 13
    geographic-based enforcement, 52, 53
    management of, 49-60
    Miranda ruling considerations for, 128-129
    municipal, police power for, 16, 22
    object-based enforcement, 52, 53
    ordinances for, 17
    press relations procedures for, 60
    priorities establishment for, 58
    process origination for, 4-5
    provisions for in regulatory process, 32
    public perceptions of, 9-10
    recision of permit, 38
    regulatory conditions of approval for, 42
    relationship of to general plan, 30
    relationship of to local zoning code, 18-19
    relationship of with compliance, 7
    scope of services for, 51-53
    security for, 42
    self-enforcing conditions for, 42
    state statutes for, 22-25
    for Tough Ten Percent, 4
    under Subdivision Map Act, 17
    See also compliance
enforcement agencies
    assessment of regulatory needs by, 29-30
    code enforcement responsibilities of, 7-9
    mission components of, 30-31, 57-59, 85
    press relations procedures for, 60
    regulatory response of, 30-35
    relationship of with municipal attorney, 86-88
    sources of agency-generated needs, 29-30
enforcement officials
    actions of following citizen complaint, 4

enforcement officials *(continued)*
    arrest and citation power of, 118-120
    case evaluation procedures for, 84-90
    comprehensive evaluation considerations for, 5, 7, 10, 13
    constitutional limitations for, 67-69, 74, 77
    duties of for obtaining inspection warrant, 77-78
    investigative responsibilities of, 63-64
    Miranda ruling considerations for, 127-129
    police officer training for, 119
    requirements for, 3-4
    responsibilities of, 7-9
    testimony of as expert evidence, 125
    training for, 56-57
    types of, 49
    See also investigation
enlargement
    effect of on conformance, 170
    See also nonconforming uses
environment
    effect on of abandoned property, 8
    protection for with code enforcement, 3, 9
    sensitive, CEQA review required for, 17
    sensitive, protecting with temporary restraining order, 135-136
    See also habitat; wetlands
environmental impacts, review of under CEQA, 23-24
environmental review, CEQA standards for, 18
estoppel defense
    elements required for, 163
    for enforcement challenges, 161, 162-163, 164
    for permit revocation, 88
    vested rights and, 163
    See also defense; permits; remedies
evidence
    evidentiary issues for criminal prosecution, 124-129
    supplying for criminal prosecution, 117, 123, 124
    See also criminal prosecution; findings
evidentiary hearings
    for probation revocation, 132

landscaping
consideration of for permit
issuance, 44
requirements for in permit
process, 42
land use regulations
in California, 16-25
challenges to in legal defense,
158-160
compliance procedures for
enforcing, 3
constitutionality issues for, 158
coordination of with implementation and enforcement, 7
landowners' responsibility under,
118
police power authority for,
13, 15, 16
procedures and processes for, 17-18
relationship of to code
enforcement, 4, 10
relationship of to zoning code,
18-19
See also ordinances; regulations
language of regulation
discussion of, 115
'maintaining' considerations, 166
'shall' vs. 'should' considerations,
37
See also definition of terms
law
appropriateness determination
for in regulatory process,
33-35
as basis for code enforcement,
13, 18, 29
common interest development
laws, 55
enabling, for municipal
regulations, 18
'municipal affairs' doctrine
compared to state law, 15
preemption and, 15
state statutes with land use
enforcement consequences,
22-25
training in for enforcement
officials, 57
See also constitutional law
law enforcement
code enforcement as, 7-9, 13
field inspection as, 67, 74
forcible entry considerations for,
101
participation of at field
inspections, 79
See also police personnel

LCP. *See* Local Coastal Plan
legal limits
on enforcement officials, 3, 13-14
See also police power
legislative process
consistency of with regulatory
framework, 32
for establishing regulations
procedures, 18
relationship of to code
enforcement, 3-4
legislature, authority of over cities,
15-16
letters
as evidence in criminal trial and
civil actions, 124-125
See also criminal prosecution;
evidence
liability. *See* strict criminal liability
licenses
defendant's burden of proof for
possessing, 127
See also ordinances; permits
liens
issuance of in enforcement
process, 103, 140, 151-152
state law liens, 152
See also fines; penalties
liquor, 23
liquor industry
warrantless searches allowed for,
73
See also businesses
lis pendens
filing of in civil action, 141-142
recording with filing of civil
complaint, 142
See also criminal prosecution
litigation
for achieving compliance, 6
impacts on of policy statements,
31
municipal attorney role in, 86-88
under common interest
development law, 55
See also civil injunctions;
criminal prosecution
litter violations
abatement practices for, 100, 111
agency response to, 49, 50, 56
Local Coastal Plan (LCP), local
government responsibility for, 24
local government
code enforcement responsibilities
of, 3
flexibility of building codes for,
21-22

local government *(continued)*
land use regulatory authority of,
16-25
See also municipalities
local policy statements
code enforcement and, 31
neighborhood preservation and, 31
See also policy statements
local regulatory needs
assessing, 29-30
See also regulations; regulatory
implementation
lofts, consideration of for permit
issuance, 44

M

'maintaining', in land use
regulations, 166
maintenance accessibility,
consideration of for permit
issuance, 44
management
of code enforcement, 49-60
relationship of to code
enforcement, 5
training for, 56-57
See also administrators;
enforcement agencies
maneuvering, consideration of for
permit issuance, 43-44
maps (certified)
for use in criminal prosecution
and civil actions, 125
See also criminal prosecution;
evidence
masonry structures, 35
See also structures
massage parlor
warrantless inspection allowed
for, 73
See also red light abatement
mediation
as administrative remedy, 93, 94,
95-96
compared to arbitration, 95
effect on of politics, 87
for gaining compliance, 6, 7, 83
See also compliance; remedies
minimum reach, establishing in
regulatory process, 32-35
ministerial permit process
compared to discretionary permit, 36, 37
definition and applications of, 37
within body of prospective
regulations, 35

ministerial permit process
    See also discretionary permit
        process; permit process
Miranda rule
    effect of on defendant's
        statements and admissions,
        127-129
    See also civil rights; criminal
        prosecution; due process
misdemeanor prosecution
    benefits and burdens of, 130
    enforcement authority for, 112
    jury trial requirement for, 124
    maximum penalties for, 115
    probationary terms for
        conviction under, 129-130
    procedures for, 110
    vs. infractions, 113
    See also criminal prosecution
mitigation measures
    authority for under CEQA, 23
    enforcement agreements for, 53
    See also California
        Environmental Quality Act
Mobile Home Parks Act, violations
    of as unfair business practice, 139
mobile homes, 53, 143
    See also housing
monitoring program
    environmental, 10
    for monitoring compliance, 5-7, 9
'municipal affairs'
    Charter city authority over, 14-15
    preemption and, 15
municipal attorney
    attendance of at *ex parte* hearing,
        78
    case preparation strategies for,
        123-124
    as deputy district attorney, 139
    participation of in office hear-
        ings, 94
    prosecution of unfair business
        practices by, 139
    relationship of to code enforce-
        ment, 4, 7
    relationship of with enforcement
        agency, 86-88, 89
    use of for prosecuting violators, 84
    See also city attorney; prosecutor
municipal code, enabling law inclu-
    sion in, 18
municipalities
    authority of for imposition of
        liens, 152
    flexibility of building codes for,
        21-22

municipalities
    general regulatory authority of, 14
    judicial abatement by, 146
    See also cities; counties

N

National Electrical Code, 22
natural disaster
    code enforcement practices
        following, 10
    See also emergency circumstances
neighborhood
    consideration of in case closure,
        85-86
    generation of regulatory needs
        by, 30
    zoning code appropriateness
        for, 37
    See also housing
neighborhood deterioration
    effect on of code enforcement,
        8, 10
    municipal authority for
        controlling, 16
    proactive enforcement program
        for, 54
    regulation enactment response
        to, 13
    strategic enforcement procedures
        for, 52, 53-55
    See also blight
neighborhood preservation
    local policy statements and, 31
    with volunteer assisted
        enforcement, 56
noise violations
    agency response to, 49, 50
    difficulty of enforcement for, 43,
        160
    See also violations
noncompliance
    permit recision for, 38
    See also compliance
nonconforming uses
    consideration of in zoning code, 19
    defenses for, 157-158, 168-171
    remedial regulations for, 35
    See also field inspection
notice of pending action, filing for
    property violations, 119
notice of violation
    procedures for recording, 103
    use of as administrative remedy,
        93-94
    See also administrative remedies;
        violations

notification
    due process requirements for, 96
    informal, for gaining compliance, 7
    judicial, for establishing existence
        of zone, 125-126
    provisions for in regulatory
        process, 32
    requirements of for adminis-
        trative abatement, 99
notify warrant
    as alternative to arrest warrant,
        120
    See also arrest warrant
nudist camp, 159
nuisance. *See* public nuisance
nursing homes
    criminal prosecution of, 118
    See also housing

O

object-based enforcement, 52, 53
    See also enforcement
occupancy certification
    invalidation of restrictions on, 21
    revocation of as enforcement
        action, 96-97
    as self-enforcing condition, 42
    warrantless inspection allowed
        for, 77
    See also housing
occupant
    authority of for inspection con-
        sent, 70
    notification of required before
        inspection, 78
    refusal of inspection by, 75
    See also property owner; tenant
office hearings
    as administrative remedy, 93, 94-95
    See also administrative enforce-
        ment hearings; hearings
ordinances
    as basis for code enforcement, 13
    challenges to in legal defense,
        158-160
    constitutional authority for
        enacting, 15
    for costs recovery, 150-151
    determining effectiveness of, 5-6
    enactment of by Charter city, 14
    relationship of to code
        enforcement, 4
    violation of establishing cause of
        action, 136-137
    See also regulations; specific
        ordinances

organization
    consideration of in regulatory
      cycle, 6
    consideration of in regulatory
      response, 39-41
    structure of, generalists vs.
      specialists, 50
    See also enforcement agencies
overbreadth
    identifying in ordinance
      challenge, 160
    See also definition of terms;
      language of regulation

P

panic hardware
    state standards for, 20
    See also fire code
parking, consideration of for permit
    issuance, 43-44
PC 836 training, for enforcement
    officials, 57
peace officer training programs
    for enforcement officials, 57
    See also law enforcement; police
penalties
    civil, 151
    for multiple violations, 130
    municipal police power for,
      16, 17
    relationship of to code
      enforcement, 7, 9
    for unfair business practices,
      138-140, 149
    for violating administrative
      enforcement order, 102, 113
    for violation of California
      Coastal Act, 141
    See also civil injunctions; costs;
      fines
permanent injunction
    for abating hazards, 143,
      145-146
    See also civil injunction;
      preliminary injunction
permit issuance
    preceding changes to zoning
      ordinances, 163-165
    provisions for in regulatory
      process, 32
permit process
    discretionary, 35-36
    ministerial, 35, 37
    nonpermit process procedures,
      38-39
    recision conditions within, 38

permit process *(continued)*
    See also discretionary permit
      process; ministerial permit
      process
permits
    defendant's burden of proof for
      possessing, 127
    determining effectiveness of, 5-6
    issuance of satisfying compliance, 4
    relationship of to code
      enforcement, 4, 10
    revocation of as administrative
      remedy, 93, 96-97
    revocation of for code
      enforcement, 6, 88
    revocation of when issued
      in error, 165
    special, 41-42
    special conditions allowed for,
      25
    See also specific permits
personnel
    consideration of in regulatory
      cycle, 6
    relationship of with code
      enforcement process, 4-5
    See also enforcement officials
photographs
    for documenting violations, 67, 143
    for jury trial evidence, 123, 125
    See also evidence
'piercing the corporate veil'
    for criminal prosecution, 121
    See also criminal prosecution
plan checks, record keeping required
    for, 44
planned unit development
    discretionary approval required
      for, 36
    permit process and criteria for, 19
    permit revocation allowed for, 96
    public/private enforcement
      partnerships for, 55
    See also housing
planners
    code enforcement responsibilities
      of, 9, 10, 13
    relationship of to code
      enforcement, 4, 5
planning, strategic planning for
    enforcement, 52
planning department
    identification of regulatory needs
      by, 29, 30
    for processing citizen complaints, 4
point system, for establishing
    enforcement priorities, 58

police officer standards and training
    (POST), for enforcement
      officials, 119
police personnel
    coordination with for
      enforcement, 51
    forcible entry considerations for,
      101
    Miranda ruling considerations
      for, 127-129
    presence of at abatement site, 100
    presence of at field inspections, 79
    See also law enforcement
police power
    for assessing civil penalties, 151
    as authority for code enforce-
      ment, 4, 13
    constitutional authority for, 15, 18
    preemption and, 15
    scope of within land use
      regulatory authority, 15-16
    See also constitutional law;
      due process
policy evaluation criteria, for
    prioritizing enforcement cases,
      84-85
policy statements
    establishing for regulatory
      response, 33, 84-86
    for evaluating case-specific
      criteria, 88-90
    local, code enforcement and, 31
    See also local policy statements
politics, relationship of to code
    enforcement, 9, 29, 85
POST. *See* police officer standards
    and training
poverty
    neighborhood deterioration and, 8
    See also neighborhood
      deterioration
preemption
    defined, 15
    determination of for investigative
      checklist, 64
    use of as enforcement defense,
      159
    See also field inspection;
      investigation
preliminary injunctions
    use of for abating hazards, 135-
      136, 142, 144
    vs. criminal prosecution, 110-111
    vs. temporary restraining order,
      144
    See also civil injunctions;
      criminal prosecution

redevelopment law, authority of for
  blight elimination, 24
red light abatement, 140
  costs recovery for, 149
  See also abatement
Red Light Abatement Law, 23
regulations
  as basis for code enforcement, 13
  challenges to in legal defense,
    158-160
  constitutional authority for
    enacting, 15, 17
  cost estimation for, 39-41
  enactment of by Charter city, 14
  enactment of in regulatory cycle,
    6, 10, 29
  enforceability vs. defensibility of,
    39
  evaluation of effectiveness of, 5, 6
  minimum reach establishment
    for, 32-35
  prospective regulations, 35
  regulatory criteria for, 35-39
  remedial regulations, 35
  state regulations, 3, 9
  See also land use regulations; law
regulatory authority
  granted to municipalities, 14
  within body of prospective
    regulations, 35
  See also police power
regulatory criteria, 35-39
regulatory cycle, described, 6
regulatory implementation
  assessing local needs for, 29-30
  consistency of with legislative
    framework, 32
  coordination of with land use
    regulations, 7, 10
  costs estimation for, 39-41
  costs implementation for, 39-41
  integration of with enforcement, 5
  of judicial abatement, 146
  local, 29-45
  process of in regulatory cycle,
    6, 31
regulatory response
  policy statement establishment
    for, 33
  process evaluation for, 45
  team approach development
    for, 34
rehabilitation. *See* repairs
relocation, for tenants of
  substandard housing, 138
remedial regulations, 35
  See also regulations

remedies
  administrative, 83-84
remedies
  administrative, permit recision
    and, 38
  civil, 148-153
  civil injunction, 83-84
  civil procedures, 141-148
  criminal prosecution, 83-84
  evaluation of in regulatory cycle, 6
  injunctive relief, 143-146
  selection of, 83-90
  under State Housing Law, 137-138
  See also administrative enforce-
    ment hearings and civil
    injunctions; compliance;
    criminal prosecution
rent control
  municipal authority for
    enacting, 16
  See also housing
repairs
  as alternative to demolition,
    98-99
  completion of satisfying
    compliance, 4
  for deteriorating neighborhoods, 8
  effect of on conformance, 168
  to substandard housing, 138
  See also abatement; demolition
residential zone
  business use not allowed in, 77
  conflicting uses in, 9
  See also housing
restaurants, 122
rezoning of property
  as discretionary action, 36
  as prospective regulation, 35
  See also zoning
road construction, as 'municipal
  affair', 14-15
rotational training
  for enforcement officials, 57
  See also training
rubbish abatement liens
  for recovering abatement costs,
    152
  See also abatement; liens; litter

S

safety
  civil actions for protecting,
    110-111
  local government responsibility
    for, 10, 16
  See also public welfare

sanitarians, code enforcement
  responsibilities of, 9
search. *See* field inspection;
  investigation
security
  for permit enforcement, 42
  See also enforcement;
    permit process
seismic safety
  remedial regulations for
    increasing, 35
  summary abatement provisions
    for, 98
  See also emergency circumstances
self-enforcing conditions
  for discretionary permits, 42
  See also discretionary permit
    process
sentencing
  in criminal prosecution,
    129-132
  See also criminal prosecution
setback regulations, enforceability
  of, 37
'shall' vs. 'should'
  in ordinance language, 37
  See also language of regulation
sign standards
  abatement provisions for, 35, 53,
    170-171
  compliance procedures for
    enforcing, 3
  investigation scoring formula
    for, 58
  municipal authority for
    regulating, 16, 31
  object-based enforcement for, 52
social factors, relationship of to
  code enforcement, 9
staff. *See* personnel; specific titles
standards of measurement,
  establishment of for zoning
  code, 19-20, 56
State Building Standards Code, 115
State Housing Law
  authority of over municipalities,
    20, 22-23
  contempt actions for violations
    of, 148
  cost recovery provisions of, 149
  enforcement provisions of,
    137-138, 144
  evaluation of in enforcement
    process, 7
  housing standards of, 115-116
  See also housing
State Planning and Zoning Law, 18

state regulations
  effect of on local codes, 3, 9
  See also regulations
statute of limitations
  as defense to enforcement
    prosecution, 166-167
  See also defense
stop work order
  use of as administrative remedy,
    93, 94
  See also administrative remedies;
    building permits; cease-and-
    desist order
strategic planning
  as enforcement tool, 52
  See also planning
strict criminal liability
  provisions for in code
    enforcement, 117-118
  See also criminal prosecution
structures
  continuous violations of, 114
  discretionary approval required
    for, 36
  masonry structures, 35
  nonconforming uses of,
    168-171
  See also building code; housing
Subdivision Map Act
  enforcement provisions for
    violations of, 116
  evaluation of in enforcement
    process, 7
  regulation and enforcement
    under, 17, 18, 44
subdivision of land
  as discretionary action, 36
  violations of as unfair business
    practice, 139

T

team approach
  for regulatory response, 34
  strategic planning for, 52
  See also coordination
temporary restraining order (TRO)
  use of for abating hazards,
    135-136, 142
  vs. preliminary injunctions, 144
  vs. criminal prosecution, 110-111
  See also civil injunctions; crimi-
    nal prosecution
tenant
  authority of for inspection
    consent, 70
  field inspections affecting, 69

tenant *(continued)*
  Fourth Amendment protections
    for, 70
  notification of for violations, 4, 9
tenant
  relocation of from substandard
    housing, 138
  See also occupant; property
    owner
terms. *See* definition of terms
timeliness concerns
  effect of on customer service, 65-66
  effect of on permit recision, 38
  for enforcement procedures, 84
  for laches defense, 161-162
  See also deadlines; statute of
    limitations
Tough Ten Percent, 4
traffic congestion, 13
training
  for enforcement officials, 56-57
  See also enforcement officials
trespass
  effect of on inspection, 71
  See also field inspection; forcible
    entry
trial
  for criminal prosecution, 116
  See also criminal prosecution
24-hour notice
  requirements of for inspection
    warrant, 78
  See also due process; notification

U

unfair business practices
  defined, 139
  injunctive relief available for,
    138-140
  See also businesses
Unfair Business Practices Act, con-
    tempt actions provisions of, 148
Uniform Building Code
  abatement provisions of, 98
  allowance for additions to, 21
  authority and purposes for, 20
  continuous violations of, 114
  enforcement provisions for, 3,
    112
  evaluation of in enforcement
    process, 7
  permit revocation provisions of,
    95, 96
  See also building code
Uniform Fire Code, 21, 112
  See also fire code

Uniform Housing Code, 21
Uniform Mechanical Code, 21
Uniform Plumbing Code, 21
Unlawful Liquor Sales Abatement
  Law, 23
use permits
  relationship of to code
    enforcement, 4
  revocation of as enforcement
    action, 96
  self-enforcing conditions for, 42
  See also conditional use permits;
    permits
uses
  discretionary approval required
    for, 36
  reasonable judgement standard
    for, 39
  See also nonconforming uses

V

vacant buildings, inspection
  procedures for, 71
variances
  process and criteria for, 19
  See also zoning code
vagueness
  identifying in ordinance
    challenge, 160
  See also definition of terms;
    language of regulation
vested rights
  estoppel and, 163-165
  See also estoppel defense
violations
  continuous, 114
  documentation of in field
    inspection, 67
  evaluation of by enforcement
    official, 4, 9, 63-64, 88-90
  identified by citizen complaint, 4
  identifying with agency
    declaration, 65
  investigation of in regulatory
    cycle, 6
  multiple, 130
  plain view identification of, 70-71
  satisfying conformance for, 59
  site-specific, 76
  substantial compliance allowed
    for, 85-86
  target area 'sweep' for
    identifying, 54
  as unfair business practices, 139
  voiding without field investi-
    gation, 64-65

violations *(continued)*
    See also complaints; investi-
        gation; specific violations
violators
    arrest provisions for, 120
    due process guarantees required
        for, 96
    evaluation of for enforcement
        prosecution, 88
    hybrid penalties for, 113-114
    identification of for prosecution,
        117
    recovering costs from, 53-55,
        138, 148-153
    refusal of inspection by, 75, 153
    relationship of with enforcing
        agency, 66
    See also property owner; tenant
volunteers
    for assisting neighborhood
        enforcement, 56
    for facilitating mediation, 95
    See also enforcement;
        neighborhood; personnel

W

water quality regulations, effect
    of on local codes, 3
weed abatement liens
    for recovering abatement costs,
        152
    See also abatement; liens
Western Association of Fire Chiefs, 21
wetlands
    monitoring of restoration for, 53
    protection of in conservation
        element, 31
    See also environment; habitat

Y

yards
    aerial surveillance of, 72
    forcible entry into, 101
    inspection procedures for, 69,
        70, 71, 77
    privacy expectations within, 72
    See also privacy rights

Z

zones
    establishment of in zoning code,
        18-19
    proving for criminal prosecution,
        125-126

zoning code
    adoption of establishing enabling
        regulations, 17
zoning code
    due process considerations for
        prosecution of, 122
    enabling component elements, 19
    local, scope of, 18-20
zoning investigators
    code enforcement responsibilities
        of, 9, 56
    See also enforcement officials;
        investigation
zoning ordinances
    changes to subsequent to permit
        issuance, 163-165
    compliance procedures for
        enforcing, 3
    determining appropriateness of, 37
    determining effectiveness of, 5-6
    police power authority for, 13,
        15, 16, 17
zoning variances, process and
    criteria for, 19
zoning violations
    agency response to, 49, 50
    See also violations

SUGGESTION FORM

Through their own careers and the 'war stories' recounted by those attending their training sessions, Joe Schilling and Jim Hare are keenly aware of the ongoing explorations among code enforcement practitioners into the areas of management, field investigation, and litigation strategies. This book is a first effort in assembling a comprehensive guide to code enforcement, for which future editions would benefit from the observations and comments of its users. Do you have a practice tip you want to share? Do you have a differing interpretation of a rule or case in this book? Have you found a typographical error or a bad citation? Is there something that you think we should add? Please take a moment to tell us!

My comments relate to page(s)_____

_____

_____

_____

_____

_____

_____

_____

_____

Please mail this form to the authors, in care of Solano Press Books
Attention: Code Enforcement, P.O. Box 773, Point Arena, CA 95468

Other Titles from Solano Press Books

Your Definitive Guides to the Latest Changes in CEQA, Redevelopment, and Land Use Laws

Guide to the California Environmental Quality Act (CEQA), 1994 Edition (Code C)

By Michael H. Remy, Tina A. Thomas, James G. Moose, and J. William Yeates

An understandable, in-depth description of CEQA's requirements for adequate review and preparation of environmental impact reports (EIRs). The book also includes the entire Act, updated through December 1993, the entire text of the most current CEQA *Guidelines*, and an appendix with summaries of important cases.

Successful CEQA Compliance: A Step-by-Step Approach, 1994 Edition (Code Q)

By Ronald E. Bass and Albert I. Herson

A practical user's guide that explains how to proceed, in a step-by-step fashion, from the beginning to the end of the environmental review process. It summarizes the California Environmental Quality Act and CEQA *Guidelines*, focusing on the procedural and substantive requirements of the law.

Mastering NEPA: A Step-by-Step Approach, 1993 (Code N)

By Ronald E. Bass and Albert I. Herson

A step-by-step analysis of the provisions of the National Environmental Policy Act and the environmental review process. Intended as a user's handbook, the book includes the authors' recommendations for successful compliance, with charts and illustrations clarifying key points.

Redevelopment in California, 1994 Edition (Code R)

By David F. Beatty, Joseph E. Coomes, Jr., T. Brent Hawkins, Edward J. Quinn, Jr., and Iris P. Yang, with A. Jerry Keyser and Calvin E. Hollis

A guide to California's Community Redevelopment Law and the authority given cities and counties to establish and manage redevelopment agencies and to prepare, adopt, implement, and finance redevelopment projects. The book includes a comprehensive analysis of the Community Redevelopment Law Reform Act of 1993 and a new presentation on the economics of successful redevelopment projects and plans.

California Land Use & Planning Law, 1994 Edition (Code L)

By Daniel J. Curtin, Jr.

A well-known, definitive summary of the major provisions of land use and planning law that apply to California cities and counties. This book not only includes the latest statutes and the most recent federal and state court decisions and Opinions of the California Attorney General through 1993, but also revises Curtin's *Subdivision Map Act Manual* which will no longer be published as a separate document.

Putting Transfer of Development Rights to Work in California, 1993 (Code TR)

By Rick Pruetz

With the aid of numerous case studies, this book describes how TDRs can be used to protect open space, agricultural land, natural resources, historic properties, and areas of historic value.

Guide to California Planning and Land Use Law: A Wall Poster, Second Edition (Code PO)

By M. Lauren Ficaro and Thomas C. Jensen

An ideal quick-reference guide graphically displaying California's planning and environmental laws and permit procedures as of January 1, 1994.

Public Needs & Private Dollars—A Guide to Dedications and Development Fees, 1993 (Code X)

By William W. Abbott, Marian E. Moe, and Marilee Hansen

An excellent legal and practical guide to understanding how exactions can be used by local government to provide necessary public works, facilities, and services.

Guide to California Planning, 1991 (Code G)

By William Fulton

In a lively and readable fashion, this book describes in detail what land use planning is supposed to be and how it actually works in California, including the processes and laws that must be observed, and how they are used for better or worse. Prepared for members of the general public and students who wish to understand the fundamentals of the current practice of land use planning in California.

Land-Use Initiatives and Referenda in California, 1990 Edition with 1991 Supplement (Code I)

By Michael P. Durkee, M. Thomas Jacobson, Thomas C. Wood, and Michael H. Zischke

This book summarizes the constitutionally established power of initiatives and referenda and the limits on their use at the local government level to effect land use policies and projects and to enact slow-growth or no-growth measures in California.

Solano Press Books 1994 Order Form

(Contact us after December 15, 1994 about the availability and prices of our 1995 editions)

QTY	CODE	TITLE	UNIT COST	TOTAL
_____	CE	*Code Enforcement: A Comprehensive Approach*	$38	$ _____
_____	C	*Guide to CEQA,* 1994 Edition	$55	$ _____
_____	CS	*Guide to CEQA* — 1994 Executive Summary Supplement	$15	$ _____
_____	CX	*Guide to CEQA* Package (Book plus Executive Summary)	$65	$ _____
_____	Q	*Successful CEQA Compliance,* 1994 Edition	$42	$ _____
_____	L	*Curtin's California Land Use and Planning Law,* 1994 Edition	$42	$ _____
_____	R	*Redevelopment in California,* 1994 Edition	$42	$ _____
_____	RS	*Redevelopment in California* — 1994 Executive Summary Supplement	$15	$ _____
_____	RX	*Redevelopment in California* Package (Book plus Executive Summary)	$52	$ _____
_____	G	Fulton's Guide to *California Planning*	$30	$ _____
_____	I	*Land-Use Initiatives and Referenda in California*	$28	$ _____
_____	N	*Mastering NEPA*	$35	$ _____
_____	X	*Public Needs and Private Dollars*	$38	$ _____
_____	TR	*Putting TDRs to Work in California*	$25	$ _____
_____	PO	*Guide to California Planning: A Wall Poster,* Second Edition	$22	$ _____
_____	PS	*Guide to California Planning: Poster* — Desk Reference Supplement	$10	$ _____

SUBTOTAL OF ALL PUBLICATIONS   *(LINE A)* $ _____

PREPAID ORDERS —

Select only one of the following two discount options, if eligible:

- **Less 15%** of **all** publications ordered, if three (3) or more different book titles (not Supplements) are included in your order (.15 x line A) $ _____

- **Less 15%** for **students** (photocopy of current photo student I.D. required) (.15 x line A) $ _____

LESS AMOUNT OF ONE of the above discount options   *(LINE B)* $ _____

COMBINE TOTALS: MERCHANDISE AND DISCOUNT (LINE A MINUS LINE B)   *(LINE C)* $ _____

Sales Tax Add California sales tax of 7.25% (California only) (.0725 x Line C). You pay the sales tax at point of purchase [Mendocino County], not at the rate in effect at your location. $ _____

Shipping Add $3/book for shipping (but not more than $12 total for any one order) $ _____

Supplement Shipping Add $1/copy of CS, RS, and PS (but not more than $10 for any one order) $ _____

Poster Shipping Add $6/poster $ _____

Handling Add $6 handling charge if order is not prepaid $ _____

Foreign Sales Shipping: Add $10/order to ship via surface; $20/book to ship via air $ _____

GRAND TOTAL $ _____

PHONE ORDERS: (707) 884-4508 OR FAX THIS FORM TO: (707) 884-4109

IF PAYING BY MAIL, SEND THIS FORM AND A CHECK PAYABLE TO:

Solano Press Books, PO Box 773, Point Arena, CA 95468

SHIPPING INFORMATION

VISA, MASTERCARD, AND AMERICAN EXP[RESS] ACCEPTED!

Phone or fax your order, and receive it faster. Unle[ss] are ordering for a government agency, university o[r col]lege, library, or other official public agency (in wh[ich] case, include your purchase order number), comp[lete pay]ment must accompany your order, or you may pay [by cred]it card. We cannot bill individuals and private busi[nesses] that do not have an established credit history with [us].

UPS SHIPPING:

Since orders of more than one book may be se[nt] please also enter your UPS shipping address, if a[ppropri]ate. Allow 10 to 14 working days for delivery. If y[ou need] faster delivery, call us. There may be an extra [charge] depending upon the size of your order.

ALL SALES ARE FINAL. NO RETURNS FOR C[REDIT]

SOLD TO

CUSTOMER # (MAY BE FOUND IN UPPER LH CORNER OF ADDR[ESS])

PHONE (   )

FIRM/AGENCY

STREET

CITY

STATE   ZIP

IF PAYING BY VISA/MASTERCARD OR AME[R]ICAN EXPRESS: ❏ VISA   ❏ MC   ❏ A[mEx]

CARD#

NAME ON CARD

EXPIRATION DATE

SIGNATURE

SHIP TO

PHONE (   )

FIRM/AGENCY

STREET

CITY

STATE   ZIP

Notes